A Grand Strategy

Countering China, Taming
Technology, and Restoring the Media

William J. Holstein

edited by Michael Slizewski

Brick Tower Press

Brick Tower Press
Manhanset House
Dering Harbor, New York 11965-0342
bricktower@aol.com
www.BrickTowerPress.com

Copyright © 2021 by William J. Holstein
First Edition
Library of Congress Cataloging in Publication Data
Holstein, William J.
A grand strategy, countering china, taming
technology, and restoring the media.
Includes index.
1. Intelligence and Espionage—United States. 2. History
Asia/China. 3. Political Process—Media and Internet. I. Title.

ISBN: 978-1-899694-98-3

A Grand Strategy

Countering China, Taming
Technology, and Restoring the Media

Table of Contents

Author of:

"The New Art of War: China's Deep Strategy Inside the United States" 2019.

"How =the ThinkPad Changed the World...And Is Shaping the Future" 2017.

"Has the American Media Misjudged China?" 2014.

"The Next American Economy: Blueprint For a Real Recovery" 2011.

"Why GM Matters: Inside the Race to Transform an American Icon" 2009.

"Rags to Riches: The Story of Cintas." 2002. With Richard Farmer

"The Japanese Power Game: What It Means for America," 1990.

Introduction

I have grown into a curmudgeon—and I do not use the word in the narrow dictionary sense of someone being a miser or a scrooge. A curmudgeon is someone who does not fit neatly into polite bureaucratic structures, and who is indomitable in spirit. A curmudgeon scoffs at the labels that people with small minds like to use. A curmudgeon tells you things you don't want to hear.

The experience of being curmudgeon-ed is akin to hearing fingernails on a chalkboard. You want desperately to get out of the room. You want to hate the curmudgeon.

But then he starts to charm you. It happens gradually. The more he develops his arguments, and the more flavorful detail he lays on, the more you come to realize the curmudgeon is right, about certain things at least. Now you love the curmudgeon.

The first part of the process is spitting out the truths that few want to hear, starting with: we Americans are losing ground to a centrally orchestrated strategy by the Chinese government to strip us of our technological, economic— and therefore strategic—advantage. No war will ever be necessary, as some Jeremiahs are proclaiming. The Chinese government will have developed such technological, economic—and therefore military—power that we will not be able to even contemplate the possibility. Our institutions have been unable to formulate a response not only because of our own intellectual confusion about China's rise under President Xi Jinping, but also because our computer systems have been thoroughly hacked, and spies have been implanted in our companies and governmental institutions. Some of our leading institutions, such as think tanks, Hollywood studios, and universities, have been co-opted. The simpletons who have led our response to China have been completely out of their depth. The world's most populous nation of 1.4 billion people is driving a Mack truck through our midst, and we are confused about who's driving.

The rapid spread of the coronavirus demonstrated how deeply interwoven our societies have become, yet we have failed to understand the Chinese Communist system and its values. I do not buy the theory that the Chinese Communist Party intentionally unleashed COVID-19 on the world, but they certainly have taken advantage of it to push their agenda and their interests far more aggressively than at any point in the "engagement" we have had with them for some forty years. I was there in southern China when it started.

The next set of truths revolves around technology—and there is a profound connection with the previous set of truths. I have lived through and written about the incredible technological revolution of our times. As a child, I had access to a mere three television stations, all in black and white. On Sunday nights at 8 p.m., you could watch anything you wanted as long as it was the Ed Sullivan show. Sullivan introduced Elvis, the Beatles, and other great musicians. He had a dominant "platform," much as the technology giants do today.

There were no remote controls, so you had to physically get up to change channels. All the television shows that could be watched in a given day filled up just one part of a newspaper page. The milkman brought milk to the back door. It was a big deal to make a long-distance phone call. There was no Internet, no semiconductors or computers, no smartphones, no automatic answering machines, no space program.

Imagine such a primitive life! I might as well have been living in a mud hut. The Internet, which has taken hold over the past twenty years or so, has created some incredible capabilities, such as Google Translate and Google Maps. We can go anywhere in the world and know where we are and how to communicate.

At the same time, we can spend hours a day looking at stupid pictures of dogs and playing endless games of Solitaire.

But as recent headlines attest, the Internet also has had more pernicious effects: billions of people can post on Facebook, YouTube, Twitter, Instagram, and other services, and their messages go directly to other people. There is little or no buffer, other than a few meager algorithms and toothless do-little monitors. Foreign governments and other bad actors can exploit these sites—and do, on a regular basis.

The addiction to social media and online gaming has become so intense that young peoples' ability to develop true human intimacy is threatened. Their views of sexuality, according to published reports, are shaped by the massive cesspool of pornography available on the Web. Some teenagers have been bullied on social media and committed suicide as a result.

In some ways, our smartphones have become the opiate of the masses, as Karl Marx once suggested that religion was. If we don't get enough "likes" when we post a picture on Instagram, we are disappointed. The world does not love us anymore.

More broadly, the explosion of social media threatens the way we organize and govern ourselves as a nation. The shattering of any political consensus in America is partly the result of what the technology has done to us. The attempted insurrection against Congress on Jan. 6 was the culmination of these trendlines. Mobs fueled by social media and a handful of political leaders were mobilized to storm the Capitol and livestream their actions to viewers, sometimes for profit. It was a moment of stunning clarity. We were atomized.

We now can clearly see: the Big Tech platforms can literally make or break our democracy. They can shape what people feel is an accurate reflection of reality. They can either lead us into a technological future that is equitable and well-balanced in view of our societal goals, or they can seek to simply make money.

They can help America respond to China's technological challenge—or they can try to play both sides.

What makes this discussion so important is that the pandemic has made Big Tech more powerful than ever—and new waves of technology are starting to wash over us, such as artificial intelligence, 5G wireless communications, virtual and augmented reality, genetic engineering, quantum computing, the Internet of Things, and many others.

We have not truly been able to understand the impact of the technology that already has been introduced, much less figure out how to manage it—and even more powerful and transformative technology is being unleashed.

Here's a nasty twist: we as a society have doubts and hesitations about AI, drones, genetic editing, and other technologies that have Orwellian connotations. But China is spending vast sums of money on these technologies. They care little about privacy or social implications. If we continue to dither, they will inherit the future. Pure and simple. We will become a de facto colony, having to buy advanced products from them, such as Huawei's 5G telecommunications systems and Zoom, WeChat, and TikTok, all based on algorithms and all of them intimately connected with China's surveillance state. To avoid that, we have to figure out a way to thread the eye of the needle by figuring out quickly how to develop and commercialize new technologies while minimizing the chances of misuse.

Technology thus has become the central battleground in the global struggle between the United States and China over whose systems and whose values will prevail. It is a technological arms race that far exceeds the Soviet challenge in scale and complexity.

The last set of irritating truths is about our media, which traditionally has been the bedrock for how we communicate with each other, and how we as a society make decisions. An eternal truth about the media and democracy is this: if people are well-informed, they tend to make the right decisions. But if their information flows have been diluted or corrupted or hijacked, they almost certainly make the wrong decisions.

The mainstream media's critical role of playing arbiter or gatekeeper—to help sort out truth from fiction, to help interpret the flood of information that exists in the world—has been marginalized, if not almost eliminated. There is much blame to go around. It could not have happened without average people allowing it to happen. If someone believes in QAnon websites more than they believe *The New York Times* or *The Wall Street Journal,* they have consigned their minds to the control of algorithms that scour the world for whatever information feeds and reinforces that person's innate set of attitudes and perceptions. The algorithms know your browsing history and your purchasing patterns. They know what you respond to—which articles you read and videos you watch, and which ones you don't. They measure how much of an article or video you consume. Then they go looking for more of the same, because that's how they make money. If these types of services are the sum total of your exposure to information, the game is over. You never will be truly well-informed by being exposed to other points of view or information that challenges any of your beliefs. You will forever exist in your very own "content pod," your own dream world.

Of course, the practitioners of the media also have erred, and I say this as someone who has been involved in the media for half a century. We have not found a way to protest, much less halt, the wave of money grubbers such as Gannett and GateHouse Media and Alden Global Capital and Sam Zell, who took over and destroyed thousands of local newspapers and other media outlets. These guys make the media barons of previous eras, such as William Randolph Hearst, look like absolute choirboys. Every media organization where I was on staff—United Press International, *Business Week, U.S. News & World Report, Business 2.0*, and *Chief Executive* magazine—either went out of business or was sold for pennies on the dollar. (When I recite this litany to other journalists, they invariably say, "Please don't come to work here.")

We practitioners also bear some of the blame, because we have cooperated in our own marginalization by easing away from the role of being the trusted gatekeeper, the modern-day Walter Cronkite, one of my heroes. We have done that partly to survive economically. Hate and division obviously sell. I would not say we have completely abandoned the role of attempting to offer some measure of intellectual leadership to the American people. But we have allowed some of our media institutions to be ideologically typecast as liberal or conservative or some other perhaps more extreme identity. And increasingly we measure our success by how many clicks an article gets on the Internet or how high the ratings are for a television news show—not by whether a news item broke fresh intellectual ground or framed an issue in a compelling way.

How ironic it is that journalists have essentially failed at public relations—explaining to the public why what they have traditionally done is important and valuable. But because the media has failed to maintain that trust, there can be no genuine debate about the irritating truths I have raised. We are incoherent in our so-called debates about China or technology or the quality of our democracy. It took way too long to develop a cohesive response to the coronavirus. And we also haven't been able to come to grips with such obvious major issues as climate change, the crisis in our educational system, deep inequality, frequent massacres, our aging infrastructure, or a rising wave of obesity and drug misuse. Any such discussion can be usurped and disrupted by a sudden Tweet and a sudden sensational allegation that may prove unfounded. We can be labeled in the blink of an eye—and labels destroy the prospect for real dialogue. That is called being "delegitimized." Our national debate has been broken.

Moreover, we have been so consumed with partisan politics—with one "side" trying to destroy the other "side"—that we have lost focus on what we want America to be. Emperor Nero gets a bad rap for fiddling while Rome burned, but what we are doing, or not doing, is occurring on an even more massive scale. Now that you are edging for the exits, I am going to start the process of entertaining and charming you and then proposing a grand strategy to respond. It's nothing less than a miracle that I have reached curmudgeon-hood, having been born in South Charleston, West Virginia. It wasn't even Charleston itself, which is decidedly modest. It was in a poorer neighborhood down the Kanawha River, where a large number of chemical plants were located because of lax environmental enforcement. I was the seventh generation of my family to live in West Virginia, where we hid from most of the rest of the world. We were hillbillies long before "Hillbilly Elegy" came along, and erudite readers on the left and right coasts started to understand what people in "flyover" mountains actually thought or felt.

My paternal grandparents were Papa (pronounced *pappah*) and Mama (pronounced *mam-mah*). They lived in Tornado, West Virginia, not far from a poetically named place called Nitro because of all the chemicals manufactured there. Potatoes were "taters," tomatoes were "maters," and mosquitoes were "skeeters." That side of the family was primarily Methodist. But my mother's parents, from the shining metropolitan complex of Milton near Huntington, were Baptists. They looked down on Methodists because they allowed dancing and card-playing on Sundays. That set of grandparents was Pap Harry and Ninny Jack.

I was named the fifth William in a row—either out of some form of family loyalty or absence of imagination, I'll never know. To differentiate me from my father and to avoid having me called "Little Bill," my mom suggested calling me "Billy Jack" (my middle name being Jackson, her maiden name). Fortunately, Dad stopped that.

Instead, they decided to call me Jack. I was perfectly happy with that name until a teacher on the first day of school in the second grade read out the names of every student aloud and asked what we wanted to be called. "William Holstein," she said. "What do you want to be called?"

"Jack," I said proudly.

"Okay, William."

I didn't have the stones to correct her. That started a lifetime of confusion. My extended family called me Jack. Professionally, I was known as Bill. When the two universes of family and professional contacts mingled, there was always confusion over what to call that guy over there.

There was also confusion over where we were from. My father and grandfather assumed they were German descendants because Schleswig-Holstein is a province in Germany and one of the relatively few areas of Germany with access to the sea. I discovered the answer to the identity question in a book called *The Swedish Holsteins*. A guy named Mathias was a Swede and was part of a Swedish occupation of northern Germany. The Thirty Years War broke out, and the Germans beat the Swedish interlopers. So in about 1640, Mathias and family sailed to Philadelphia. Being Swedes, they had no last name. So the immigration officers gave them the name Holstein, because that's where they came from. The distinctive black-and-white Holstein cattle were developed in the same geographic area. No, Holstein people are not related to Holstein cows.

How was it then that I, as a young almost-Billy Jack, found myself covering China's economic modernization without speaking any more Chinese than being able to ask for a beer and a restroom where I could deposit the recycled beer? I simply stumbled into the middle of one of the biggest stories in history. How did I survive doing stupid things while covering the Soviet invasion of Afghanistan? I heard Soviets were being attacked in Kabul's bazaar, so I decided to check it out by myself. Bad call. Or how could a boy from South Charleston take part in the incredibly important fight about whether Microsoft had violated antitrust laws by "choking off the air" to Netscape? Allowing Microsoft to wiggle off the hook set the stage for today's behemoth tech platforms. How could I become World Editor of *Business Week* magazine at the height of its influence and power? I took part in the great debates about the fall of the Soviet Union, the reunification of Germany, and the challenge being mounted by Japan in the late 1980s. What gave me the legitimacy to do all that?

Part of the explanation is that I rode an incredible series of waves. I was a journalist during a true golden era of the media business. United Press International literally showed me the world over ten years, including postings in Hong Kong and Beijing. When I was at *Business Week* (1985–1996), it was an era in which journalists based in New York could actually travel and touch what was happening on the ground not only internationally but also in America. I made repeated trips back to China, Hong Kong, Japan, and South Korea, as well as to Germany and Russia. I began to develop a body of real-world knowledge rather than the sort that comes out of textbooks. I probed why so many American factories were closing in the face of primarily Japanese competition at first, and then later, how many factories were simply being moved to China.

Over time, I tried to understand what aspects of the American economy were best-positioned to withstand international competition. I studied and wrote about innovation inside both large and small companies. I interviewed hundreds of CEOs. I came to understand the connections between the decisions they made and the overall vibrancy of a city's, state's, or nation's economy. I helped come up with the concept of "hot spots" for *Business Week,* referring to the concentrations of technology-based activity that exist in places such as Silicon Valley or Cambridge, Massachusetts.

After *Business Week*, I spent five years at *U.S. News & World Report* and crisscrossed the country once again, looking at how Austin was managing an emerging digital divide between rich and poor, and how Omaha was using advanced telecom-munications to turn itself into a technology hub. I made trips to Finland to learn how Nokia was creating "wireless wonders," meaning wireless telephones, and to China, to write about the debate over whether the Americans should continue granting it most-favored nation (MFN) trading status.

Some people may think I am a narrow specialist, an Asian junkie, but our entire world order has been Asianized. China and Japan are now the second and third largest economies in the world, respectively. I literally watched it happen.

As we did after Pearl Harbor in 1941 and throughout World War II, and as we did after the Soviets launched their Sputnik satellite in the mid-1950s, we need to mobilize our resources to channel our energies into confronting China, whose popula-tion outnumbers us by four to one. The vision of globalization that many of us advocated for decades—in which we assumed that it did not matter where a company manufactured or sold its goods—has been proven wrong by Chinese domination of pharmaceuticals, medical supplies, rare earths, and other critical goods. While we were dreaming sweet dreams about the open flow of trade, investment, people, and technology across national borders, creating wealth and prosperity for all, Chinese Presi-dent Xi Jinping has been devising a strategy to use those inputs to subdue America and build a China-centered world order. And democracies tend to be slow to react to emerging authoritarian regimes, particularly when a democracy is distracted or confused.

In essence, today we need a smarter brand of Ameri-can capitalism and governance. We have to adapt our models to become more cohesive in the face of a centrally coordinated strategy being carried out by the monolithic Chinese Communist Party.

We will need to enlist our technology giants in this global confrontation. The antitrust actions filed against Google and Facebook will be useful in shaping their behavior, but the ultimate goal should not be to break them up. The goals are to moderate their monopolistic practices, persuade them to fulfill their responsibilities to clean up the social media cesspool, ease the pressure against established media, and get serious about helping America compete against China—rather than selling advanced technologies to the People's Liberation Army or security forces. (Microsoft, for example, helped create the entire leadership of China's AI industry, which may be ahead of America's in some respects.)

The American media's role in the grand strategy is that it must help move our democracy out of gridlock to recognize the scale and nature of the challenges we face—not just China, but also at home. The two sets of problems are clearly linked. To cite just one example, we need more people trained in computer and scientific skills to cope with China's techno-monolith, and that serves a domestic need as well as in terms of creating more well-paid jobs. Another: we need to bring some manufacturing home to ease our dependence on China. Doing so would create high-quality, good paying jobs.

As the old cliché goes, a crisis is a terrible thing to waste— it's possible that after the coronavirus has inflicted its grim toll, Americans will be more inclined to have serious conversations about what values and institutions really matter. The traditional political gridlock about the role of government in our society and economy could be eased after we see that an effective government, working with the private sector, is essential to national survival.

I don't pretend to be a genius or a revolutionary. I'm not competing with Mother Teresa for sainthood. I promise never to run for president. I have merely put modestly new ideas together in a modestly interesting way. The sheer accretion of detail in this book is meant to both entertain and inform.

I was struck by what David Attenborough said in his excellent documentary on climate change, in which he featured footage of himself as a young man in various wilder-nesses and ocean reefs that have suffered over the years. He said he was making a "witness statement" of just how pro-foundly those landscapes had changed. In my cultural con-text, I wish to testify, to bear witness, that my experiences bear directly on the challenges we face today. The fact that I have deep experience in covering both China and technology means that I understand the nature of China's technology-intensive strategy better than a traditional foreign policy analyst might. The fact that I've been a journalist for fifty years means I understand the role of the media in shaping big debates. I don't need the latest TikTok app tattooed to my forehead to impart a measure of wisdom about how long games are played out in the arc of human history.

And because I am an unmitigated curmudgeon, I can offer a clear-sighted vision of what we must do about these prob-lems. Having been a permanent outsider, you can rest assured I am not in the hip pocket of any political party or industry or weird religious sect. I will speak to you as only a curmudgeon can, with scant regard for sacred conventions or pecuniary interest.

To resist China, which is in the process of imposing a measure of control over us, we must overcome our internal divisions and coalesce around a great challenge. We have many fissures among us, because we believe in allowing competitive interests to flourish. But it is time to manage those separate inter-ests as part of a coherent strategy to demonstrate conclusively that America as a concept is not over, as China's top diplomats are arguing.

In the final analysis, experience truly matters. Over the course of the following pages, I will include a generous helping of my adventures not directly related to China, technology, or the media—covering the sinking of the Edmund Fitzgerald; being put under house arrest by the Soviets in Afghanistan; avoiding would-be kidnappers in the southern Philippines; covering Pope

John Paul II on two memorable occasions; confronting CIA agents working on secret listening posts on the Sino-Soviet border; playing Monopoly with KGB agents in Beijing; forcing my way into the Forbidden City in the Chinese capital; inadvertently smuggling a gyroscope from a Soviet missile from Germany into Moscow; and others. Those stories will enliven the stew.

PART ONE

Setting the Stage

1   A Restless Spirit

I've often wondered why I devoted my life to understanding the world and its many peoples, languages, and economies. My ancestors in the hills of West Virginia did not display the slightest interest in how the rest of the world worked. People simply stayed up in their hollows, or "hollers," as they were pronounced in West Virginia twang. Why did I, as a 24-year-old UPI correspondent in Lansing, Michigan, decide that I wanted to become a foreign correspondent? Was it a sudden moment of insanity?

Of course, it goes back to my upbringing and the kind of environment that my father, William Reed Holstein, created for me. It was World War II and then the post-war economic boom, accompanied by the expansion of the national interstate highway system, that propelled people such as my father out into the world and sent his family and him around the country. As a result, I was much more a product of suburban Middle America, rather than the hills, but a certain cultural limitation marked my youth. I never sampled Chinese food until I got to college, for example. I knew Jewish people in high school, but did not understand that they were Jewish and what that meant until many years later.

Dad served in the US Navy during World War II and told stories to his three children about taking trains across North Africa (to avoid the German-controlled Mediterranean) to get to Egypt. He must have met Berber tribesmen, because Dad would open his mouth and demonstrate how their teeth had been filed down into pointed fangs to make them look fiercer. From Egypt, he was involved in the invasion of southern France, which evoked adventure in faraway places. After being in Europe, he was sent to the Pacific, where once on his supply vessel in Okinawa getting ready for the presumed invasion of Japan, he had a pistol and thought he heard someone swimming toward his boat. Nothing happened, but again, it inspired the imagination.

We moved a great deal because my father worked for the chemical division of B.F. Goodrich, and it was an era of corporate mobility. I got used to moving through different sets of people. It became ingrained in me. *Oh, here is a new set of people,* a club, if you will, and they have their own sets of rules. So my goal became to engage with these people for a finite period of time and try to understand their rules. But I knew on some deep level I would be moving on through. Having been born in West Virginia, I lived in three places in northern Ohio, then Southern California, then back to high school in Louisville, Kentucky, and on to East Lansing, Michigan to go to Michigan State University.

In my experience, the vast majority of humans are born in one area and tend to stay in that general region, in their zones of comfort. They maintain relationships from childhood or high school. They are rooted.

But I became the exact opposite—someone who is just passing through. I have no friends from my youth. I tend to gravitate toward "bridge people," meaning they bridge the differences between two cultures, such as Japan on one hand and the United States on the other. I am attracted to outsiders and people who don't easily fit into stereotypes. It's no wonder I never developed the behaviors that might endear me to elite institutions in New York or Washington. I have always been "other."

My family drove a lot on vacations, taking advantage of the new interstate highway system as it was being built. From Southern California, we would go on family vacations to Zion National Park, Bryce Canyon National Park, Yellowstone National Park, and Joshua Tree National Monument (now Joshua Tree National Park), a family favorite. There were no Game Boys or Nintendos. We would play Twenty Guesses. We would also tell stories. Storytelling was a big part of my family's culture. Today, it is called creating a narrative. That's just fancy talk for telling a story. Knowing how to tell stories ended up shaping my entire career.

Dad, brother Allen, and I would leave Mom and Mary Ann at home and go on long drives from Louisville out to Yellowstone and Glacier national parks, or south to the Smokies, or east to the Red River Gorge in Kentucky. Then we would get lost in the backwoods for a week at a time, backpacking. I learned a lot about how to prepare for any trip or any mission, and how to find the things I needed in the towns we passed through. Before we left home, Dad would go to the local American Automobile Association (AAA) office and get guidebooks and maps. He also taught us that you could learn an enormous amount about a town from the Yellow Pages, a book containing phone numbers of everybody and every business in town, and from the local newspaper. If you had those tools, you could figure out how to get what you needed.

Technology Notes:
The only cameras we had in the 1950s and early 1960s were Polaroids You waited a minute after taking a picture before pulling a layer of paper out of the camera, revealing the photograph—"Modern" single-lens cameras did not arrive until I was in college and required silver halide film that you had to take to the drugstore to get developed over twenty-four or forty-eight hours. And the only music in the house in my early days came from my father's hi-fi, which about the size of a two-drawer filing cabinet. It was mono. Stereo eventually came along. There were only records, no CDs or DVDs.

The transistor radio came along in time for me as a preteen to listen to the Beatles and the Beach Boys on KRLA, the radio station that played all the music that was bursting onto the scene. Dad brought home another amazing machine. It was a tape recorder. About the size of a breadbox. I got tapes and tape recorded my favorite songs. There was no Spotify. The idea that anyone could listen to music on a telephone would have been seen as preposterous.

We used to have very large sets of World Book encyclopedias in our home. It seems incredible now to think that humankind believed all important knowledge could be contained in a set of books. My mother even went door to door selling World Books because she was able to convince parents that the encyclopedias would help their children in school.

The black-and-white Xerox machine was invented in 1959 and gradually became the household name it is today. But I didn't have any contact with one until I was an adult. To make copies of tests for her math students, Mom had to use a mimeograph machine. The color Xerox machine came along in the 1970s, a marvel to behold!

To do research for either a journalistic story or a college paper, you had to consult microfiches, which were black-and-white film images of old newspapers. You would go to the library and ask for the microfiche of a certain newspaper for a certain date, and then put the roll of film on a machine that allowed you to scroll through the newspaper, page by page.

Typing up papers was always difficult because if you made a mistake you had to go back and redo the whole page. This was before IBM unveiled its Selectric electric typewriters with a self-correcting ribbon. Books called dictionaries were essential because there was no spell-check.

If you needed to make a telephone call, and you were away from the home or office, you had to find a telephone booth, which was a glass-paneled kiosk that had a telephone in it that was hard-wired to the overall telecommunications system. You had to be ready with coins to pay for the call.

End Technology Notes

* * *

Dad also always had lots of newspapers and magazines in the house. *National Geographic, Time, Readers Digest,* and *The Christian Science Monitor* were in the house when we lived in California and Kentucky.

Another internationalizing influence was that I studied French for five years beginning in the seventh grade when I was still living in Southern California. I continued when we moved to Kentucky. There, Mrs. Butler was one of those teachers who left a major impact on the students who chose to stay awake. She was passionate about the existential work of Jean-Paul Sartre; we read *Huis clos (No Exit)* and others of his work in French. It was a powerful intellectual shot in the arm. Old conventions and ideologies seemed to be crumbling. This was the 1960s, and powerful forces were erupting in our society.

In sum, I was programmed to be restless and to have a burning curiosity.

***

The Vietnam War wasn't a war such as today's conflicts in Afghanistan or Iraq. There was a draft, and young men were being called upon to serve in combat. It was not an academic exercise. It was a real threat to my life, as I saw it.

I was 17 in Louisville, Kentucky, during the summer of 1969, preparing to go to Michigan State in the fall. I would turn 18 on September 24, after I was off to my freshman year. That forced the issue of my draft board status to be resolved that summer.

My dad had given me books about the Viet Cong and how cruel they were. They would ram chopsticks into the ears of their enemies and place poisoned stakes in the rice paddies for American troops to step on. I didn't understand why the war was important or why I would ever want to be involved in anything like that.

On a trip with my Teens Who Care club (a mental health volunteer group), a Swedish guy on a school bus asked me if I would really register for the draft so that I could go off and fight in Vietnam.

He referred me to a counseling service for draft dodgers, to put it bluntly. I had the same draft board that Cassius Clay had. The draft board were a bunch of real hardliners who forced him to be drafted. He later took the name Muhammad Ali.

When my father learned I was going to file for CO status, he went ballistic. This was probably the most intense confrontation I ever had with him.

"You're ruining your life," he said. In his day, that would have been right. People who declined to enlist to fight Hitler and Hirohito were seen as cowards and shunned professionally and personally.

But I filed for CO status and went off to college. I never had to appear before the draft board, because President Nixon's draft lottery gave me a high number and assured that I would most likely never be called upon. By the time I graduated in the summer of 1973, American involvement in the war was over. We had pulled out. The last American helicopters had left.

Starting in the winter semester of my freshman year (it was a three-semester system), I got an internship on *The State News*, the student newspaper with a daily circulation of 40,000. I did things like going to get coffee in the rain for the top editors or running stories over to the pre-press shop, where the stories were laid out on a board. We used offset printing technology.

I began looking around at the things that were happening on campus. I noticed a great deal of anti-war activity—meetings of the Students for a Democratic Society (SDS) and anti-ROTC gatherings, for example. (The Reserve Officers Training Corps trained students to become soldiers after they graduated.) There were so many threads of the whole anti-war movement, including women's rights and African-America rights. They were all wrapped together. Having filed for Conscientious Objector status, I obviously was against the war. But I tried to maintain critical distance in covering the stories around me.

Incredibly, the newspaper was not covering these issues. It's an age-old problem in news organizations: they are set up as bureaucracies with different desks and different beats. They often are slow to respond to issues or stories that challenge their bureaucracies, because that is uncomfortable and forces difficult decisions about turf and personnel and budgets.

By spring semester, I was a full-time reporter, and I kept on covering the same stories. There was a People's Park on campus where a lot of pot was getting smoked and LSD dropped. People were sleeping in tents. There was incredible ferment.

On May 1, a Friday night, I was at the International Center, where students were protesting. President Nixon had just expanded the war by invading Cambodia. The presence of ROTC on campus was thus a hot issue. The International Center was a scene of chaos, because nobody was in charge and there were competing agendas. But the anti-war voices seemed to be the most persistent.

Hundreds of people were there, but no other reporters from *The State News*. Speaker after speaker got up and spoke passionately about the issues. Finally, one young man got up and said, "Like my back's up against the wall. I'm tired of not doing anything. I want to do something. I wanna go out into those streets."

That's how incoherent it all was. But people streamed out and took to the streets. I went with them. They broke into different groups. I was with one group on Grand River Avenue, which formed the northern border of campus, when police fired tear gas at us. That was my first taste.

I was with another group at the Administration Building, which had a great deal of glass—glass doors, glass windows, etc. Here I found young men ripping up stanchions that held chains that protected patches of grass in the plaza in front of the building, trying to smash in the glass doors of the Administration Building. I didn't understand how trashing the building was going to have any impact on the issues. There always seems to be a fringe of violent, destructive people who take advantage of protests.

I wrote up a detailed blow-by-blow report and presented it to George Bullard, the editor of the paper, on Sunday. It was in the style of "First I saw this, then I saw that." We had to get ready for Monday's newspaper.

He read it and came out of his office to the main newsroom and said to me, in front of others, "This isn't what I want. I don't care where you went and exactly what you saw. What does it mean? What does the Administration have to say? Put this in context."

It was one of the best lessons I ever learned in journalism. I did what he asked of me and my byline, and only my byline, was bannered on the front page of the paper the next morning, Monday May 4. It was the same day that the National Guard killed four students at Kent State University in nearby Ohio. It seemed like all of America's campuses were erupting. Student demonstrators were on the cover of *Time* magazine, which was still very influential, and their protests were prominently displayed in newspapers and other forms of media. I was completely hooked on the power of journalism.

***

I probably learned more outside the classroom at Michigan State than I did inside. It was an enormous bureaucracy of 40,000 students. My passion was *The State News*, and I spent thirty to thirty-five hours a week at it. I did all sorts of jobs, ranging from photo editor to wire editor, reading all the copy from United Press International and the Associated Press about the Vietnam War. I worked my way up to being campus editor.

By 1972, I had started thinking about the role the media played in American society. I had spent the summer of 1971 at the *(Louisville) Courier-Journal* and would spend the summer of 1972 at the sister afternoon newspaper, *The Times*. I saw how the Bingham family owned and operated the newspapers as well as a local television station. The *Courier-Journal* was seen as one of the finest regional newspapers in the country. Its reporters often went to work for *The Washington Post*, one of the best national newspapers. The Binghams, led at the time by Barry Bingham, felt an obligation to the community to provide quality journalism, a kind of noblesse oblige.

The Binghams did not want to lose money on their newspapers, but they did not insist on the 18 to 20 percent rates of return that a new wave of corporate owners, such as Gannett, would soon start imposing as they bought up family-owned newspapers. Ownership of the media was becoming more concentrated.

I was attracted to the work of Ben Bagdikian, who wrote *The Information Machines: Their Impact on Men and the Media*; A.J. Leibling, who wrote *The Press*; Marshall McLuhan, who wrote *Understanding Media* ("The media is the message"); H.L. Mencken, who wrote *A Gang of Pecksniffs*; and I.F. Stone, the fiery iconoclast who ran his own newsletter for decades. This is when I discovered the curmudgeon phenomenon.

As a journalism major, I started writing a paper about the ownership of the media. I had met Al Neuharth, the chief executive officer of Gannett, at a journalism convention in November 1971 and asked for his cooperation in allowing me to research Gannett's role. He turned me over to Vince Spezzano, his Director of Promotion and Public Service. We corresponded by letter. "The topic (of my research paper) is the impact of the ownership of the media on the viewpoint expressed, both editorially and in the news columns themselves," I wrote to Spezzano. "In other words, does the form of ownership of a newspaper or electronic outlet affect the particular bias of that medium's coverage?"

Spezzano naturally insisted that the publishers and editors of every Gannett newspaper made their own decisions about what to print and how to print it.

I didn't buy it. In my paper, I argued "… that the role of the press in a free society as a purveyor of a wide diversity of viewpoint and as a relatively objective disseminator of information is hampered by its development into 'big business.'" Other chains that were emerging at the time included the Knight newspapers, and the Chicago Tribune, Hearst, and Newhouse groups. I quoted Liebling, who suspected that the large chains would use their clout to promote pro-business agendas.

"It is a kind of Catch 22," I concluded. "As long as the media is controlled by a few whose interests focus more on profit than on the integrity of the news, the media is not likely to take up questions of concentration. And the longer the issue is blithely ignored, the worse becomes the need to place the matter before the eyes of each and every American."

Looking back, Liebling (and I) were only partly right. As we have seen by the dramatic collapse of more than 2,000 local newspapers across the country since 2007, the real issue was not that the new corporate owners imposed any ideological dogma, but rather that they squeezed the newspapers for bigger profits. They kept firing journalists, shuttering virtually all afternoon papers, and homogenizing the news of any local flavor and color. It became a vicious downward cycle: Newspapers did not have the money or ambition to provide compelling local coverage. They did not have a mission, so they became increasingly irrelevant. People did not see the need to read them, which inflicted more damage. The loss of classified advertising to the Internet was another savage blow.

So the beginning of the collapse of American local newspapers could be glimpsed nearly fifty years ago. Under the influence of the Lieblings of the world, combined with my own experiences, I came to regard journalism as being sacred. It was the air our democracy breathes. Or at least, it used to be.

***

I got my first real taste of going global when I needed eight more credits to graduate. I applied for a summer program at Exeter College at Oxford University in England and spent eight weeks in England, Scotland, Wales, and Holland. Kids were there from twenty countries.

One of the great traditions at Oxford was debating. I decided to stage a debate about Watergate, the political scandal involving Richard Nixon that was dominating the headlines from America. My opponent argued that it was the end of American democracy. I argued that it was a positive sign of American democracy and am pleased to think I was right, because Nixon resigned a year later.

Upon returning from Oxford in August 1973, I started at UPI in Detroit, but within a matter of weeks, it was clear UPI wanted me in Lansing. There I was thrown in with Paul Varian, the bureau chief. Paul was a heavy smoker and was able to punch telex tape while a cigarette burned in his mouth. He was able to flick off the ash at just the right moment.

One of the first requirements of the job was learning how to punch a telex machine and how to read the tape. It was like learning Braille or Morse code. Depending on what key you hit on the keyboard, the machine would punch a certain pattern on the tape. There was room for five dots across the tape. The tape would then transmit your story to Chicago, which was our regional hub, for possible relay to New York and the national wires. We controlled only the Michigan wire. My main job was covering the State Senate, but I also covered other parts of the government, such as the state's Department of Natural Resources. We wrote most of our stories on manual typewriters before punching them out on the telex. Varian was good enough that he could simply sit down at the telex and start writing.

I began to discover what it was like to be part of a global organization. I had heard that Carl Gerstacker, chief executive of Dow Chemical in Midland, wanted to have an island where he could put his headquarters so that his company would not be beholden to any government. I thought that was pretty far-fetched and approached him for an interview. To my surprise, he granted it, and I wrote about his island aspirations. The story was printed all over the country, including in such major newspapers as *The Chicago Tribune* and *Detroit Free Press*. It was my first exposure to an issue that I would follow for life—the connection between the United States and its largest companies, the multinationals. Much later, I would write a cover story for *Business Week*, "The Stateless Corporation," an examination of many American CEOs who agreed with Gerstacker on some level that their actions should not be constrained by any US government body.

I also got huge pickup for a human interest story. I discovered a little old violin maker in downtown Lansing, which was a gritty auto manufacturing town aside from the state government complex, and went to see him with a photographer. I described how he made violins "… with deft movements" of his aging hands. Clearly, he would be the last in a line of violin makers. Who would have dreamed that Lansing, Michigan, would have a violin maker? The story went national.

***

Technology Notes:
We went to drive-in movies. Most drive-ins have now disappeared except for some reinvented for the pandemic era. A family would drive in, park at a designated spot, take a microphone speaker positioned on a post, and place it inside the car, wires and all. That would allow us to hear the movie, which was projected up on a large screen. Hundreds of cars might be parked, all filled with families.

Photography used to be limited to professionals who made the investment to buy an expensive camera. It was in my freshman year that I first saw a single-lens reflex camera, which a Japanese exchange student by the name of Kaz had in the dorm. It was a Nikon. I bought it from him for a nominal sum and was an avid photographer for years. It was expensive to develop the film into paper-based photographs, so my family used slides for our personal pictures. We had to have a slide projector to watch the slides in a darkened room. I also learned how to develop black-and-white photos in a darkroom.

Newspapers used to be printed using hot lead. I saw it in action at the *Courier-Journal*. Men in the printing shop had metal trays at about waist level where they would take whatever the editors had submitted to them, usually through pneumatic tubes, and line up pieces of lead to mirror what the editors wanted. This process was called typesetting. If a headline said "Extra," the printers would have to find a capital E followed by the other four letters. They would thus construct each page of the newspaper in hot lead. The next stage was positioning the trays to allow big sheets of newsprint to run over big presses and absorb the images from the trays printers had painstakingly prepared. The air smelled of ink.

End Technology Notes

***

The late Charles W. Bell, or simply Bill Bell, became the Detroit bureau chief soon after I started in Lansing. I loved this guy. He was a big-time correspondent who had covered wars in the Congo and other major stories in Africa. He had been based in Rome and covered the pope as well. He covered the massacre of Israeli athletes at the 1972 Olympics in Munich. I didn't realize it at the time, but he also had hung out with Jack Kerouac and others who were credited with launching "the Beat Generation" in Paris. He was brilliant and funny and a great storyteller. He was always pumped up and excited about a breaking story. He was then transferring to Detroit from London, which is not exactly the kind of move that most correspondents would want. I didn't know what happened until later, when he told me this story.

When Bill was London bureau chief, Rod Beaton, the president of the company, wanted to fire someone in the bureau on the business side of the house, meaning a salesman. But he wanted it to look like it was a resignation or something other than a hatchet job. So he ordered up a farewell party for the individual and flew to London for it. Incredibly, he decided that he wanted to give the departing person a set of knives as a parting gift. But he had time to physically procure only one of them. The rest of the set was en route. This was long before Amazon.

The party was a noisy affair, with lots of different conversations going on, when Beaton suddenly made the presentation of the single knife to the fired employee.

At that precise instant, all the noise abated, and Bill blurted out, "And the rest of them are sticking out of your back."

Everyone heard it, of course, including Beaton. And that's how Bill Bell ended up in Detroit.

Flash forward to 1975. I think Bill helped trigger my audacious decision to write a letter to my lords and masters in New York on Aug. 18, 1975. "My objective," I announced grandly, "is to be a foreign correspondent. I speak French and would welcome the opportunity to learn another language if necessary. My primary interest is in the southern half of Africa, an area that I have studied in college … Of course, I'd be delighted to talk about any location from Hong Kong to Stockholm. I am single, highly mobile, and eager to move on." Soon thereafter, Bill wrote in support of my appeal to be transferred to the Cables Desk, which was where all incoming foreign copy arrived for editing and distribution on the American news wires. It was where "wanna-be" correspondents were groomed.

There are many lessons in this story. The news business has always been based on instincts and energy more than on one's grade point average in college. The senior people in UPI were watching me and testing me and giving me an opportunity to obtain crucial experience. Without me recognizing the pattern, people became mentors. This training and nurturing have largely been wrung out of news organizations today because of the economic and technological calamities that has befallen so many of them.

One day in November 1975, while their eminences in New York were considering my fate, Bill called me in Lansing to say a ship had sunk in Lake Superior during a storm. The nearest city was Sault Ste. Marie (pronounced *Soo-Saint-Marie*) on the remote Upper Peninsula. It would have been a four-hour car drive for me to get there, but that was not good enough. Time meant everything. We knew that a Lansing radio guy, Walt Sorg, had a pilot's license and access to a twin-seat airplane. Bill told me to call Walt, and he agreed to fly me to Sault Ste. Marie for a fee.

I found the headquarters of the rescue effort and checked into the nearest motel. I'm not aware that any other journalist actually went to Sault Ste. Marie to "get the dateline," as we called it. The same story could have been written from Detroit or Cleveland on the basis of telephone calls, but to get the dateline, a news organization had to put a person on location.

Using a landline phone and calling long distance, I phoned in mere tidbits to Bill Bell, because there was not much to discover. The 729-foot *Edmund Fitzgerald*, carrying iron ore pellets from Wisconsin, had simply disappeared. All twenty-nine crew members were missing and presumed dead. Search and rescue guys came in with oil-soaked oars, life preservers, and other minor paraphernalia, but no one could offer any explanation as to what happened. The Great Lakes can be more dangerous than the world's oceans. They are not as deep, and that means waves can be more destructive.

I couldn't see what Bill was writing on the basis of my fragmentary reporting—this was way before the advent of mobile phones or mobile computing—but he obviously hit it hard. It wasn't until decades later that, on the basis of an Internet search, I saw that *The New York Times* ran a UPI story on the sinking with the Sault Ste. Marie dateline on Nov. 11, 1975. There was no byline on it, but it must have been my story, because I was the only UPI person on the ground. It was a big deal to get a UPI story into *The Times*, because they tended to prefer the AP. *Newsweek* picked up the story, and Gordon Lightfoot made it the subject of a hit song in 1976, "The Wreck of The Edmund Fitzgerald." Much later, investigators concluded that the ship must have split in the middle and that both the front and rear sections plunged straight to the bottom.

My coverage of the sinking could have been what sealed my transfer to New York. I was being launched, it turns out, after a short lifetime of being prepared—of being "weaponized," in modern parlance. It wasn't until years later, as a result of my work with the Overseas Press Club Foundation, which discovers and launches young correspondents, that I realized I fit the profile so many correspondents do—they've lived in multiple places, have been exposed to other languages, show keen curiosity, and are willing to go nearly anywhere at the drop of a hat.

2   The Big Apple Opens the Wide World

I transferred to New York in January 1976 not knowing a soul in the Big Apple. I soon realized I was at the heart of an enormous real-time information collection and distribution system, foreshadowing today's Internet. I had enjoyed a preview of the power of this machine in Lansing. But now, here in New York, foreign news arrived from all over the world, and news from America went everywhere else. Computers had only recently been introduced. We had global connections and global power, which was intoxicating. It was a 24/7 operation, long before that became a widely used phrase. UPI headquarters was in the old Daily News Building at 220 West 42nd Street, where the big globe in the lobby served as a backdrop for the *Superman* television series.

"Steve" is what everyone called Editor-in-Chief H.L. Stevenson. His real name was Hubert Lamar Stevenson, but he hated those two names, and no one dared call him anything other than Steve or H.L. Steve, a hard-driving southerner, seemed to be a god.

Stevenson enforced a strict code of conduct on the wires. No angry or overly emotional messages were allowed. If someone in a distant bureau made us angry, we could write an angry message if that made us feel better—but "Never hit the 'send' button," we were told. It was still a world of "cables," meaning telexes that would print out line by line and pour in. They also would show up in our computers, which was a new innovation for the company and the industry. That made it much easier to edit copy. It was the first time I ever worked with computers aside from a computer programming course in college. We needed big air-conditioned rooms with technicians to keep the computers operating.

There was a system of desks to manage all the flow of information. There was a "slot" person on each desk, meaning the person who made the ultimate decisions for that desk. Editors sitting around the rim of the desk would do the actual editing, but then the slot would read and approve the story before distributing it to the next desk, depending on what the ultimate destination was.

Technology Notes:

Traveling was more difficult back in the day. You might have to go to an actual airline office to purchase a ticket. You also could send a messenger. Or else you could get your travel agent to obtain the paper ticket and mail it to you. There used to be lots of travel agents; they survived by taking a percentage of the travel costs, but that industry has retreated dramatically. I think only high-end travelers looking for special experiences use travel agents these days. Everyone else does it online.

Banking also has been transformed. When I first moved to New York, we had to take our physical paychecks downstairs to a bank and deposit them. We could get cash only from a bank teller after standing in line. Citibank introduced its first ATMs while I was living in New York. Think how many bank tellers have lost jobs as a result of the ATM phenomenon.

Because there were so few ATMS, and even fewer internationally, if you wanted to travel you needed to buy traveler's checks from American Express or a bank. You wanted to avoid carrying hundreds of dollars of cash, so the checks could be cashed at most banks outside the United States. These checks now have largely disappeared.

You had to have a physical checkbook with checks to pay your bills, and you had to actually balance your check-book—meaning adding up deposits and then subtracting checks you had written. It was the only way to know how much money was in your account.

If you wanted to know what temperature it was when you woke up in the morning, you had to buy a thermometer and hang it up just outside a window. You could not consult your smartphone. The same for seeing in the dark—you needed a separate device called a flashlight.

End Technology Notes

***

As I had learned in Lansing, some important stories were marked "urgent." A certain number of bells would ring at the machines that newspaper editors monitored for our stories. A "bulletin" was just one sentence and was even more urgent than an urgent. After marking a story as urgent or as a bulletin, correspondents and editors would race to add to details in "adds." Then would come a "1stld-writethru" ("writethru" being shorthand for "write through"), meaning we would add up all the existing details and add new details in perhaps a smoother writing job, which is what a "first lead" or 1stld was. A "2ndld-writethru" might follow. The chase was thrilling.

At first I worked days and was assigned to the New York International Desk, or NXI. NXI decided what news from America would go to the rest of the world. Daytime hours were highly caffeinated, and the big room buzzed with energy. NXI was seen as a less prestigious desk than New York Cables, but I was transferred there after a few months. We decided what to present to the American public, via the General Desk, which controlled the A wire, the dominant domestic wire.

There was a separate Latin American Desk (called LATAM), which handled copy in Spanish going to and from points south of the border. There was a New York Local Desk, a business news department, a photo department, and a radio operation. UPI, owned by Scripps Howard, was way ahead of its time in creating all the elements of a modern media organization. (Little did we know that Scripps Howard would one day sell us because we did not make enough money.)

Critically important was that there were experienced humans at each choke point in the news flow. Each desk, in view of their experience, made decisions on the basis of what they concluded would be most appealing to their different audiences. Most of these "gatekeepers" had much more experience than I did. We also had standards of coverage. We always wanted two sources to confirm a story when the veracity of information was in doubt. If we made an error, we put out a correction. There was accountability.

No higher authority told us what stories to distribute or how. The system of "logs" was the only criteria for deciding in retrospect whether we had made the right judgments. Every day bureaus throughout the United States would send messages to New York with their accounting of what stories from the wire services ran in their local newspapers. The Los Angeles Bureau, for example, would write: "Sinking of cruise liner, 1; Bangladesh ferry disaster, 2." 1 meant UPI and 2 meant AP, which we called "Rox"—as if the nickname somehow concealed the identity of which organization we were talking about. The Houston and Chicago bureaus and others would do the same, and so forth. Someone on the relevant desks in New York would add up the numbers, so we would know that we beat Rox 15-2 on the cruise liner but lost 0-17 on the Bangladeshi ferry disaster.

One other thing I learned from Stevenson was that the culture of the people using a network was just as important as the physical network itself. Through his hiring decisions, he created a mix of third-country nationals (Brits, mostly, and representatives of their former colonies, such as South Africans and Australians) and young, eager people from middle and southern America, like me. There were very few Ivy Leaguers at the time. All of us "Unipressers" were highly motivated, and we had an underdog mentality against the establishment—particularly against the AP. We were a tribe. There were intramural squabbles and personal animosities, to be sure, but in general we trusted each other.

Today, there is very little filter between Americans and the flood of information that comes their way via Facebook, Instagram (which Facebook owns), or Google or Twitter or LinkedIn (which Microsoft owns). These platforms have made enormous sums of money by presenting free, user-generated "content" that has not gone through any genuine type of vetting process. Facebook says it has algorithms that do the work, and they have hired some human monitors, but that system has not truly worked, as demonstrated in Washington in January.

* * *

Sidebar:
THE THIRD WORLD DEBT CRISIS

One of the things I loved doing on the Cables Desk was looking for patterns in the news flow that not everybody else could see. Call it early machine learning or a pattern recognition algorithm.

When I spotted an interesting pattern, I would do what we called a "roundup." Roundups were elective. They were not included in the job description of spending X number of hours editing copy. Not many other people did them. But I enjoyed the power of asking different bureaus to give me reporting on a certain subject, and then I would add it up in combination with my own reporting. It sounded really good to say, "Most analysts contacted in a worldwide survey by United Press International concluded [this or that]."

One of the most spectacular wins for me was the Third World debt crisis, which I, in effect, created at the age of 25.

I did a roundup on lending by Western banks to Third World nations. The top of the story read: "The West's top political and financial leaders are voicing concern that major banks have jeopardized their stability by lending too much money to financially troubled and politically unstable nations."

To my great surprise, *The Washington Post* picked up the story on March 13, 1977, under an equally benign headline: "Concern is Voiced Over Global Lending." Presto! The Third World debt crisis was born. It never really went away. Today one hears about "emerging market debt," particularly in reference to Latin America.

I didn't do the roundups to win brownie points and win the transfer to a foreign post. I was genuinely fascinated by how easy it was for me to get the knowledge I wanted. I did roundups on arms sales in the Middle East and on Soviet aspirations to find a warm weather port and hence access to Persian Gulf oil—things I knew very little about. I wrote about climate change and international trade. The key was asking the right questions of the right people.

End Sidebar

***

I started on the Cables overnight, a surreal world in many ways, because I started as the third person, the most junior, arriving at 1 a.m. and working until 8:30 a.m. The second slot started at 10:30 p.m. and got off at 6 a.m. The overnight Cables editor started at 9 p.m. and got off at 4:30 a.m. Altogether, there were three of us on the overnight NX CBLS shift. The logic was that the lead editor needed more time to figure out what stories to schedule for that news cycle, so he or she arrived at 9 p.m. The others arrived in time to actually edit the stories and handle the avalanche of news that started to break at around 4 a.m. or 5 a.m., which was the middle of the day in Europe and the end of the day in Asia.

One exciting character was Mike Keats, who was Beirut bureau chief, and who would later play a big role in my life. A complex war was raging in Lebanon between the Christians and Muslims. Beirut was divided into two camps with a so-called Green Line with checkpoints running through it. Keats would call in frequently at 4 or 5 a.m. New York time with updates on the fighting. He would have to cross the Green Line. "I told them I was the bloody Australian ambassador," he said one morning, obviously irritated. "And they still shot out my tires."

Another dominant figure was Walter Logan, the foreign editor. Walter's stories about covering World War II in Asia were fascinating. At one point when the British and Americans were supporting Chiang Kai-shek in Chongqing (formerly romanized as Chungking) as Chiang's Nationalists fought the Communists, the only way to get military assistance and other supplies to him was to fly over the Himalayas from India. That was called "flying the Hump," which Walter did. He got drunk in the caves of remote China with Chou En-lai (now spelled Zhou Enlai), one of the most internationally experienced Communist leaders. Walter once got into a poker session in a Shanghai hotel room on the Bund with American military men and won a Navy cruiser parked below in the Huangpu River, although he never took possession. He never filed an expense account in four years of covering the war because of his ability to make money on the side. "I was a hustler," he confided years later before he died.

All around me in New York, I found fascinating things to explore. I heard about Tibetan Buddhist lamas who had come from India, where the Tibetans fled after the Chinese invaded their territory in the 1950s. They were attempting to spread their religion among young Americans and to seek support against the Chinese Communists. I went to listen to them talk about how it was important to memorize detailed images of various gods, which would have required hours to actually do. I decided Tibetan Buddhism was not practical in a modern, Western lifestyle. But I wrote a story about the lamas, as the Tibetan religious leaders were called, and it was printed widely.

Socially, I was set up on a blind date with Cathy Fox through my French teacher. After I got off the overnight at 8:30 a.m., I would go to the home of Madame Leibaud and practice speaking French. Ever the optimist, I wanted to be ready for the transfer to Paris! An avid matchmaker, Madame Leibaud called Cathy's mother to see whether Cathy would meet a man who was not Jewish. Cathy spoke French, had lived in France and Switzerland for a year, and had written her college thesis on Simone de Beauvoir, who was Jean-Paul Sartre's companion. The introduction was made. One thing led to another, as they say, and we moved in together in 1977.

That did not stop my explorations. We traveled together to Haiti on holiday, and I wrote freelance stories about Baby Doc Duvalier taking power in Haiti after the death of his father.

But the biggest source of learning was probably the job. The big game was the Cold War between the Americans and Soviets, as they were called at the time. Pretty much the whole world was divided between US and Soviet spheres of influence and power. Many lives were being lost in this global game of chess, and it was fascinating to observe it playing out globally. The superpower confrontation was particularly acute in Africa after the retreat by European colonial powers. One example was the civil war in Angola. The Americans backed the National Union for the Total Independence of Angola (UNITA) while the Soviets, Cubans, and their allies supported the People's Movement for the Liberation of Angola (MPLA). Everywhere around the world, conflicts were put in the context of the Americans against the Soviets.

About a year after arriving in New York, in 1977, I was promoted to be in charge of the NX CBLS overnight shift, going in at 9 p.m. I suddenly had real power inside this global communications network. I was struck by the story of a young black man, Steven Biko, being beaten to death by South African security forces in August of that year. Our guys in Johannesburg had written a small story about it, but it struck a chord with me. I had a sense of moral outrage. I saw it through the prism of race relations in the United States. So whenever there were developments in the story, I would lead the "sked" (i.e., schedule) with it, meaning I put it at the top of the foreign news report for afternoon newspapers (which still existed). Editors of both morning and afternoon papers liked the Biko story and printed it. I was winning in the logs, which was the only criteria for success. No higher-up told me to promote the Biko story, nor did anyone question my judgment.

Time passed. There had been no offer of a foreign posting. I grew restless. I was living with Cathy, and it was a serious, deep relationship. I didn't want to walk away from it, but I wanted action.

So in September 1978, I sweet-talked the South African consulate into giving me a visa to go to South Africa. I thought the stories in that part of the world were the most exciting. A UPI buddy, Ken Englade, agreed to put me up in his home in the posh, verdant suburb of Sandton and let me use his VW Beetle to get around. (It was tricky because the South Africans drove on the British side of the road, meaning the opposite side of where Americans drive. The manual gear shift was to the left of the driver's seat, which took some getting used to.) Sandton was a scene of complete racial segregation: maids, gardeners, and house servants were all African or colored. Busses were completely segregated. I tried riding a non-white bus. They let me on, but it was profoundly uncomfortable.

The clear analogy, at this point in my trip, was the Deep South in the era of slavery and then segregation. I wondered how the Afrikaners had held on so long. (The Afrikaners were descendants of the Boers, the people from Holland who conquered the area. Other whites were either English or Jewish, and they did not particularly like the Afrikaners.)

Then I rented a car and started driving around the country. I drove through Kruger National Park and saw many wild animals, passed by the border crossing to Mozambique and entered Swaziland, which is where the Swazi tribe lives. It is surrounded on all sides by South Africa and Mozambique but is a separate country. Britain granted it independence in 1968, and it had its own king, Sobhuza II, the "lion" of Swaziland.

I thought I had arrived on a different planet when I stopped for gas and went into a kind of a mini-market. The people were speaking a click language, the likes of which I had never heard or even imagined. I had studied a few languages, and there was nothing I could recognize.

The next day, I drove to Durban, a larger city back in South Africa on the Indian Ocean. There I had made contact with an older English couple, Manny and Rosemary Ladlau, who would extend courtesies. (I was introduced through the UPI bureau in Joburg.) Here I realized I was in a very different racial setting. The locals were all members of the Zulu tribe, who were known for their ferocious warmaking capabilities. They also had their own king.

The Ladlaus had a beautiful home, a veritable mansion, with a swimming pool and a guest cottage for me. Mr. Ladlau had 850 acres of land, 700 of them planted in sugar cane. The soil was very rich, and the area received abundant rainfall and sunshine.

The racial dynamics were very different in Durban than in Joburg because of the presence of about 1 million

Indians, whose ancestors were brought from India by the British. (Mahatma Gandhi spent part of his youth in South Africa.) Mr. Ladlau had 100 Zulus doing the tough work of tending and cutting the sugar cane, but his top men were Indians. They had separate living quarters, and there were clearly tensions between the two groups. Mr. Ladlau told me that when the Zulus in the area rioted, as they did from time to time, they would go for the Indians first. "They're in a hell of a spot," he said.

From Durban, I flew to Cape Town and stayed with yet another older couple I had been introduced to. Cape Town, on the southern tip of South Africa, was near the Cape of Good Hope, and its Tabletop Mountain offered sweeping views of the ocean at the very bottom of the African continent. Here the local people were the Xhosas, and they also spoke a click language; they could not communicate with the Zulus unless both parties spoke English. There was a strong Malay presence, again because of the British, and I heard the muezzin cry (the call to worship) from a mosque for the first time. The Malays played a similar role to that of the Indians in Durban; they managed the African laborers.

By traveling a bit, I had developed a much more complex picture of South Africa, one that was not defined entirely by white versus black. Joburg was the major city with the sharpest black/white divide, and it was also the home of the largest colored population, mostly in Soweto, a kind of ghetto located outside of Joburg. These were people whose ancestors had intermarried at some point. The pure Africans did not accept them, nor did the various whites. They were another piece of what was actually a highly complex mosaic of races.

The truth on the ground is always more complex than when surveyed from afar. That was what we call "ground truth" today, and it is under assault as news organizations have retreated. Throughout history, Americans consistently make the mistake of trying to interpret events in faraway lands through the prism of their own cultural or political context. Editors sitting behind computers in New York or Washington try to explain events without ever having set foot in the country they are writing about. My trip to South Africa was the first time I ever experienced that disconnect.

In Joburg, before I had started my travels to Durban and Cape Town, I had been in touch with Alistair Sparks, editor of *The Rand Daily Mail*, which was an English-language newspaper, as opposed to the dominant Boer language newspapers. (*The Rand Daily Mail* has since disappeared.) I was looking for a job. Sparks agreed to give me a tryout when I returned from my travels and assigned me to a reporter named Richard Walker.

Richard and I learned one morning that Nthato Motlana, a prominent surgeon from Soweto, was going to give a talk that evening at the University of Witwatersrand. He was a leading critic of apartheid, and I discovered much later that he had been friends with Nelson Mandela. Richard and I decided to cover it. But that afternoon the government banned him, meaning no one could come within a certain distance of him, and he couldn't be quoted. To an American, the power to simply ban someone was Orwellian, but it was standard practice under apartheid.

Richard and I decided to go to the university anyway to see what would happen. We stood on the edge of the campus. Sure enough, Motlana approached the campus and stayed within the technical rules of being banned. He kept everyone in his entourage at the required distance. He walked up to the edge of the campus and handed his speech to the school's chancellor. Then he walked away, with his right fist in the air. It was a dramatic statement of defiance.

The next morning, I was all gung ho to help write a story about how Motlana, being banned by the government, nevertheless walked to the edge of the campus and made a dramatic gesture of defiance.

But Richard consulted with *The Rand Daily Mail*'s lawyers and broke the news to me. Under the ban the government had declared, we could not write about the incident at all without the newspaper being fined or penalized. It was a stark lesson. Alistair Sparks did offer me a job on the night desk, so now I was truly torn. I had discovered that working for *The Rand Daily Mail* or any other South African news outlet was going to be an exercise in frustration. It would be much better, I told myself, to work for a foreign organization like UPI. I told Alistair I would think about it and let him know. I flew the seventeen hours back to New York.

On an intellectual level, what I had learned in South Africa was that it was fantastically more complex than a mere white-black confrontation. On a personal level, I was in a real dilemma. I told Cathy I had the job offer. I went sideways for a while. It was agonizing. I asked Cathy to marry me, and we scheduled a wedding for January 22, 1979. It wasn't clear what Cathy and I would do after we were married, or where we might go.

***

Sidebar:
THE SELECTION OF POPE JOHN PAUL II
It was October 1978, and I was working the overnight. We were gearing up for the naming of a new pope. Pope John Paul I had died, and the cardinals were meeting to select his successor. Jack Payton was Rome bureau chief and a veteran of watching for the white smoke to come up out of the building where the cardinals were meeting. That was the signal that they had made a choice.

This was going to be one of the most competitive stories between UPI and AP. It would be a "flash" that went around the world. It wouldn't be a bulletin or an urgent that was sent out by the General Desk. Whoever took the call on the Cables Desk would hit the button, and it would go around the world. We had prepared a dozen biographies of the key candidates so that when news broke, we would be able to pump out background about the new pope.

One night, about 6 a.m., we got word from Jack Payton that the white smoke was going up. It was October 16, 1978. I could have gone home after my shift ended at 4:30 a.m., but it was exciting to see how this was going to play out. The day shift guys started to arrive at 6:30 a.m. It must have been 8 a.m. when the call from Jack Payton came in. He was going to call in the news because it was faster than transmitting it by cable.

The old timers knew how dangerous this was. If the editor handling the call made a mistake and sent out an errant flash around the world, UPI would be humiliated and the editor in question would face dire career consequences. The older guys had pensions to protect, retirements to look forward to. They needed a sucker. They had me. They gently coaxed me into position to take the call.

I didn't understand any of the dangers. Besides, we had all twelve biographies ready to go with all the right spellings and background details.

I got on the phone with Jack. It was a bad connection. He said, "The new pope is Karol Wojtyla."

I looked at all the biographies—and that name wasn't there.

"How do you spell that?" I asked. The older guys hovering over my shoulder must have been crapping their pants.

Getting Karol spelled right was relatively easy. But the last name was a killer. I had never come across anything quite like it. W-O-J-T-Y-L-A. I went through it with Jack at least two times. Then I wrote "New pope is Karol Wojtyla." I hit the button and those five words went around the world. He took the name Pope John Paul II.

I got it right. After having been up all night and being in serious need of sleep, somehow my youthful adrenaline and raw ambition had saved me from perdition. Maybe this was part of the explanation for how I got the call to go abroad just a month later. I was a junkie. And I never forgot how to spell W-O-J-T-Y-L-A.

End Sidebar

***

One day in November, H.L. Stevenson called me on my landline in our apartment on 19th Street. It was about 4:30 p.m., and I had just awakened in preparation for going to work that night. The wedding invitations arrived that day in the mail. Steve said, "Bill, we need you in Hong Kong."

I was elated, of course, and called Cathy at her office where she worked for a literary agent. "Guess what?" I said excitedly. "We're moving to Hong Kong." We advanced the wedding date to January 6 and got on the plane to Hong Kong on January 22, our original wedding date.

Decades later, after we had raised two children, I made the startling discovery that Cathy had told Walter Logan, with whom we socialized, about my job offer in South Africa. UPI knew! She may have forced their hand.

Recalling this crucial period in our lives, she asked me, "What would you have done if I said I wasn't going to Hong Kong with you?"

"I would have gone anyway," I said truthfully.

"I know," she replied.

3   Stumbling Into China's Modernization

It was a moment of truly historic proportions. The United States and China, archenemies who had fought a bitter war on the Korean Peninsula and a kind of proxy war in Vietnam, were going to open their doors to each other. After Jimmy Carter and Deng Xiaoping announced the normalization of relations in late 1978, my bosses at United Press International knew they were going to need more correspondents on the ground in the region, which is what triggered Stevenson's call to me. The older, more experienced correspondents, Bob Crabbe and Aline Mosby, got the plum assignments of going into Beijing (still called Peking at the time) to open a bureau and start covering what seemed like one of the world's great stories. Everyone assumed that awards would be won. Maybe even Pulitzers.

I was going to Hong Kong to assume a more modest role. I was going to be deputy Asia editor, supporting Mike Keats, who had transferred from Beirut to become editor for all of Asia. I would help run a desk of about a dozen young editors who handled copy from all over the region and fed it into the global news wires. Other pieces of my job were to cover southern China and to "parachute" in on big breaking news stories in the region.

Mike and Bill Bell had covered stories together in Africa and had been good buddies for decades. I like to think that Bill put in a good word for me, because Mike was pre-disposed to like me and believe in me. This was the power of a mentoring network.

Cathy and I found a small apartment, and I could walk to the UPI office through a district called Wan Chai, made famous by the myths surrounding prostitute Suzie Wong. This was a very authentic Chinese area, where I could smell the odors of fruits and vegetables I couldn't identify and hear mah-jongg tiles being played within the apartments overhead. In the cooler days of February, merchants would sell snakes, because snake soup was supposed to help you feel warmer. The merchant would hold one end of a snake in his left hand and step on the other end of the snake on the ground. Then he would use a knife in his right hand to slit open the entire length of the snake.

The British colony consisted of the very rugged Victoria Island, where most foreigners lived, but going north onto the mainland, the colony also included two districts called the Kowloon Peninsula and the New Territories. The British had seized all these slivers of land from the Chinese at a time of Chinese weakness in the 1840s. There was no love lost between the two sides as a result. To this day, Chinese students learn how that was the beginning of their "century of humiliation" at the hands of foreigners.

The debate in those early days of China's opening was whether the Chinese could modernize themselves economically. After all, they had been consumed by class struggle. "Seize Class Struggle As the Key Link" had been one of their slogans. It meant that they defined their most important objective as eradicating the former elites, meaning landowners, intellectuals, and others whom they perceived as having betrayed the common Chinese people. Perhaps ten million people had been killed during the Cultural Revolution of 1966–1976, which ended only three years before my arrival.

The first time I saw China was at the Hong Kong border. Looking out from the New Territories in the north across a heavily fortified border (fortified to keep desperately poor Chinese from sneaking into Hong Kong), I could see an area called Shum Chun (in the local Cantonese language) or Shenzhen (in the national language, Mandarin). For as far as the eye could see, barefoot Hakka girls in their distinctive conical hats (the Hakkas were a distinctive ethnic group in China, sort of like the gypsies in Europe) were using switch sticks to get their water buffalo to walk down dirt paths between rice paddies. That's all that existed in the part of Shenzhen I could see—endless green rice paddies.

This was going to be one of four Special Economic Zones (SEZs) where the Chinese would start experimenting with capitalism, or at least their version of it, and seek to lure in foreign investment. The Chinese have a long history of using their southern regions as places to experiment. If an idea went bad, it could be cut off and eliminated without "infecting" the rest of the country. If it worked, it could be replicated elsewhere.

Until the experiment with modernization started, the central government and its various ministries—all controlled by the Communist Party—made the vast majority of economic decisions. Each ministry was like a god. If a ministry told a state-owned industry to make 500,000 black shoes, that's what the factories did, whether the Chinese people wanted those black shoes or not. Indeed, walking through state-owned department stores in Canton, I could see that the Chinese were not really interested in many of the things on sale. But no private sector economic activity had bveen allowed.

I began to get a sense of the sheer pressures of population. Most Americans have never experienced the presence of so many people in confined spaces unless they've gone Christmas shopping at Bloomingdale's in New York in the pre-COVID era. You could feel the immense human power in a train station as several thousand peasants lugging their possessions on their shoulders charged off a train. I began to think that if that incredible concentration of human power could be focused on getting rich, as Deng had urged, it just might work.

One experience helped convince me it just might work, and ironically, I never wrote about it for UPI. It was only later that I understood the significance. I went to one of the SEZs in Zhuhai, also in Guangdong Province. The locals had decided that they wanted to build a port. The only problem was that a mountain of about a couple of thousand feet was in the way. The southern coast of China is very rugged physically. Without a single piece of power equipment, the Chinese were taking the mountain down. They had guys at the top with picks and shovels and then a system of wheelbarrow operators who would go up and down the mountain on trails that had been cut for them. It was a beehive of activity. The Chinese knew that if they threw enough people at the job and worked on it for long enough, they would prevail.

This was meaningful on at least a couple of levels. If the Chinese could agree on their objectives and focus their human power on them, they would be able to achieve a great deal economically. I was becoming a student of how people organize themselves. On another level, I began to understand how the Chinese thought: Americans would want Caterpillars to knock the mountain down in weeks or months. We would want quick gratification. But the Chinese knew they had strength in numbers. And they also had long-term horizons. Mao Tse-tung (now spelled Mao Zedong) once said the Chinese people could wait for 10,000 years.

Canton, which the Chinese soon renamed Guangzhou, to reflect what they traditionally had called it—not what missionaries and colonists had called it—was about a two-hour train ride north of Hong Kong, mostly through rice paddies and villages. I stayed in the cavernous, Soviet-built Dongfang Hotel and covered the Canton Trade Fair, which had been one of the only consistent points of contact between China and the outside world for decades. China had been almost completely sealed off.

At the trade fair, the Chinese offered goods to foreigners, but few were particularly sophisticated or attractive to Westerners. We had a much higher technological standard. Perhaps more important to me was wandering the streets to get a glimpse of how the Chinese were living. Everyone—men and women—wore

Mao suits, either light green or dark blue. The women had no cosmetics or high heels. Everyone looked pretty much alike as they rode their bicycles through the streets. There were no private cars. At night the streets were dark, because there were no streetlights. It was haunting to witness thousands of bicyclists making their way through the dark streets, almost as if they were ghosts.

I had many encounters in which I would attract crowds of Chinese just to look at me. Many had never seen a white man before. I sported a beard at that time, which was also novel to the southern Chinese (who have very little facial hair), and I had a camera, watch, nice shoes, pens, and all the things you would expect an American correspondent to have. I was not exactly a style maven, but I had a pair of light blue jeans that had a pocket for pens just above the knee. I often kept a pen there. Imagine the incredulity the Chinese felt in staring at me, a white man with a beard and a pen on his knee!

I just kept writing about what I saw. "Slowly, almost imperceptibly, China's new modernization policy is changing the lives of the shop owner, housewife, and taxi driver," I wrote in one story. Let me quote a chunk of that story, because it is revealing:

"A walking tour of downtown Canton one bright Sunday morning," I wrote, "shows how China's march to modernization is lifting the straight jacket of nearly 30 years of Maoism.

"The foreigner finds crowds of Chinese gawking at billboards advertising movies featuring kung-fu style violence and Western love stories—hardly the stuff of class struggle.

"Turning right on Chiehfang Road, the stroller finds a bustling shopping and residential area. Youths wearing blue jeans and open-necked shirts with gold pendants hanging on their hairless chests congregate on some corners, smoking cigarettes. One sports a red-and-white travel bag emblazoned 'Marlboro.'"

Shopkeepers all had abacuses, and their fingers would fly over the beads to add up how much someone owed.

Until this time, most China-watchers had been stuck in Hong Kong and could only make guesses about what was happening in China on the basis of the official Chinese media. At the UPI office in Hong Kong, we had a service called Foreign Broadcast Information Services, where the US government monitored local Chinese radio stations and translated their programming into English. Travel by Western reporters had been virtually impossible or tightly restricted until China decided to open its doors.

Thus, through some fluke of history, I was one of the first Western journalists to actually be on the ground in the place that was most important to China's early modernization efforts. In one dispatch, I wrote, "The central preoccupation of the man in Canton's streets is not socialist class struggle; it is the acquisition of watches, televisions and other luxuries."

For my coverage, I won the Overseas Press Club award for best economic reporting from abroad. I had simply reported on what my eyes saw—and what could not be seen by my older and wiser colleagues in Beijing, where very little changed for a decade or more. (That award is what started my decades of involvement with the OPC and OPC Foundation.)

China's opening was a key moment in the process called globalization. You could say that globalization started after World War II, because the Americans wanted to cement the Europeans and Japanese into a trading order that would guarantee a measure of stability. Hence the Marshall Plan. Richard Nixon and Henry Kissinger had started the process of normalizing relations with China to deprive the Soviet Union of a key ally. Carter, a Democrat, had actually signed the deal. But Ronald Reagan took over in January 1981 and proclaimed that it was time to open our borders even more broadly and to allow and encourage our businesses to go global. Globalization was not a Republican plot or a Democratic plot. There was bipartisan political accord, and certainly large businesses and many leading economic thinkers supported it.

The assumption was that it would continue to undermine the Soviet Union, which it ultimately did, and that Americans who were displaced by waves of imports coming in from China and other low-cost locations would be reabsorbed into other jobs and other industries. This was a key (and it turned out to be flawed) assumption. We never demonstrated the political will or wisdom to organize our educational institutions to provide the training and retraining that would be necessary, which is why so many Americans have been left behind.

There were other critical assumptions about China. In this general time frame, we believed that the Chinese people would demand greater political power as they gained wealth and became more middle class. We allowed ourselves to believe that the Communist Party would tolerate some level of "civil society" at the local level. Dissidents started popping up and lawyers got training, and there were signs that the party would tolerate that. This was the "peaceful evolution" theory. The Chinese system would evolve over a long period of time toward a more Western-style system, and the Communist Party would gradually be marginalized. State-owned enterprises would be gradually replaced by private sector companies. Wouldn't all that be only natural?

We also assumed that China would be a "responsible stakeholder" in the world order we had created with our European and Japanese allies. Like the Christian missionaries before us, we assumed our values were superior and would prevail.

***

What a crash course I received about how the world operated! In June 1979, Keats and I flew to Tokyo to coordinate coverage of the G7 economic summit. I covered the news conference where President Carter, German Chancellor Helmut Schmidt, French President Valéry Giscard d'Estaing, British

Prime Minister Margaret Thatcher, and the leaders of Japan, Italy, and Canada spoke about their wish that the Organization of Petroleum Exporting Countries not increase oil prices any further. OPEC was still very powerful.

Being in Tokyo started a lifelong engagement in Japanese issues. Tokyo's sophistication was head and shoulders above anything I had seen in China. Keats and I joked that the Japanese were a nation of extremists. They had such tight security that I couldn't jog anywhere from my hotel because policemen would intercept me about every ten yards. They shut down expressways and highways for security reasons. Guards inspected the undercarriage of buses going to the airport using long poles with mirrors on the end to spot any bombs. I had never witnessed such extreme security.

Back in Hong Kong, I spent a fair amount of time covering the Vietnamese boat people exodus. The Vietnam War had ended in 1975, but there were still a lot of Vietnamese who may have been affiliated with the Americans or French and who wanted to—or needed to—get out of Vietnam. To take advantage of them, ethnic Chinese triads, or gangs, purchased old freighters and other vessels on their last legs. In exchange for gold, they loaded up Vietnamese refugees at a place called Vung Tau, on the coast south of the former Saigon, now named Ho Chi Minh City. The ships would head to Hong Kong on the assumption that Hong Kong, being British-controlled, would provide some shelter and assistance in relocation. But the Chinese captains often abandoned the ships and there was often not enough food. I would get calls early in the morning from the Brits at the Government Information Service telling me another boat had been found and was being towed in. I'd go to see. I never boarded, but I heard that older people had died. In one particularly gruesome incident, the boat people had run out of water and started to drink sea water to survive. That killed many of them.

The Brits put the Vietnamese in refugee camps while they awaited resettlement, mostly to the United States. The British and their Hong Kong Chinese government didn't want the Vietnamese to try to become absorbed into Hong Kong's population, in part because the colony was already crowded. Conditions in the camps were better than on the boats, but still fairly grim.

Then the Vietnamese government began cracking down on its ethnic Chinese citizens (there are ethnic Chinese living throughout Southeast Asia, and it is a constant issue for all those countries.) It also started cracking down on Roman Catholics, who adopted the religion under French control of Vietnam. Rice rations were cut. Thousands of these targets were kicked out of their homes and were therefore homeless in the streets. "If a lamp post had feet to move, it, too, would want to leave Vietnam," I quoted one 37-year-old woman as saying.

I knew my way around the camps, and one day the author Joan Didion and her husband came to Hong Kong. They found me through Cathy's publishing connections, and I gave them a tour. I remember the expression on her face as we saw an old Vietnamese woman cut the throat of a chicken and drain the blood into a container. It was a vivid scene, and she described it in one of her novels.

In some ways, the Vietnamese boat people exodus set the pattern for the mass migrations we are seeing today: desperate people paying "snakeheads," or middlemen, to put them on vessels, only to be abandoned at sea or left to wash up on remote islands. Then they are re-victimized by being forced to stay for long periods in squalid camps.

4   The Soviet Invasion of Afghanistan

It was in the last week of December 1979. When I emerged from my morning shower, Cathy told me, "Keats just called. Pack a bag. You're going to India tonight. The Soviets have invaded Afghanistan." Neither one of us realized I would be gone for a long time.

It was such an important story because the Soviets were trying to find a way to obtain access to a warm water port and to the oil fields of the Persian Gulf. Americans depended heavily on Middle East oil. A Soviet military presence in Afghanistan might alter the global balance of power—particularly if the Soviets used it as a platform to keep expanding toward the Persian Gulf.

New Delhi was about an eight-hour overnight flight from Hong Kong. As I moved through the streets, I could certainly tell I was no longer in the prim and proper British colony. Cattle and other animals wandered the streets (cattle being considered sacred by Hindus). Piles of cow manure were everywhere. I guess they were sacred too.

I could see and hear from speaking with diplomats and journalists who had lived in Delhi for years that India had a fascinating history and an incredible variety of religions and ethnicities. A visit to the incredibly beautiful Taj Mahal certainly reinforced that largely superficial observation. But I was focused on getting things done and communicating to the rest of the world. India wasn't a place where doing that was easy.

Overall, I spent about ten days trying to get into Afghanistan, moving back and forth from India to Pakistan, as we American journalists tried to figure out a way to get in. The land route through the Khyber Pass was closed. The closest city of any size close to the border was Peshawar, where an InterContinental Hotel was located, so I spent time there.

There were at least two other American correspondents in town, and I spent time with them. Jim Sterba of *The New York Times* and Tyler Marshall of *The Los Angeles Times* were both significantly older and more experienced. Plus they worked for prestigious publications, and I was a lowly wire service guy.

About the only official source of information in Peshawar was Doug Archard, who was the US consul general and almost certainly CIA. He had extensive contacts with different people coming and going across the border and would speak on background, meaning no attribution. He invited the three of us over for New Year's Eve.

Before we went to Archard's home, we had to file our stories at the telex center at the InterContinental. The Pakistani guy who worked there was stoned out on the very powerful hashish that was available in the area and could barely find the keyboard. It was not a problem for me, since I knew how to punch tape. I transmitted my story.

But Sterba and Marshall, who soon arrived, did not know how to punch tape, and they were confronted with an impossible situation. The Pakistani operator would never have been able to transmit their stories. So they asked me to do it for them. I felt like that vaulted me ahead in their estimation of me. I was useful.

The three of us hacks spent New Year's Eve at Archard's home watching a Jane Fonda movie after dinner. We all were so struck by the insanity of the moment—watching Jane Fonda with a CIA guy—that we didn't talk very much. The only joke of the evening was a grim one: "If World War III breaks out, it's going to be right on top of us."

***

I made several trips to the border, where I watched Afghan refugees pour out of their country, marveling at what they looked like. There were some people with red hair, the Afridis, which might have meant they were descendants of the Greeks or the Huns. (Later, in Kabul, my driver would jokingly call me a Nuristani. In the Nuristan region, there were people who looked just like me.)

Some women were almost completely veiled, with only parts of their heavily tattooed faces showing. These people were from a different world. The Pakistani government laid on a helicopter ride for reporters to survey the refugee situation. Thousands of Afghans were camped out in tent cities near the border.

One of the stories we heard in Pakistan was about a journalist traveling in Afghanistan with an Afghan military convoy. The *mujahideen*, or holy warriors, the name we had given to the rebels fighting the Soviets, cut off the convoy on a mountain road, blocking with logs both its forward access and its retreat. They then were able to rake the convoy with their weapons and easily prevailed. They captured the journalist, who they assumed to be a Soviet. The *muj* couldn't tell the difference between English and Russian faces or the languages.

So they marched the journalist up the hill and tied him to a tree, where they were going to disembowel him. He was screaming the entire time—"Journalist" and "Walter Cronkite" and everything he could conceivably think of to communicate to the bearded men that he was an American correspondent. Nothing worked. They were about to carve him up when he finally shouted "BBC."

"Aah," the men said as they stroked their beards and repeated the name, BBC. That did it. They finally understood who he was—and released him.

So once we were allowed to board a flight in New Delhi for Kabul, we all knew of the dangers of being mistaken for a Soviet. The first phrase we learned was, *"Rusee neestum, man Amerikaaee astum."* It meant, "I'm not a Russian. I'm an American." It

was in the Dari language, the Persian derivative that was the closest thing Afghanistan had to a national language.

The bazaar in Kabul was the first one I had ever seen.
Perhaps that's why I made such a serious mistake. I had heard
that the Soviets were having a tough time in the bazaar. I had
reported that some Soviet civilians and troops had gone into
the bazaar and simply disappeared. Others had their throats cut.
Their assailants were never found.

I took a taxi to the bazaar and went in. In retrospect, I find
it amazing that I did this. What was I thinking? The streets were
very narrow and were lined with shops on both sides. The streets
were also muddy, and you had a sense of being in the middle of a
lot of people looking out from behind windows or from between
cracks in the doors. It extended in all directions in a maze largely
unchanged since Kabul was a stop on the Silk Road.

It was late January and early February, so it was cold. Afghan
men wore blankets that they wrapped around their shoulders in
such a way that you could not see what they had in their hands.

After walking into the bazaar for just a few minutes, I
sensed two big Afghan men behind me. Were they following me?
I wasn't sure, but it didn't feel very comfortable, because I could
not see what they had in their hands beneath the blankets they
were wearing. If they whipped open the blankets and had knives
in their hands, I would be a dead man in a hurry. "A Westerner
walking into the bazaar gets penetrating stares from dozens of
hardened faces belonging to merchants selling dried fruit, spices,
nuts, carrots and blackened bananas from the backs of donkeys
or from tiny open-air shops that line the streets," I later wrote.

Then I became aware that people sitting in the dust were
making odd motions of their necks and heads in the general
direction of my feet. They were spitting at me, I realized.

The two men were still behind me. Realizing that I had
foolishly put myself in harm's way, I made a U-turn and got out
of there. They parted to let me pass.

The next day I hired an Afghan guide to take me in. He walked about ten steps ahead of me and told everyone that an American journalist was touring the bazaar. The reception was entirely different. A blacksmith invited me to sit cross-legged on a rug by his anvil and gave me the sweet green tea that the Afghans drank. "Russians no good," he said, through my guide. "Americans our friends. Japanese our friends. But Russians our enemies."

"Russians do not walk here," the blacksmith said. "They come only in tanks."

Another shopkeeper put it this way: "Who's a guerrilla? I'm a guerrilla. Everyone's a guerrilla. The Russians will never know."

So the Soviets were in control of Kabul, but they weren't in control of the bazaar. I wrote about my experience, but I don't think any newspaper editor printed the story. I had risked my neck for nothing. Some of the biggest risks I took did not result in journalistic victories Avoiding death did not make for an interesting read. If I had gotten myself killed, *that* might have made the papers—but, as one cynic later pointed out, there would have been no one to write the story.

Partly because I realized I had made a mistake, I started teaming up with Jim Gallagher of the *Chicago Tribune* and Pepper Martin of *U.S. News & World Report*. I was a wire guy who didn't compete directly against either of them. And a newspaper guy didn't compete against a magazine guy. So we could cooperate. Plus, like Jim Sterba and Tyler Marshall, they were decades older and had much more experience.

Because the Soviets and their lackeys had tried to convince us that there had been no Soviet invasion, many journalists tried to get out of Kabul into the countryside. The three of us decided to go to Jalalabad to see what was happening in that region. It seemed like it would be a day trip, down and back.

Jim, also bolstered by the fact that he spoke Russian because he was based in Moscow, arranged to rent a taxi in Kabul for the two- or three-hour drive. It was an old Mercedes. We started out down on Route A01 through the Kabul Gorge, which is very distinctive with its steep cliffs of rock. There was very little vegetation. Just rocks shooting up on both sides of the valley. The road followed a river down below.

The driver, whose vehicle was accustomed to only short drives around Kabul, had a flat tire, and we had to get out of the car to let him fix it. Standing there, I became aware of feeling my ribs and wondering what it would feel like to have a bullet rip into them. I scanned the rocks above us but couldn't see any signs of movement. The driver fixed the flat and we were got back in.

As we proceeded down through the gorge, we came out into a much flatter plateau. This area represented much greater danger. We could tell it was ambush territory because of the burned out vehicles along the road. In one place there was simply a blackened patch of pavement where a vehicle had burned. We also could see the logs that the *mujahideen* used to block the road.

This area was populated, and we attracted perhaps twenty villagers as the Mercedes suffered a second flat. The villagers all wore their robes in ways that made it impossible to know whether they were armed or not. Gallagher, unfazed, somehow convinced a truck driver to take the three of us into Jalalabad while the driver contended with getting his flat tire fixed.

The town of Jalalabad seemed largely deserted. The Indian government maintained a consulate, and we had lunch with the Indian consul there. He told us that the region was very unsettled, and that the Soviet troops stayed on their own base east of town. The *mujahideen* were in charge after 5 p.m., so it was unsafe to travel back to Kabul if we waited much longer. Naturally eager to avoid running through ambush alley, we found our driver and headed back to Kabul.

But at the last checkpoint before getting on the road itself to Kabul, the driver suffered a third flat. This was unbelievable. It meant we were trapped in Jalalabad.

There was one hotel in Jalalabad, and we retreated there. They had cold Czech beer in the lobby, and it tasted great. The hotel knew it had a problem on its hands, because the *mujahideen* would learn that three white men were at the hotel, and they would come for us in the night, assuming we were Soviets. So the hotel hired their own guys in robes, whom we saw in the lobby as we drank beer. They worked the actions on their Kalashnikovs to make sure that they were ready. This was both alarming and reassuring—alarming because they were preparing for a fight. Reassuring because they were on our side.

Sure enough, during the night, I peered out the window and saw our guards talking to other men about 200 yards away, at the entrance to the hotel parking lot. We all assumed that our guys had explained to the *muj* that we were Americans. It worked.

***

A few days later in Kabul, Jim and I were moving around, checking the traps so to speak. We decided to stop by the American embassy to see what was happening. We knew there would be a press briefing at 2 p.m. for the twenty or so American media types who had descended on Kabul from all directions.

We met the young man who was defense attaché in the lobby. He was pale and looked shaken. What's wrong? He told us that the 10th Motorized Rifle Division of the Soviet Army, with 10,000 men, had been spotted making a move for the Persian Gulf in the southwestern part of Afghanistan, near the Iranian border. This was a worst-case scenario, because it threatened a confrontation between the Americans and the Soviets over control of the Persian Gulf. This could be the start of World War III. We had a one hell of a story on our hands.

We raced back to the hotel and wrote our stories. I wrote the word "Bulletin" at the top of my mine.

The next question was, how could we file our stories? There was one flight out to New Delhi at 4 p.m., so we took a taxi to the airport. People were already gathering to get on the flight. By now it was about 1 p.m. We persuaded one of the passengers to take our stories, in separate hotel envelopes, and hand them to the UPI office assistants who would greet the flight with a big UPI sign when it landed there. There were no telephone or telex links. This was called "pigeoning" a story.

We headed back for the briefing, but we realized we had a competitive problem. What if the other guys were able to pigeon their stories on the same plane?

At the appointed hour, the chargé d'affaires sat down and began telling us what the defense attaché had told Gallagher and myself hours earlier. Everybody knew it was a big story. But Gallagher and I started asking irritating and repetitive questions, drawing it out. We never discussed this as a strategy to prolong the briefing, but once one of us did it, the other understood the game. What was the name of that province again? And what did "motorized" mean? Nobody could leave, because what if we learned something they didn't get? Gallagher and I extended the briefing by fifteen minutes or so, but it was enough. No one else was able to get their stories on that plane.

I learned later that my story was on front pages around the world. This was one of the sweetest scoops of my career. The Associated Press just didn't have the story with the dateline. To make matters worse for them, the next day we were snowed in. It only took a few inches of snow before Kabul airport became impassable. The AP coped by sourcing the information from intelligence sources in Washington. Obviously, satellites had picked up the troop movements. But the AP didn't have the Kabul dateline.

A couple days later, the Afghan government announced that we American journalists were going to be put under house arrest and deported. They took our passports. Several of us filed stories on how we were being put under house arrest, and those stories got out.

The Afghan flunkies did not impose any real controls. We were free to come and go from the InterContinental as we pleased. The bar and restaurant still functioned. Massages were available at the spa in the basement.

Then we got snowed in again and were incommunicado. We were in Kabul for forty-eight hours with the outside world not hearing a word from us. The only negative thing the Afghan government did was put up tables in the lobby. Women working for the government wrote in our passports in the Dari language. We were being expelled for interfering in the internal affairs of a sovereign country. What a laugh. We had interfered in Afghanistan's internal affairs? What about the 80,000 or 100,000 Soviet troops? It was only when I reached New Delhi that I realized the world had been worried about American journalists held incommunicado in Kabul.

The story shifted back to Pakistan, where the world was meeting to try to figure out how to respond to the Soviet invasion. There was an Islamic summit attended by the Saudis and other Arab states. Everyone suddenly wanted to be friends with Pakistani President Mohammad Zia-ul-Haq, whom I chatted with on the sidelines of one of the meetings. He had been seen as a cruel strongman, but now he was seen as the lynchpin to resisting the Soviets.

One of the big stories was the visit of Jimmy Carter's national security adviser Zbigniew Brzezinski. He had been born in Poland and was a fierce critic of the Soviet Union. A number of us went with him one day to a Pakistani military position in a two-story mud outpost near the Afghan border, where we had to climb a series of ladders to get up top. This is where Brzezinski took an AK-47 from one of the soldiers and pointed it toward Afghanistan and hence the Soviets. The photo of him doing that was plastered all over newspapers around the world. It was a gesture of defiance.

What did not make the newspapers was that a number of us, possibly including Brzezinski, could have died that day. There was a heavy machine gun position in another area of the outpost facing toward the border. The machine gun was pointed out of a large window.

When Brzezinski walked in, the Pakistan soldier manning the weapon wanted to impress us by firing off a barrage. He was on his haunches low behind the gun.

As he fired, the recoil started knocking him back into the room while he was still firing. He had lost his balance, but he hadn't taken his finger off the trigger. This could have been seriously bad if the bullets started ricocheting around the room. But fortunately, a couple of other soldiers were able to grab him and stabilize the situation. If they hadn't, the stories that day about Brzezinski could have been very different.

I ended this six-week journey in Karachi, a dark and scary city on the Pakistani coast where Danny Pearl of *The Wall Street Journal* would later be beheaded on video. The Iranian revolution was occurring literally next door, and Americans were being held hostage. I was exhausted, but in a half-hearted way, I suggested on the telex to the UPI office in Hong Kong that I should take the hop to Tehran, a mere five hours away. Someone there was smart enough to recognize that I was finished. This is one of the central hazards of being a correspondent—you get hooked on the juice and don't know how or when to stop.

5 The Philippines: Into The Heart of Mindanao

In February 1981, Pope John Paul II was to visit the Philippines, a devoutly Catholic country because of four centuries of Spanish occupation prior to American and Japanese occupations. This would be my second fateful encounter with His Holiness.

I was going to coordinate the coverage from the UPI office in Manila. Edith Lederer was sent from Hong Kong to do the same thing for the AP. I assume her setup was very similar to mine: I had correspondents or locals at each stop the Pope was going to make. At one university, they had mounted television cameras so I could actually see what was happening there. I had the perfect angle.

When the Pope got to the university, I saw a young man push out from the crowd behind ropes and kneel down and try to kiss the Pope's hands. Security guards wrestled him back. Then the Pope beckoned and the young man was able to kiss his ring.

Almost immediately, I started getting "rockets," or urgent messages, from UPI bureaus in Los Angeles and London. "Rox bunning papal assassination attempt. How please?" one read. The AP had put out a bulletin saying someone had tried to kill the Pope. This was every UPI person's worst nightmare.

I had no evidence there had been an assassination attempt. So I opened a sidebar to our main story about the Pope trying to appeal to President Ferdinand Marcos to ease up on his authoritarian grip. After checking with my people on the ground by telephone, I was sticking to my guns.

What usually happened in these situations was that editors at US newspapers and television networks would call up the two wire services and demand to know who was right. But that did not seem to happen. Nobody from UPI in New York or Hong Kong called me. I was on my own.

I assumed the AP would have to put out a correction. I kept piling on detail in my running sidebar about the young man being allowed to kiss the Pope's ring.

I didn't know the final outcome of the day's coverage when I retreated to the Manila Hotel that evening, where most of the press corps was staying. At a bar near the swimming pool, Lederer, whom I know to this day, made a kind of apology to me. I wasn't sure what it was about. AP people didn't often make apologies to UPI people.

It turned out that AP never put out a correction. Instead, they put out a 1stld-writethru. It started: "An assassination scare today marred the visit of Pope John Paul II to the Philippines …" They swept the coverage, even though they were the ones who had created the assassination scare! We got shut out.

I agonized about that for years, so bitter was the taste of defeat, until I realized that editors probably preferred an assassination scare story. That's what sold newspapers. Sometimes fake news is better than the real thing. Perhaps that was just a tiny taste of what was to come. (Decades later, I asked Lederer what happened. She speculated that an AP reporter standing near the pope might have seen the young man charge toward the pope and concluded it was an assassination attempt. The reporter did not have as clear a line of vision as I did from the camera overhead. That seems plausible, but still does not explain why the AP never ran a correction.)

***

I liked the Philippines because it felt a bit like home. English was the second national language after Tagalog, and there were many cultural echoes. When I showed up to play tennis early one morning with the UPI bureau chief, Fernando "Boy" Delmundo, he was drinking Coca-Cola!

Manila had the terrible Tondo slum, where human waste flowed through open sewers, but the area around the Manila Hotel, overlooking Manila Bay, was lovely. The hotel was the headquarters for both the Japanese military who occupied the Philippines during World War II and for Gen. Douglas MacArthur when he stormed back ashore.

But there were deep mysteries about what was happening on the southern island of Mindanao. On the desk in Hong Kong, we had handled several stories that piqued my interest. One was the story of an American missionary, Lloyd Van Vactor, who lived in the area of Marawi City, on top of a volcano on Mindanao. He had been kidnapped by unknown persons, and his wife had died during his captivity. He eventually was released but stayed on.

There were also many stories that went like this: "An unidentified group of armed men ambushed another unidentified group of armed men, killing six." Who were all these armed men engaged in this shadowy conflict? I knew Moro separatists were fighting for Islamic causes because this area of the Philippines was largely Muslim. Then there were the New People's Army, which had Communist inclinations.

Later that year I got an assignment to write a profiler, or a "situationer," about where the Philippines was headed under President Ferdinand Marcos. I wanted to go to Mindanao to see the situation for myself. How could I offer a definitive assessment of whither-the-Philippines if I hadn't even set foot in the most troubled region of the country? I got in contact with Van Vactor, and he said he would put me up.

Because we were going to be leaving the Tagalog-speaking part of the country, I signed up someone whom Delmundo recommended. He spoke Visayan, the language group that dominates Cebu and the surrounding area. I also took a staff photographer. The three of us flew to Cagayan de Oro and then took a taxi to Iligan, which is the city that marks the dividing line between Christian and Muslim territory.

The three of us needed a different taxi driver now, one who could drive up the side of an enormous but extinct volcano into the crater, where there was a lake, Lake Lanao, and a village. Van Vactor lived nearby.

At the taxi stand in Iligan, different taxi drivers shouted at us to get the job, but one of them struck me as particularly skilled. In English, he said, "You can call me Peter. Or you can call me Mohammed." Great, I thought, he can pass as either a Christian or a Muslim.

We piled into his car, and up the volcano we started. There were army checkpoints along the way, but Peter/Mohammed knew how to pull through the checkpoints and then walk back and pay the guards about fifty cents. He knew the players. He knew the system.

When we reached the crater, we found Van Vactor's compound. It was a modest place behind high linked chain fences topped with barbed wire. It was a veritable fortress.

I wanted to go see the village, so the four of us intrepid souls piled back into the car. It was not a very densely settled village. Wood huts were spread about. When we started walking, one woman pulled out beautiful fabrics with designs I had never seen. I wanted to buy one. I started talking about that with her.

Within a few minutes, the guys on my team started to get nervous. They started giving me gentle nudges with their elbows. Let's go, they said. But I wasn't done with my transaction.

Their intensity level soon got kicked up a notch. I relented and agreed to go.

Somehow, they had picked up signals that the bad guys were coming. The bad guys must have heard that a foreigner was in town. I would have been an attractive captive, worth a lot of money. I never knew whether the woman offering the beautiful fabrics was part of the conspiracy. My colleagues from Manila would not have been able to pick up the signals. It must have been Peter/Mohammed who recognized the pattern. It was an example of how picking the right taxi driver or translator can save a correspondent's life.

In retrospect, I had done some things right. I had built a small team of people around me. The odds of surviving any difficulty are dramatically enhanced if you are with a group of some sort. The mathematical odds shift. Also, I actually listened to my local guys. Some correspondents insist they are famous and American and hence invincible. As a result, some have gotten killed or kidnapped. You have to go into dangerous situations with a low emotional center of gravity. Don't assume you know more than the locals. The locals can see signals you cannot.

That night at Van Vactor's home, he entertained me while the others found shelter elsewhere in the compound. Another guest was a general in uniform. He was there to be social, it appeared. I assumed he was a general in the Philippine army, but he could have been a general in any of the armed forces in the area. As I discovered, in addition to the Moro and NPA guerrillas, various sultans had their own armies, and different police forces were heavily armed. So in addition to the army, there were four other different groups of unidentified armed men killing other groups of unidentified armed men.

Ultimately, I wasn't able to use any of this material for my story. It was all too murky, too chaotic. Once again, I had risked my life to go into an area that did not produce a clear story.

I heard that someone threw a grenade into Van Vactor's compound shortly after we left. No one was injured. But the message was clear. Van Vactor left not long afterward. There was no point to trying to spread Christianity.

6 Covering the Middle Kingdom, 1981-1982

One day in early 1981, Beijing Bureau Chief Ray Wilkinson called Mike Keats and resigned. From the newsroom, I could see Keats behind a plate of glass that formed one side of his office. He caught my attention, and with his big first finger he beckoned me to enter.

"Ray Wilkinson just resigned," he told me, "and as I cast my great eye about the room, it fell upon you."

That was all it took to change our lives once again. So it was that I found myself in charge of covering the Middle Kingdom. Trying to cover China in any kind of comprehensive way was extremely difficult, if not outright impossible. One problem of course is that it had one billion people at the time and was a large, diverse country geographically.

But the other problem was that China considered journalists to be spies, just by another name. They sought to greatly limit and monitor our access to real people. These pressures were more perceptible in Beijing than southern China, because it was the capital city.

We lived in a gated diplomatic compound called Qijiayuan, one of three in Beijing at the time. Some foreign students and intellectuals lived in northwestern Beijing near the university, but diplomats, business people, and journalists lived primarily in the three diplomatic compounds with People's Liberation Army guards at the gates. No Chinese were allowed to come in unless they had official business. We were on Chang'an Avenue, which led into Tiananmen Square.

Compounding the isolation was the staff. Mr. Zheng was my translator, but he was really the de facto boss of my Chinese staff. Mr. Kang was the driver, and he would become my pal because I could practice Chinese with him as we made the rounds in the company's white Volkswagen station wagon to pay bills and such, usually around midday. We also had a cook, housekeeper, and telex operator. Every Saturday they would have a meeting to discuss me and what I was doing. It was a conspiracy, and Mr. Zheng was the ringleader.

Mr. Zheng had had experience with my two previous bureau chiefs, Crabbe and Wilkinson. Crabbe was a savvy Asian hand because he had lived in Japan. But his wife developed medical problems, and she could not receive proper care in Beijing. Wilkinson had transferred in from Nairobi. Although he was an experienced hand at covering conflict and war in Africa and the Middle East, he simply didn't get the China story. So Mr. Zheng didn't have much respect for American bureau chiefs.

I was determined to get my money's worth from him, however. After I learned enough Chinese, I began picking out headlines from the Chinese newspapers that looked interesting, and I asked him to translate them for me. The symbols for America, or "pretty country" in Chinese, were easy to pick out, and so too were the symbols for China, or "middle country" or "central country," hence the term Middle Kingdom. Whenever I saw America and China together in a headline, I asked for it to be translated. Zheng labored over it mightily, because he had to type out the translations on a typewriter. That was difficult for him, and it took him hours. The fact that I was learning Chinese was giving me leverage.

Of course, language was not the only problem. The way the Chinese had set it up was that correspondents would be stuck in their offices watching the Xinhua wire roll in with propaganda. Xinhua (literally "new tongue") was the official government propaganda machine. We were discouraged from moving more than twenty-five miles outside Beijing because we had to do battle with at least three different sets of bureaucracies to get permission and make arrangements. One was the Information Section of Foreign Ministry. Another was the Public Security Bureau, or police. Then we had to do battle with China Travel to book flights and hotels.

Of course, we assumed that our telephones were monitored, our telexes were read, and our mail was intercepted. And we knew that our walls were bugged. We knew that because my No. 2, Paul Loong, and I needed to figure out how to respond to complaints from our wives that the cook, Mr. Shih, was spitting in the sink. The Chinese were notorious spitters, and it really bothered our wives.

We had a meeting in our living room, and the four of us agreed that the next day I would call the Diplomatic Services Bureau to demand a new cook. That was awkward, because the Chinese liked to maintain the fiction, if not the reality, that they made all decisions about who worked for us. They would not allow us to be rapacious capitalists and fire people. So it was going to be difficult. But lo and behold, the next day Mr. Shih walked in and quit. The listeners had heard us and maneuvered to head off a diplomatic tussle.

I knew where the listeners worked. Every day at the back of our diplomatic compound, dozens of Chinese arrived by bicycle and entered low-slung buildings that must have been filled with monitoring devices. They were the first wave of the people China employed to monitor foreigners and keep outside influences at bay. (Today, millions of Chinese are employed monitoring the Internet and preventing unwanted information from reaching the Chinese.)

In short, I knew firsthand what it was like to live in the grip of a totalitarian regime. I might know from the newspapers that the Central Committee of the Communist Party was meeting, but it was impossible to learn where the meeting was or what they were talking about. That was infuriating.

Diplomats often were a source of insight, but not always. One of the sensitive issues between the US and Chinese governments was (and remains) whether the US military could have direct contact with the People's Liberation Army. The two governments were feeling each other out and looking for points of leverage. If diplomatic relations were on a positive footing from their point of view, the Chinese would allow military-to-military contacts. If things were tense, they would not.

I knew State Department people at the Embassy as well as the defense intelligence attachés. The State Department people were trying to shape coverage of the issues, whereas the Defense guys played it straight. One day the defense guys told me that military-to-military contacts had been suspended. I wrote that.

The next day at a diplomatic reception, a State Department guy named Jay Taylor said to me, "I didn't tell you to write that."

Needless to say, I resented his presumption that he could tell me what to report. The State Department was trying to manage tensions over Taiwan. They had their agenda; I had mine.

We got some tidbits when visiting dignitaries came to visit and meet with senior Chinese officials. When someone of the stature of Alexander Haig came, he and a gaggle of us reporters would be ushered into the presence of Deng Xiaoping. Deng was a very small man, and he spoke a Sichuan Province dialect that regular Mandarin speakers couldn't understand. So he needed a special translator. That dialect trick also might have allowed him to think more carefully and take longer to answer questions. He spat liquid tobacco into a spittoon. He was a crude man in appearance. But he had been a brilliant survivor.

Studying the language was the most difficult intellectual challenge of my life—bar none. Mr. Li was my teacher. He was a very gentle soul, an intellectual, and about 60 years of age. I suspected he could have been the kind of person who was persecuted during the Cultural Revolution. We never spoke a word of English. It started by my spending about a month trying to learn how to hear the different sounds the Chinese make. They also had four tones, and if you got the wrong tone, it changed the meaning of the word. You really had to immerse yourself in it to soak up the sounds and the tones.

Mr. Li would come every weekday morning at 8 a.m. for about an hour, and I would practice writing Chinese characters in the evening. The first time I was ever able to communicate in Chinese was when I was with Mr. Kang in the car and saw an intense knot of people standing together in the street. The denizens of Beijing tended to cluster around an accident. I knew how to ask, "What's happening?" Mr.Kang responded, *"Dui wo, mei-you guanxi."* ("To me, there is no connection.") I got it.

Guanxi is a tremendously important concept in China. There are so many people that you have to define who matters to you—in other words, with whom do you have a connection? *Guanxi* also applies to trying to get things done while battling the infuriating Chinese bureaucracies. If you have *guanxi*, a connection, you can take the back door. That was called *"zou hou mer."*

The language allowed for great ambiguity, at least partly because of the bitter ideological struggles of the Cultural Revolution and other ideological campaigns. People had to avoid speaking what they regarded as the truth, because that might get them killed. It was acceptable to say, "The situation isn't very clear." Or, "No one knows." Or, "It's difficult to say." The one phrase that perhaps best exemplified this ambiguity was "Horse, horse, tiger, tiger." If someone asked you for your opinion, you could say *"Ma ma hu hu,"* which meant, "It could be a horse, or it could be a tiger. I don't know."

The language also reflected poverty. One common greeting was, *Chi hao le ma?* Have you eaten well? Getting a meal had not been easy for millions of Chinese. Starvation had been used as a political weapon. In shops that often ran out of products, shopkeepers also repeated the word *"meiyou."* We have nothing. And by implication, with a shrug of the shoulders, there is nothing that can be done about it.

The language was deeply tied to history. Chinese speakers could make cultural allusions to poets or emperors who lived hundreds of years ago. Stanley Ginsberg, an American who arrived to represent the Aga Khan when he came to China, became a friend. He was the most fluent foreign speaker of Chinese I had ever heard. He once remarked, "Chinese is not a language you can master. It is like an ocean in which you can merely swim." That might be applied to the whole country itself. You could never truly master China.

As I spent more time in China, I obviously had more opportunities to hear from individual Chinese who often were eager to practice the English they had learned on Voice of America. The very early morning hours, starting at about 5:30 until 7 a.m., particularly in warmer weather, was when the Chinese were out in the parks or on the Bund doing their graceful *tai chi* exercise or walking their birds. Old men would walk with one bird cage in each hand, swinging them back and forth. The birds needed their fresh air.

The Cultural Revolution was a period of absolute insane class struggle. Mao unleased the young Red Guards against all symbols of authority. Relying on his Little Red Book for inspiration, the Red Guards sought to destroy the "four olds"—old customs, old culture, old habits, and old ideas. Children who belonged to the Red Guards would smash their own family heirlooms. They were focused on sniffing out anyone who had bourgeois, capitalist, or landlord tendencies. Millions were struggled to death, meaning they were persecuted in public to the point that they either committed suicide or died in detention camps. There were also massacres in the streets.

I'd get glimpses of the chaos from chats with young Chinese people. As I walked with one young man in Shanghai, we passed a building and he exclaimed, "Oh, here is where our music teacher jumped to his death." His students, including my conversational partner, had struggled him so aggressively that suicide

was the only way out. Another acquaintance, Mr. Mao (no rela-
tion to Mao Tse-tung), told me about how his father-in-law had a
heart attack during the Cultural Revolution. Mr. Mao took him to
the hospital, but they were denied entry because the father-in-law
was *"fan ge ming,"* a counter-revolutionary. He died in Mr. Mao's
arms.

I heard most of the stories while walking in Shanghai.
Why did we walk? Everyone was concerned about security. Sitting
still wasn't safe. When I walked with one of my friends in particular, his brother followed us about ten yards back to make sure the
police weren't tailing us. The key way to tell was if someone was
wearing leather shoes as opposed to the cloth slippers with rub-
ber soles that most Chinese wore. If someone wore leather shoes,
they were cops.

One of the hardest things about China was to adopt a
balanced view of the place. Some foreigners "fall in love" with
it. Others "hate" it. There are many things that are highly admi-
rable—the language, the culture, the rich sense of history, the
food, and the temples. But there are also terrible things about
China—Communist Party control, the surveillance, the gulags,
and female infanticide. I tried not to swing to either extreme
and be either pro-China or anti-China. I couldn't form a single
moral judgment about the place.

Sidebar:
DANCING TO GLENN MILLER IN SHANGHAI

Cathy and I first went to Shanghai in 1981. We stayed at
the Peace Hotel on the Bund, which was the series of impressive buildings overlooking the Huangpu River. They were
built by the colonial powers that had once controlled Shanghai and much of the rest of coastal China. We were struck by
the Bund but also by the shops elsewhere that reflected a different sensibility than what we had seen in Beijing. The Peace

Hotel had been built in 1929 by an Iraqi Jew by the name of Victor Sassoon. Many Jews from the Soviet Union and elsewhere had migrated to Shanghai, which bore the nickname the Paris of the Orient.

It was a walking town, unlike Beijing, and we wandered through it. As we strolled through the boulevards of the old French Quarter, we saw wedding shops, for example, featuring models wearing Western-style wedding gowns. Shanghai had been a flourishing crossroads of many different cultures. Now it was seedy and slowly sinking into the mud because the Communist Party's leadership in Beijing did not trust Shanghai and was starving it for funding. Shanghai's party was seen as a rival to Beijing's complete control.

On one of our first nights at the fading Peace Hotel, we saw a band of older Chinese men probably in their late 50s and early 60s setting up to play in the lobby. Called the Old Jazz Band, they were playing Western big band music. We were stunned. It turned out that the men had buried their instruments and music during the Cultural Revolution so that they would not be identified as being counter-revolutionary.

The band launched into a robust version of Glenn Miller's "In the Mood," and the place erupted as dozens of tourists and visitors surged onto the dance floor. No one could believe we were listening to Glenn Miller and dancing in China.

The first time we saw this band, the musicians were wearing Mao suits, which had become the universal dress code. But on our second trip to Shanghai, they appeared in Western shirts and ties. They must have also buried this clothing, lest they be accused of being pro-foreign tools.

At a time when the vast majority of Chinese were still wearing Mao suits, the band was a kind of touchstone, a way of judging what was happening deep under the surface of Chinese society.

Many years later in the 1990s, when I went back to Shanghai on assignment for *Business Week*, I returned to the Peace Hotel to see what had happened with the band. Like so many other things in China, everything had changed. The band had gone on the road and had been replaced by an affiliated group of younger men playing the same music. Now there was a cover charge to listen and the hotel had been completely refurbished. The place had gone commercial in a big time way. It was just a small reflection of China's mad dash for modernization.

End Sidebar

***

George and Lucia Terkerov were our KGB babysitters in Beijing. In theory, George worked for the Tass news agency as a reporter, but the way that he and Lucia sought to draw us in and compromise us made it clear that they were working for the KGB. Everyone in the American press corps had KGB babysitters.

George and Lucia also were "responsible" for Brad and Hideko Martin, and the six of us would often socialize. Sometimes we would go to their apartment, also in the Qi Jian Yuan diplomatic compound where we lived, and eat pizza and play Monopoly. The Soviets, to our surprise, were excellent capitalists and won most every game. They displayed a maddening desperation to get ahead; no sooner did they got a monopoly than they would pour all their money into getting houses and then a hotel, to make it more expensive for other players to land there.

Then late in the evening George would get out his guitar and sing emotional, gypsy-type songs while we drank excellent wine from Soviet Georgia. Lucia was said to have been a doctor back in the Soviet Union. Two children, almost certainly not theirs, were in the apartment. It was a make-believe family.

The Soviets regarded themselves as the *lao gege*, the older brother, in the Sino-Soviet relationship, because in the early days after the Chinese Communist revolution in 1949, the Chinese were flat broke and were suffering through upheavals like the Great Leap Forward. The Soviets had the technology and the medicine the Chinese lacked. George said things like: "The Chinese have our trucks and our medicines. They are nothing without outside help. If it is not us, then it is you."

The Chinese had almost nothing to boast of culturally, in George's view. "How can you compare the cultural life in Peking and Moscow? We have the Bolshoi. They have nothing."

Henry Kissinger and Richard Nixon had opened talks with the Chinese for the express purpose of damaging the Sino-Soviet relationship and isolating Moscow. The Soviets obviously did not like that and were determined to reverse the situation.

I had never known any Russians. I knew George was playing a dangerous game, but I was just so fascinated that I went along. This was one of the many situations in my life in which being stupid and straight kept me out of trouble. George was in his forties and was trilingual, speaking Russian, Chinese, and English. He was more experienced and smarter. I suspect he had been trained in how to be personable and charming.

George invited me to go the Soviet Embassy one day to play tennis on their outdoor court. I did not engage in outdoor activities very much because of the air quality, but I decided to go and try to have fun. We were both average players. But we played other games. He would ask me to get electronic schematics for consumer products when I went for R&Rs to Hong Kong. The Soviets were barred from going to the then-British colony, and George was trying to establish a pattern in which I provided him with completely harmless documents, but then he would tiptoe into more sensitive territory. I never did any of that.

But I did bring in cases of Johnny Walker Scotch from Hong Kong and trade them for the excellent Georgian wine the Soviets flew in under diplomatic immunity. Sometimes I owed him money, sometimes he owed me money. I was careful not to get into a situation where I owed him very much for very long.

The name of the biggest game was disinformation. The Soviets wanted to poison the American perception of China. And they had allies in the Soviet bloc. One was Sunil Roy, who worked for Press Trust of India (PTI). He was an odd little Bengali who filed his copy through UPI and our telex operator, which meant I could see it if I wanted to. Sometimes in the evening he would come in with half-cracked stories and transmit them to PTI in India, and then he would try to persuade me to "match" them, meaning write my own similar version for UPI. I suspected he had some sort of relationship with the Soviets and never fell for that trap. At that time, the Indians had deep relations with the Soviets.

The KGB also tried sexual entrapment—the old honey trap. Another fellow traveler of theirs was Lafdal, a big, gregarious Mauritanian diplomat who loved to throw parties. It was late in 1981 when Cathy became pregnant. She went to Hong Kong for medical care sometimes. Lafdal must have assumed that a young guy with a pregnant wife who was out of town would be tempted by Chinese women. One time, he invited me to his apartment, and there was an attractive young Chinese woman. He introduced us. Then he said he had to run an errand and disappeared. She and I chatted for a few moments in rudimentary Chinese, but I concluded it was pretty useless. I didn't know who she was or what she wanted, so I left. It wasn't until later that I put it all together. She wasn't wearing shoes. That was supposed to be the tip-off to me that she was available. Fortunately, I was too naive to figure it out.

Then Lucia tried to entrap me sexually. One other evening, I had to go to a *Far Eastern Economic Review* event because one of their stars, David Bonavia, had written a story that Deng

Xiaoping had been ousted from power. If true, it would have been incredible that he was the only guy in town reporting it. The event was a few blocks north of Qi Jia Yuan, so I walked over. Lucia walked over as well, which was odd, because she did not present herself as a journalist. After the event, at which Bonavia came across as a bumbling fool, I walked home, and again Lucia joined me. She was acting funny. She was all perky and bright. She was putting the moves on me. I shrugged it off.

The Terkerovs ultimately failed to persuade us to hate the Chinese or compromise us so that we owed them something, but not for the lack of trying. Years later, after we both had left Beijing, Brad Martin and I tried at different times to find George Terkerov, but he seemed to have vanished into thin air.

***

Sidebar:
CHASING THE CIA IN XINJIANG

Tony Walker was one of my pals in the Beijing press corps. A lanky Australian with a great sense of humor, he worked for *The Age* of Melbourne. One day he proposed that we team up and go on a reporting trip together to Xinjiang Province, the westernmost province of China, inhabited mostly by the Uighurs, an ethnic Muslim minority. It was definitely the frontier, right up against the border with the Soviet Union.

To get there, we had to fly to Lanzhou and change planes to get to Urumqi, the capital of Xinjiang. In the Lanzhou airport we were surrounded by Chinese travelers, but then we saw two other foreigners, both men. One man was about 45 years old, tanned and in good physical shape. His bespectacled companion was in his late twenties or early thirties and was a bit round in girth. We made no contact.

Upon arriving in Xinjiang, it turned out there was only one hotel fit for foreigners, the Balou, literally "eight floors." It was the tallest building in the town. Tony said it felt like a different world than Beijing, and it did. Once again, Tony and I found ourselves bumping up against Mr. Tough Guy and the Nerd. We identified ourselves as reporters. Little Nerd boy just about wet his pants, but Mr. Tough Guy, who gave off a military air, politely explained that they were on a rug-buying trip.

Tony and I went ahead and tried to scout out stories. We went to Turfan on the edge of the Gobi Desert. This was a stop on the old Silk Road. Our hosts were Muslim and did not drink alcohol, but they made a lovely local wine available to us as they entertained us one evening sitting beneath a grape vine arbor and watching young women dance, dressed in the local tribal fashion. It was incredibly hot. Cold Chinese beer never tasted so good.

Back in Urumqi, day after day, we'd see Tough Guy and Nerd at breakfast. Their body language didn't invite conversation, so we didn't really try. We were simply watching them, and they were watching us.

We spent some time trying to make contact with Uighurs, hoping to understand how they were so different from the Han Chinese, but it was difficult. One problem was language. They hated speaking Chinese, and we could speak only limited Chinese, but certainly not their language. It was not very conclusive reporting.

One day at the hotel, we saw a real, honest-to-goodness American cowboy. He had one eye that worked, and one that was stuck in orbit. In a room, he told us how he was there working on putting out an oil well fire as part of a Red Adair team. Of course, the Chinese would never want the media to know that they had a fire in an oil well, but Tex, let's call him, spilled out many of the details. He also described how he smuggled vodka in from across the Soviet border into this Muslim area where booze was not readily available. He was able to buy watches and trade them for vodka.

On one of the last days of our trip, Tony and I were having breakfast and started talking about Tough Guy and the Nerd. We could see them across the room. Nothing they had said made any sense. We didn't see any carpets being bought. They just seemed to be camped out in the hotel. Tony prodded me, suggesting I walk over and demand an explanation. Which I did.

As I approached their table, the Nerd did the wet-pants thing again, but Tough Guy was all smiles. I told them nothing they said made any sense. "Who are you really?"

"You know, the great thing about being an American," said Mr. Tough Guy, "is that you don't have to say nothing to nobody you don't want to."

I obviously wasn't going to learn anything, so I turned and walked away, but Tony and I developed a theory. The CIA's listening stations on the Chinese border must have had a technical problem that needed repair. They needed the technical know-how of Nerd. They sent along a babysitter in the form of Tough Guy. The reason they were simply camped out is that they were waiting for us to leave. Whatever they were doing must have been highly classified. The last thing they wanted was for us to break a story about CIA listening stations!

Taking off from Urumqi airport was memorable. The plane was full of Han Chinese returning to Beijing. They hated living in Urumqi, where the locals hated them, and couldn't wait to get out. One thing they loved about the region, however, were the succulent *Hami-Gua* melons. Every passenger seemed to carry three or four aboard and stuff them into every compartment and corner. When the plane started down the runway, it was obviously straining with the extra weight

of the *Hami-Gua*. If I had met my maker that day in a plane crash, it would all have been because of the damn melons.
End Sidebar

***

My frustration about not being able to understand what was happening in China exploded one day in an incident I am not proud of. But it revealed my state of mental health.

Cathy told me that an old college friend of hers, Linda Marshall, was coming to town with her husband, Ken. The husband was an actor and was playing the lead role in an Italian move about Marco Polo. The filming was taking place inside the Forbidden City, the vast secretive compound of temples and plazas. I obtained the official approvals from the department Linda pointed me to—and received permission to visit the area where the filming was taking place. Because I was so fond of my Chinese teacher, Mr. Li, I asked him to come with Cathy, Linda, and myself. The next day we set out in our Volkswagen for the East Gate of the Forbidden City.

When we got to the gate, the officials in charge would not let us enter. I couldn't understand why. I was humiliated.

The next day I found another department with oversight of the East Gate and applied for a second set of papers. I got them and went back by myself.

Again, officials tried to stop me. I heard one say, *"Bu yao jizhe."* ("We don't want journalists.") There was a J on my license plate, so they knew my status from that, if not from the paperwork.

I flipped out. I got back in the car and started bumping it forward with an official standing in my way. He was obviously concerned that I was going to flatten him and jumped out of the way.

I drove past him into the Forbidden City and found where the filming was taking place. I was chatting with Leonard

Nimoy, who had a role in the movie, when I saw an older Chinese official, in his fifties, come charging through the entrance to our area. He stormed up to the Italian director, who very nonchalantly pointed to me. He was with an interpreter, which was lucky for both of us.

He was obviously furious. I saw the kind of hate in his eyes that American GIs must have seen as they fought Chinese soldiers in the Korean War. He started saying angry things, and I couldn't understand anything because he was essentially spitting out his words, but the translator took the edge off by saying something like, "The director expresses regrets that you have been inconvenienced."

I replied in English, and the translator once again smoothed it out. The director finally stormed off. But I could have been expelled from China for the incident if the East Gate director had chosen to report me to the Foreign Ministry. It is one of the peculiarities of the Chinese bureaucracy that petty gatekeepers think of themselves as emperors in their own right. They make their own rules. They don't answer to anyone. (There are many stories about interpreters saving the day in crucial moments. All of them could be true.)

The air quality in Beijing was awful. It was because of entirely different reasons than today, when millions of vehicles are creating foul air. Back then, when virtually no Chinese citizen possessed a car, there were three causes: The Shougang steel factory was on the west side of town and the prevailing breezes came from the west. That meant the effluent blew into town. The Communists believed good socialists should not be alienated from their own pollution. The second reason was the widespread burning of coal during cooler months. And thirdly, winds from the Gobi Desert, the same ones that brought the steel plant effluent, also brought clouds of dust from the desert each spring. Our *amah*, or housekeeper in Cantonese (but *ayi* in Mandarin), would often spend the whole day trying to collect the dust that seeped through the windows of our apartment that the Soviets had built in the 1950s.

I tried to run only once during my sixteen months or so in Beijing, including two winters. It was clear from the physical impact on my lungs that I couldn't do that.

On more than one occasion, I developed asthmatic bronchitis. The drip in the back of my throat would reach down into my bronchioles. The suffering was most acute at night, and I often got up at 4:30 or 5 a.m. because I couldn't sleep.

Because the UPI office was located in our sprawling apartment, it was only natural that I would drift into the bureau at very early hours. The Xinhua telex machine was located there, and it was the practice of the propaganda masters to let their barrages loose in the middle of the night so that everyone would wake up and see them. Only I saw them much earlier than my competitors. (AP bureau chief Victoria Graham lived in much the same setup on the third or fourth floor of our building. I never once set foot inside.)

China and the United States had re-established diplomatic relations at the beginning of 1979, and Americans were genuinely interested in China, partly because of the personality of Deng Xiaoping. But relations remained strained over continued military and economic support for Taiwan, which China regarded as its own renegade province. We had agreed to a "one China" policy with Beijing, but we never spelled out whom we regarded as the legitimate government. It was called "strategic ambiguity."

China's anger at the US was the subject of many of these early morning statements. I started writing small stories about how the Chinese were demanding that the Americans take a particular action on Taiwan or risk a serious deterioration in the Sino-American relationship. I kept racking up small victories in the logs: 6-0 or 7-0. If that many American editors had not printed the stories, I would have stopped writing them.

I never understood why the AP did not try to match me more consistently. Were the State Department guys at the Embassy telling Vicky Graham to ignore the Xinhua blasts because they interfered with State Department policies?

The other possible explanation was that I was simply up early and was writing stories before Graham had put on her face and had her morning cappuccino and croissant. Graham hated me for many reasons, and the Taiwan wins were just one. The two news organizations attracted different sorts of people. A UPI person just wanted to win in the logs. AP people sometimes took on greater pretensions. They were more than just wire service reporters. They had stature. I sensed that Vicky thought of herself as the doyenne of the American press corps.

I knew that millions of Chinese party members were reading my stories, because *Cankao Xiaoxi*, or *Reference News*, reprinted my stories each day in Chinese as part of a summary of what all Western journalists were saying about China. It was odd that a 29-year-old correspondent for a wire service was getting such visibility, but the Chinese believed UPI was the most important news agency.

The way I survived my health issues was by taking advantage of the Chinese practice of *xiu xi*, or nap. In those years in China, the entire nation shut down for an hour or ninety minutes every day after lunch so people could sleep. Offices had to have rooms where staff could nap, and we had a room for our translator, driver, cook, amah, and telex operator. By napping with Cathy, my health could recover somewhat.

Aside from health, my other major concern was persistent rumors that UPI was about to be sold to Reuters or some other organization. I didn't want to get stranded in China with no job. Back in New York, meanwhile, Paul Varian, who had been my boss in Lansing, had moved to New York and become foreign editor. I never understood how that happened, because he had no foreign experience.

But with Cathy back in New York preparing to give birth, Varian called me and said he wanted me to move back to New York and become his deputy. He needed someone he could trust and someone who had foreign experience. I realized that the game in Beijing was up. The next morning at my Chinese lesson, I cried as I tried to explain it to Mr. Li.

I wonder what would have happened to me if I hadn't had a wife and hadn't wanted a family. I might still be in China. My fascination was that deep. They say there are two types of foreigners who live in China. Some are deeply affected by the experience, whereas others leave and are not interested in ever going back. I was clearly in the first category. But with Cathy about to have a baby and hearing frequent rumors about UPI being sold, I accepted reality.

Brad Martin threw me a farewell party, and a woman I didn't know came from the Information Section of the Foreign Ministry, which was the key body that managed relations with correspondents.

"Thank you for helping us," she said to me.

I was flabbergasted. The Americans did go to the negotiating table with the Chinese, and they came up with three different installments of the Shanghai Communique, which sought to clarify American support for Taiwan. But the thought never occurred to me that my stories played any role in pressuring the Americans to negotiate. I was merely taking advantage of my bronchitis to make life uncomfortable for Vicky Graham.

I didn't realize it at the time, but this was the end of my time as a foreign correspondent in the sense of living abroad. I was one of the lucky ones. I had a series of mentors who mentored me and gave me chances to either screw up or excel. I had six years of training in Lansing and in New York before setting foot in Hong Kong. I wasn't just thrown into the deep end of the pool. My lords and masters knew what they were doing.

I also was lucky in the sense that I was married—and the marriage worked. Single male correspondents sent abroad often suffered from a lack of balance in their lives—particularly, it seems, the ones sent to Asia. They drink too much and chase too many Asian women (or men). Or they work too hard and ignore their health. Single women, although rarer, also face psychological pressures.

Cathy was an ideal correspondent's wife, because she kept herself busy, made friends easily, organized social gatherings, and helped me keep connected to our families back home. (We exchanged letters and tape-recorded messages through UPI in New York, which couriered mail to us in Beijing. Telephone calls were very rare.) Correspondents who don't have spouses or companions are less happy than those who do. I've known correspondents at age 37 or 38 who are still alone, while all their friends are married and having babies. They sacrificed years of their personal lives.

Some news organizations used to have husband-and-wife teams, where both were correspondents. That was more expensive than sending out single correspondents, but it was a more stable arrangement in terms of personal balance. It seems, however, that as the news media's economic model has crumbled, fewer organizations send out couples. In fact, more and more of them rely on stringers and freelancers, who are already on the ground and who already speak the local languages. Maintaining emotional balance is their own problem.

I also had support networks when I was in dangerous places—either older correspondents or else drivers, translators, photographers, and the like. But the *Chicago Tribunes, Newsdays* and *Baltimore Suns* are gone now. The ranks of foreign correspondent networks today have been badly depleted.

I regret that I had only three and a half years on the ground, but it wasn't necessarily a bad thing that I was summoned home. Some correspondents who spend fifteen or twenty years on the road suffer bad health or dental problems and have broken marriages. (My own marriage ended when Cathy died of cancer in 2006.) Some of these scribes have been away so long from headquarters that they don't know how to act as part of an organization. Couples who have children while on the move sometimes experience discipline problems or other problems of adjustment to new cities and new languages.

The bottom line was that being a correspondent shaped my entire life and career. I had found my community, my club, my cause.

7 Back to America

Coming home is more difficult than most correspondents and their editors recognize. If you've been out of the country for years, you don't recognize the names of movies or actors that other people bring up at cocktail parties. You've missed the latest trends in music. When you start talking about something you saw or lived through, people look at you like you're from another planet, which in many ways we were. There was an enormous gulf between us and our old friends.

I wrote a funny little note about coming home that was never published anywhere. It started: "The Chinese eat dogs, but urbane New Yorkers walk contritely behind their canines carrying 'poopie-scoopers.'

"Most Chinese work the land under a harsh sun and wonder about their next meal. New Yorkers actually pay money to perform physical labor (at gyms) and sit under lamps that darken their skin.

"A correspondent, returning to the United States after three years in China and Hong Kong, is struck by Americans' stunning wealth, which gives them a standard of living most of the world's inhabitants can scarcely imagine."

All very drole. But figuring out how to create new lives took big energy. Son Jason was born in June 1982, and we had to figure out where to live. We bought a two-bedroom condo. Suddenly, I had a kid and a mortgage.

While rumors about UPI's future kept flying, I buried myself in my job as Varian's deputy. I was now a grizzled veteran at the age of 30. Paul and I worked well together. We trusted each other's instincts. So it was that on September 14, 1982, we were both working in the afternoon when news rolled in that Bachir Gemayel had been assassinated by a bomb blast in Beirut. The Lebanese civil war was in the headlines; Gemayel was the Christian Phalangist leader and Lebanon's president-elect. His assassination would plunge the nation back into turmoil. Paul broke that story with a bulletin.

Somehow, Stevenson got wind that something had happened to Princess Grace in Monaco. She was the former Grace Kelly, a world-renowned figure. I called Paris looking for bureau chief John Moody but couldn't reach him. It was late evening Paris time, and there were no cell phones. Then I had an idea. Let's just call the royal palace. Jacques Clafin on the desk spoke fluent French, much better than mine.

Clafin reached a palace spokesman who read a statement in very somber tones—Grace's car had shot off a cliff and she was dead.

I knocked out a bulletin on this story and scrambled for further details.

It was a frenzy with two major breaking stories, but Paul and I knew exactly what to do and how to do it.

At 6:30 p.m., we turned on the television to see how the CBS Evening News would handle the news.

Dan Rather's face appeared and he said: "We have two shocking stories tonight from United Press International."

We couldn't believe it. Of course, we were elated even if the subject matters were shocking. This was the power of an international news agency at its very best. The AP must have been a step or two behind us, because Rather would have simply said, there were two shocking stories tonight. Period.

It was a moment of ultimate triumph.

Another triumph was when the Soviet Union announced that Yuri Andropov would replace Leonid Brezhnev, who died in office in the fall of 1982. The Soviet media machine started putting out the spin that Andropov loved Western jazz, and that deep down inside he was really a nice guy. Having played games with the KGB, I recognized a con when I saw it. I was able to get Zbigniew Brzezinski on the phone at Columbia University, where he was teaching, as well as a handful of other top Soviet experts. The story began, "New Kremlin chief Yuri V. Andropov crushed the Soviet dissident movement, masterminded the Polish military crackdown, and transformed the KGB into a modern intelligence agency, US experts say."

I quoted Brzezinski as saying that Andropov was "the prime moving force" behind all these repressive measures as head of the KGB for sixteen years. The story got wide play. I had gone up against the KGB's propaganda machine.

But reports about UPI's financial condition kept whipping through the newsroom. The latest was that our new owners were going to move all the New York operations to Washington to save money. That was over the top for me because of the condo and the son, and because Cathy had gone back to work in her beloved field of publishing.

It just so happened that a public relations acquaintance who represented American Express knew they were having a crisis with their annual report. I was asked to come in one weekend and rewrite it. American Express was a kind of financial supermarket, with charge cards, travel services, insurance, stock brokering, and banking. I could readily grasp what they wanted, and the writing was a breeze. I was soon offered a job for an amazing $48,000 a year as a corporate writer, compared with the $36,000 UPI was paying me after almost ten years working for them.

I knew I had to make more money. We wanted a second child. I thought that taking a corporate job was simply what journalists had to do to survive. I took the plunge and told Varian I was quitting. It was one of the hardest personal things I had ever done. It meant walking away from doing things I loved. But it was the price of growing up, I told myself.

So within a year of coming home from my adventures, I decided to enter a strange new land. It was like walking into the Kabul bazaar by myself. I was grossly unprepared.

At first, there was some adventure. My job included writing speeches (and I had never written a speech) for James D. Robinson, the chief executive officer. I also wrote speeches for Sandy Weill; his sidekick, Jamie Dimon, helped out. (Jamie, today one of the most powerful men in the world of finance as CEO of JP Morgan Chase, learned how to build financial goliaths by being Sandy's go-fer) The third major figure was Lou Gerstner, who was head of the Travel Related Services division, which included the American Express Card. He went on to become the CEO of IBM.

I had to navigate all three personalities when it came to quarterly earnings statements and the annual report. They didn't really like or trust each other, as best I could tell. And they defended different pieces of turf. I had to clear the content of any quarterly or annual earnings statement with each of them. Everything was written on Wang word processors.

It was a wild ride, literally. Like in *The Bonfire of the Vanities*. Devoted assistants scheduled limousines, helicopters, and private jets for the top guys to travel in, and I often went with them to hear how they delivered a speech. We often would have lunches in the executive dining rooms and be served like we were kings. I wore red suspenders and tasseled loafers and tried to look like I fit in.

Writing earnings releases was one thing, but the politics of writing speeches was another. Being a speechwriter was high risk. Harry Freeman, the executive president in charge of all communications and government relations, was the consummate Machiavelli. If I had direct one-on-one contact with Robinson or Weill, I was developing some measure of a relationship. That made Freeman and various aides uncomfortable. They wanted to keep me in my place.

My death by 10,000 cuts started. I kept getting poor performance reviews, which reflected on what kind of raises I got. I knew I had to get out. Cathy became pregnant again, and that added to the pressure. Once I had been stamped as a correspondent, it would have been impossible for me to make it in the corporate world. One had to speak a certain code language and display certain behaviors. The corporate world is intensely political, and the game was particularly rough-and-tumble at American Express.

One day I saw a story in magazine about a new editor, Steve Shepard, taking over *Business Week* magazine. I wrote him a cold letter. It was one of the rare times in my life that the cold-call approach worked. *Business Week* needed someone with Asian expertise, and my brief business background didn't hurt. The rule of thumb was that once a journalist crossed to the "dark side" of corporate communications, there was no coming back to the sacred path of journalism. But *Business Week*, recognizing the importance of the emerging Asia story, needed me. And they offered a competitive salary.

Daughter Ali was born in February 1985, and I made the move to *Business Week* just two months later. Cathy wanted a house in Westchester County, north of the city. The familial and financial responsibilities were mounting.

Making the transition back to journalism at *Business Week* was a miracle. I suddenly found myself at the heart of an even more sophisticated information machine than UPI. Steve Shepard had been trained as an engineer, so he understood how the mechanics of things worked, and he had learned the art of magazine management at *Newsweek*. We had separate departments headed by senior editors, who then reported to three assistant managing editors, who reported to the managing editor and ultimately Shepard. There was real expertise in these departments. In the economics department, for example, there was one fellow with a PhD in economics from Harvard. I loved to argue with the economists, because they thought the world operated on the basis of their theories. I knew it operated on the basis of real people making real decisions. Other departments covered finance, information technology, telecommunications, software, management, personal business, and so on.

Shepard knew how to get this machine to perform for him. At cover story meetings held every few weeks, we all would scramble to come up with written proposals that were distributed to all senior editors and managing editors, plus Shepard. Thirty to forty of us sat in a big conference room and debated the merits of each proposal. The best ideas floated to the top.

Then Shepard often would create a "bingo," or competition. Cover A would be bingoed against Cover B for a particular week. He would watch each take shape, creating intense competition between departments. Then as late as a Tuesday or even Wednesday when we physically closed the magazine by the end of the day, he could accept Cover A and order that Cover B be cut and run inside the magazine. Or he could save it for a subsequent week.

It was very bureaucratic and turf conscious. We joked that it was an intellectual assembly line and it wasn't pretty—like making sausage. But the process created cover stories that led the business world's debate about many themes, particularly about technology and globalizing businesses. I either wrote or coordinated cover stories including Toyota's Fast Lane, Hot Spots, the Stateless Corporation, Japan in America, Why Johnny Can't Export, and Mighty Mitsubishi.

It was more sophisticated than UPI, because correspondents would file reporting to New York, where their material might be combined with other reporting from different geographies into what UPI would have called a roundup. Then after a couple layers of editing, the story would be "fed back out" to everyone involved, and they would then send in their "feedback," meaning their responses to questions. The editorial machine had the time and inclination to put most stories through some sort of process—an intellectual puree machine—to raise the value added.

We had bureaus in most important world capitals, where correspondents could speak the local language and had years of experience. In the peak years, our editorial budget topped $200 million, an incredible number seen in today's terms, and we deployed more than two hundred editorial staffers around the world. It all depended on display advertising. Companies believed they were enhancing their images and therefore their bottom lines by buying ads in a print magazine—a quaint concept indeed by today's standards.

I used a lot of stringers, because I liked stories about geopolitical skullduggery, and it was my job to come up with stories for the International edition circulated outside the United States. (Most of these stories got into the domestic edition after being reduced in size.) Some stringers were what I called "penetration artists." They could get into most any country because they had the languages, and they knew how to operate alone in somewhat dodgy circumstances. One of my favorites was Thomas Goltz, who spoke Turkish, Arabic, and German. He could portray himself as a German or even as a Soviet to blend into Middle East destinations where someone who was identifiable as an American might have difficulty.

Another favorite was Igor Reichlin, whose father had helped the Soviet army develop nuclear weapons in remote Central Asia. Igor served in the Soviet army in Leningrad (Saint Petersburg), where he eavesdropped on NATO voice communications, but after the collapse of the Soviet Union, he was out of work. He was based in Bonn, which was then the pre-unification capital of West Germany. So he spoke fluent Russian, English, and German. When news broke that Iraqi dictator Saddam Hussein was trying to build a nuclear bomb-making capability, Igor was perfect, because he understood the different steps involved in purifying uranium. Who was supplying

Hussein the equipment he needed to go nuclear? Igor found German and other European companies that made the gear and declared they were exporting it to Hong Kong. That's what their shipping labels said.

But then we had Dinah Lee, an aggressive, tenacious reporter based in Hong Kong. She actually showed up at the Hong Kong addresses where sensitive European gear was supposed to be going. But the names of the companies supposed to be receiving the shipments were fake. The European companies must have known that their equipment was headed to Iraq and Libya and other suspect destinations. That's how we used our people and resources on a global scale.

When someone today thinks that they can obtain deep insight from social media, it's true that you can connect with many people and obtain snippets of insight into their lives in real time, pure and unfiltered. Horizontal knowledge of that sort is instantaneously available. But the kind of deep knowledge that *Business Week* could create simply does not exist on Instagram or Facebook.

***

For the first time since returning from Beijing, I now had the opportunity to travel in the American heartland. I was trying to understand the impact of East Asia's emergence on my native land. What forms of economic activity would win, and what forms would lose? Aside from the auto industry, I visited an RCA consumer electronics plant in Bloomington, Indiana, that was on its last legs. With its disappearance, the United States would lose the entire consumer electronics industry to Japan and the Four Tigers—Hong Kong, Taiwan, Singapore, and South Korea. Bewildering global forces were at work.

I discovered the world of exporting and began to see that as a positive model that created wealth for Americans and would be strong enough to resist the new waves of foreign competition. The "Aha" moment came when I got a call from Lars Nelson in Bemidji, Minnesota. He was affiliated with a state university there. This was the backwoods of Minnesota, to put it mildly, and Nelson was a backwoods hustler. He piqued my interest. He invited me out to give a speech to Minnesota exporters, which I did very nervously.

One of the companies represented in the room was Marvin Windows, located in Warroad, Minnesota, far to the north, within spitting distance of the Canadian border. I went to see their factory. It was bitterly cold—about 10 below zero. The factory was taking wood produced in the region and making windows that were sold in at least twenty countries. Their windows were very high quality, and they had invested in distributorships and marketing materials in different languages. As I recall, their revenues were less than $100 million a year.

When I got back to New York and told my fellow editors about the miracle of a mid-sized company based in rural Minnesota exporting to twenty countries, they did not believe me. The economists were particularly dismissive. It didn't fit in with their theories that only big companies located in port cities did the exporting, like Boeing, then based in Seattle. It was the start of my interest in small- and medium-sized companies that go international.

All of these themes were connected. They were all points of intersection between America and the world. As I wrote in a book proposal that never sold, "The upper tier of well-educated, well-traveled and multicultural Americans are going to enjoy many years of prosperity. For them, the opportunities are enormous.

"My fear is that broad cross sections of other Americans do not fully understand the new rules of this global game. As a result, they are going to lose and keep losing. It's not an exaggeration to say that millions of Americans, whether white or black, are becoming more like American Indians—people who are gradually pushed downward and reduced to a permanent, impoverished underclass."

In Part Two of this book, which follows, I am shifting away from telling stories chronologically, with the exception of China. Instead, I will trace the arcs of major stories for as many years as it takes to make them comprehensible.

PART TWO

THE BIG STORIES

8 The Great Japan Debate

The Great Japan Debate of the late 1980s and early- to mid-1990s is important to understand, because it set the stage for an even larger debate about China's emergence today. Japan's and China's political and economic systems are dramatically different, but they both have opaque decision-making systems that are difficult for outsiders to understand. They also both have high degrees of centralization with long-term strategic focuses. And they both have been able to use the scars of history to build support for policies that would, as the Japanese said, "Catch up and surpass the West." Moreover, Americans seem to suffer permanent confusion about the nature of change in these societies. We keep wanting to see them embrace Western values, when in fact their goal has been to revitalize and strengthen their own values and institutions.

As I traveled to the Midwest and other places, China was not on anyone's mental radar screens. The Japanese were far more advanced and seemed to be advancing steadily into the US economy. In an astonishingly short period of time, Japanese companies became highly advanced in consumer electronics, semiconductors, and all the industries where Americans thought they held a competitive advantage.

The US auto industry, which had turned out shoddy cars for years, was reeling. One fundamental problem was that management's relations with organized labor had deteriorated into open hostility. I visited one Firestone tire plant in Ohio where management and the union had not spoken to each other in years other than by negotiating contracts. Americans were fighting each other rather than uniting to rally around common interests. I could see that through the eyes of someone who had been on the ground in Hong Kong, China, Taiwan, and other places where the pursuit of prosperity was the No. 1 goal. Americans were shooting themselves in their collective feet.

There was increased tension between the governments of President Ronald Reagan and Japanese Prime Minister Yasuhiro Nakasone over a mounting Japanese trade surplus. The biggest business battle shaped up between General Motors and the Toyota Motor Corporation. GM was the largest US automaker (and still is), but it had grown complacent and arrogant about the Japanese competition. I dug into the issue in doing reporting for and editing a cover story by Tokyo bureau chief Larry Armstrong called "Toyota's Fast Lane."

One key was the concept of a *keiretsu*, a system of companies that invested in each other and did business with each other. The *keiretsu* were descendants of the *zaibatsu* that fueled Japan's war effort during World War II. It turned out that Toyota Motor had relationships with Aichi Steel Works, Toyoda Automatic Loom Works, Toyoda Machine Works, Nippondenso, and others. The Toyoda family played a role in all of them. (The Toyoda family decided to call their cars Toyotas because "Toyota" has eight strokes in the Japanese language and "Toyoda" has ten. Eight is a lucky number.)

The family was involved in Toyota because it was a relatively modern company, dating back to the 1890s. But other large groups such as Mitsui, Mitsubishi, and Sumitomo were two hundred to three hundred years old. Their founding families played a minimal role.

The *keiretsu* model had developed partly because of the poverty that Japan suffered for long periods. Capital was precious. So were materials. So the Japanese system maximized the use of capital and materials in a way that Americans did not understand. It was a pragmatic response to reality. Japanese culture also encouraged a group approach to problem solving.

To ease trade tensions, US government and industry encouraged Japanese auto manufacturers to set up shop inside the United States. The assumption was that the Japanese manufacturing advantage would disappear as Japanese managers found themselves working with difficult, recalcitrant unionized workers in states such as Michigan and Ohio. Toyota and General Motors even launched a joint venture called NUMMI, which stood for New United Motor Manufacturing Inc., in Fremont, California. GM executives got their first up-close look at Toyota's famous just-in-time manufacturing system at NUMMI, but it took them decades to imitate and improve upon it. Japanese manufacturers had perfected a system of having men on scooters going to storage areas to obtain parts for the assembly line so that the parts arrived just in time, which was called the *Kanban* system. American manufacturers stockpiled parts near the line, which was more expensive and took up space.

At this moment, in 1985 and 1986, Honda had opened operations in Marysville, Ohio, and Nissan had settled on Smyrna, Tennessee. I heard about a Hitachi automotive electronics plant being opened in Harrodsburg, Kentucky, my old stomping grounds, not far from Shelbyville, where I had spent a summer working for *The Shelby News*.

I went to check it out. On the western outskirts of Harrodsburg, a small agricultural community, was a monument to the men from the town who had gone to fight the Japanese in World War II. Some twenty-nine of them perished in the infamous Bataan death march in the Philippines, forced upon them by the Japanese. There was a tank pointed west, away from the town, dedicated to the men who had perished. The Hitachi plant was located a few hundred yards east.

I knew men gathered in barbershops to share the latest news, so I dropped into one on Main Street. "Nobody likes 'em," said Kenneth Parker, a barber and officer of the local chapter of Veterans of Foreign Wars, referring to the Japanese. "Nobody forgot what they did on December 7," a reference to the attack on Pearl Harbor.

"I reckon we got the tank pointed in the wrong direction," said Kenneth Hourigan, 73, one of the few living survivors of the death march who spent three and a half years in Japanese POW camps. We sent a photographer to take a picture of him standing by the tank and ran it in the magazine.

But both men acknowledged that the area needed jobs. "Our farm situation isn't too good," Parker said. A recession in 1981 and 1982 had been particularly punishing. Folks were grateful for the economic benefits.

So that's how the Japanese manufacturers once again surprised Detroit—they located the bulk of their plants away from highly unionized Michigan and northern Ohio and built what we called an "auto alley" stretching from southern Ohio, through Kentucky, into Tennessee. They adopted much more enlightened practices in dealing with labor, emphasizing the need to build teams. They brought their own suppliers to a great extent and implemented the just-in-time system.

One of our best scoops was the Toshiba machine tool deal with the Soviet Union. In 1987, the Cold War was at fever pitch. The Berlin Wall still stood firmly. Ronald Reagan was still president.

Jonathan Kapstein, based in Brussels, got this story started. He and I had a friendly relationship, unlike my ties to other European bureau chiefs, whom I seemed to chafe and vice versa. In May 1987, Kapstein's sources in NATO and the US military began telling him that Soviet submarines were getting around the Kola Peninsula without being detected. This was Russian territory at the northern tip of the border with Norway. The Soviets had big submarine bases up in the northern Arctic waters, but to get out into the Atlantic Ocean, they had to come around the Kola Peninsula. That was the key point in listening for them. Their propellers made enough noise that NATO and the

US could detect them when they moved. The big fear was a surge of Soviet submarines. If it were one or two subs coming around the corner, they could be managed. But if dozens started pouring out into the Atlantic, that would have been a signal that the Soviets were planning major military action.

Kapstein worked with his Oslo stringer to learn that Norway's state-owned armaments company and Toshiba Machine Co., a unit of Toshiba, had sold four computer-assisted machine tools to the Soviets for $17 million. These advanced machine tools allowed the Soviets to make smoother propellers that American sonar could not detect. I was able to draw in Larry Armstrong in Tokyo and Barbara Starr in Washington.

The headline in the May 18, 1987 issue of *Business Week* read, "A Leak That Could Sink the US Lead in Submarines."

The first two paragraphs: "It could prove one of the most damaging breaches of Western controls on military technology in years. In 1983 and 1984, Norway's state-owned armaments company and one of Japan's largest machine-tool makers, Toshiba Machine Co., sold the Soviet Union the technology to make ultraquiet submarine propellers. Unlike the often obscure impact of other high-tech leaks, this breach may already be changing the rules of undersea warfare.

"The governments of both Norway and Japan are scrambling to discover what happened. On the basis of evidence so far, Norway's Kongsberg Vapenfabrik and Toshiba Machine cooperated in delivering four computer-assisted machine tools to the Soviet Union for $17 million... 'The whole package was illegal,' says Tore Johnsen, a Norwegian police official investigating the incident."

It was a short article, but all hell broke loose in Washington. Congressmen and others started smashing Toshiba boom boxes (the name given to radio and tape recorder combinations that people carried around to play their music on) and other consumer electronic equipment in public displays of anger.

Rep. Duncan Hunter (R-Calif.) was the leader of the charge. He said, "This is outrageous behavior by Toshiba." The Senate voted to bar any imports of Toshiba products into the United States, prompting the July 1 resignations of both the chairman and president of Toshiba. Nobody seemed to get mad at the Norwegians.

Toshiba and the rest of the Japanese business and governmental community were smart enough to recognize they had a real problem. The result was the first grass roots lobbying campaign by a Japanese company on US soil. Toshiba learned how to persuade politicians and community leaders from states where it had manufacturing operations or suppliers to come to their defense in Washington. It worked. Toshiba never paid any meaningful price for what it had done. "The reason," wrote my Washington colleague Steve Dryden, "was the company has waged a textbook crisis-control effort involving not only heavy-hitting lobbyists but also grassroots support from across the US."

In fact, the Toshiba playbook emerged as key to the effort by all Japanese companies and their government to avert sanctions against them through the remainder of the 1980s and into the 1990s. They learned to game the American system. In some ways, it was the beginning of the corruption of the American political system. It could be bought.

I was concerned enough about the trend that I developed a cover story on "Japan's Influence in America," with help from colleagues in Tokyo and Washington. Japanese companies were endowing chairs at American universities, meaning that the holder of a Toyota chair or a Mitsubishi chair would teach and comment publicly in ways that promoted Japanese interests. Japanese companies started lobbying more in Washington. I went to Washington to interview James H. Lake, who had been an official in administrations of both presidents Reagan and George H.W. Bush but was now lobbying for Japanese companies. "They have the right to representation," he said. The problem with his argument was that Japan's decision-making system was so opaque and

so closed to American businesses that lobbying was not reciprocal. That didn't matter to Lake. He just wanted the money.

We wrote: "Japanese companies are spending heavily to
shape the way Americans view them. They are pouring tens of
millions of dollars into US education, from Ivy League colleges
to elementary schools in Kentucky. Museums, universities, public
television stations, and think tanks are competing for—and getting—Japanese money. The Japanese also are wielding political
power from the grass roots to the top echelons of Washington.
The same words that describe Japan's economic strategy apply to
what the Japanese call their 'soft side' activities: Systematic. Coordinated. Long term.

Lester C. Thurow, then dean of the Sloan School of
Management at Massachusetts Institute of Technology, said,
"They've learned how to play us like a violin."

***

One major debate inside the magazine, and throughout
American governmental and academic circles, was over Japan's
direction. Was Japan going to open its economy and adopt more
Western business models? Was Japan's political system going to
become more democratic and less dominated by a single party,
the Liberal Democratic Party (LDP), and a handful of old cro-
nies? Could the United States persuade Japan to take these steps
in exchange for continued access to the American market? Would
Japan soften its industrious ways as a younger generation rose,
and as the Japanese started enjoying their wealth? Would they
become, in effect, more like us?

I think my boss, Bob Dowling, was one of the leading
proponents of the view that Japan had to change. It was almost a
religious issue for him. A devoted Roman Catholic, he seemed to
conflate God with Adam Smith's "invisible hand" of the market.
Having been based in Brussels and having observed European

integration efforts, it was understandable that he might believe the invisible hand moved in mysterious ways and would ultimately push other societies to embrace American-style capitalism and democracy. He never came right out and said that, but adding up the clues, I'm convinced that is a fair summary. (He later produced a special issue of the magazine on "convergence," the notion that all the world's economies and political systems were converging toward the American model.)

We were professional enough that we were able to manage positive personal relationships even if we disagreed. In fact, it may have created higher-quality coverage because we had to examine and re-examine our assumptions.

Reflecting the hope that Japan would change for the better from an American perspective, and also reflecting the influence of the Tokyo bureau chief, Larry Armstrong, we put together a cover story package, "Japan: Remaking a Nation." It appeared in July 1987. There were several articles about whether Japan would change or not change. I think the best statement of hope came in a commentary by correspondent Barbara Buell. She wrote:

"For true *kokusaika* (internationalization) to happen, the Japanese will have to start looking beyond their differences they have with outsiders and begin thinking of themselves as part of the vast outside world ... A great nation, increasingly rich and self-confident, should do no less."

I was an editor on the project and basically went with the flow. I didn't think I knew enough to argue.

But with the arrival of a new bureau chief, Bob Neff, the magazine tilted in the opposite direction. Neff was the child of missionaries and had grown up in Japan. He used to joke that he thought he was Japanese until at age 13 or so, when his Japanese friends began to shun him. Their culture was driving them away from a *gaijin* (foreigner), he felt. Neff spoke native Japanese and was a skeptic that the warm and fuzzy feelings we had expressed in "Remaking A Nation" were on target. The Toshiba flap and the cover on Japan's Influence in America had gradually shaped me into more of a skeptic that Japan would change in any meaningful way to diminish its economic momentum.

I was about to get a more important role in the grand Japan debate. In mid-1989, wife Cathy introduced me to a book publisher who had heard about the Recruit scandal in Japan and suspected it was a decisive break in the structure of Japan's post-World War II political and economic order. The chairman of the giant Nippon Telegraph & Telephone Co., Hisashi Shinto, was forced to resign when it was revealed he had benefitted personally by owning shares of a high-flying subsidiary of Recruit, a human resources company based in Tokyo. There were hints that Prime Minister Yasuhiro Nakasone might be the next to resign.

The publisher wanted to believe that Japan was "changing." I had covered China, and the book publisher thought if I understood China, I must also understand Japan. Which was preposterous, of course. They possess entirely different systems and cultures. But the publisher did not know that, and I was very pleased to get a contract and an advance that would allow me to travel to Japan. I spent the month of July 1989 in Japan (and would spend October there as well).

While I was in Tokyo conducting interviews for the book in the summer, often in tandem with *Business Week* reporters, a Socialist woman, Takako Doi, won control of the Upper House of the Diet, or parliament. Seen from ground level, it was a mid-summer diversion that did not represent any fundamental break in Japan's system. The Diet was largely toothless, and the Upper House was even less powerful.

So Bob Neff and I were flabbergasted when we read a message from Dowling back in New York telling us that a "constellation" of events in Japan proved that its post-World War II system was breaking down. Bob had been working on a cover package called "Rethinking Japan," with my support, and some of the research I did for the book overlapped with his reporting.

It appeared in August and was a response to Japan-watchers who were heralding dramatic change in Japan. Very boldly on the cover were the words: "After years of haggling, the U.S. still runs a $52 billion annual trade deficit with Japan, and Japanese society remains closed in crucial ways. As a result, a radical shift in US thinking about Japan is under way. This revisionist view holds that Japan really is different—and that conventional free-trade policies won't work. Once, such views would have been dismissed as 'Japan-bashing,' but now they have an intellectual base."

The magazine had the power to launch, in effect, a revisionist movement. We quoted thinkers such as Chalmers Johnson, Clyde Prestowitz, Pat Choate, James Fallows, and Karel van Wolferen. Neff wrote in a commentary: "Trade hawks in the U.S. used to occupy a lonely spot on the political landscape. Dismissed as Japan-bashers, scapegoaters, or even crypto-racists, they were pushed to the sidelines during the free-trade years of the Reagan era. Now, however, there's a growing respect."

Note in these stories the intellectual confusion and the name-calling, which can be seen again in the China debate today. As I became more exposed to the issues, I became more of a proponent for the argument that the Japanese were not willingly going to do anything that diminished their ability to make money and continue to make competitive and technological gains. The burden of adjusting, of becoming more competitive, fell on us.

Just as the China debate today can be caricatured as the "panda huggers" struggling against the "panda bashers," the Japan debate pitted well-meaning Americans against other well-meaning Americans. It was "the cherry blossom crowd" against the "Japan bashers." We couldn't forge a consensus view. Our own ideological confusion got in the way. Did being a "free trader" mean it was wrong for the US government to help industries better compete? If you believed in making US industry more competitive, did that mean you were picking "winners and losers?" Picking winners and losers was seen as a form of "industrial policy" and that was not appropriate for the US government, so the argument went. And the accusation of racism also was made, as it is in the China debate.

While in Japan working on my book, I hired a translator who also scheduled appointments for me. I dug into the structure of Japanese society and its politics. I interviewed top political leaders such as former prime ministers Nakasone and Noboru Takeshita and other LDP bigshots.

I immersed myself as deeply as a foreigner could in what it meant to be Japanese. I discovered that hundreds of thousands of Koreans had been forced to move to Japan during World War II to work in mines and other heavy industries. (Korean women, meanwhile, were forced to offer "comfort" to Japanese soldiers throughout the wartime empire.) I interviewed one Korean family who no longer spoke Korean. They had been raised in Japan. They spoke only Japanese and appeared to a *gaijin* as being Japanese. But the Japanese would not allow them to be integrated into their society. Schools and golf clubs would not admit ethnic Koreans. There was another class of untouchables, called the *burakumin*. The reality was far different from the notion promulgated by the Japanese media—that Japan is completely homogenous. Many Japanese hired detectives to look into the backgrounds of people their children might be considering marrying. The detectives would search through birth records in temples to establish whether someone was a bona fide Japanese or not.

There was a fundamental difference between the Chinese and Japanese when it came to dealing with foreigners. The Chinese were confident that they could draw in and Sinicize foreigners. We'd learn the language. Fall in love with the culture. But the Japanese were much more defensive against the *gaijin*.

It also became clear to me that the Recruit scandal was actually a fight for the tens of millions of yen that flowed through the telecommunications industry into the hands of politicians who protected the industry. The corruption was institutional- ized. It was almost tribal. Japan's special prosecutors were (and remain) highly politicized and were being manipulated by Shin Kanemaru, often described as the "puppet master" of the LDP, who operated from the shadows. The scandal had nothing to do with Japan breaking down its system and veering toward some Western model.

My book came out in 1990, and I was thrust into the center of the debate. I was grateful to Susan Chira, who had been based in Japan for *The New York Times,* for reviewing my book with the headline "Japan Without the Shouting." That's what I was trying to do—explain the realities of Japan to Americans in ways they could understand and act upon.

Japanese companies and governmental bodies had their hired American guns who took part in the debate, which raged for years. It built toward something of a climax in 1995 when President Bill Clinton pushed his US Trade Representative Mickey Kantor to threaten tariffs on Toyota's luxury Lexus autos if Ryutaro Hashimoto, the head of the Ministry of International Trade and Industry (the ever powerful MITI), did not make ade- quate trade-opening concessions. Hashimoto was famous for dis- playing his *kendo* swords to demonstrate how tough he was.

A "deal" was announced, and Clinton declared a victory for free trade, but in effect the Americans blinked. The Ameri- can demand for the Lexus and other Japanese goods from deal- erships, employees, and general consumers was so great that Americans as a whole did not care about the trade deficit or the competitive challenge. They just wanted their Lexus sedans.

So there was never a national strategy to respond to Japan. Certain actions helped re-establish a bit of balance. The Plaza Accords of 1985 forced up the value of the yen, which made Japanese goods more expensive in world markets but did not fundamentally solve the problem of the competitive and trade imbalances. President George H.W. Bush, a Republican, created

SEMATECH in 1988. This was a government-industry consortium designed to make sure American semiconductor companies retained their technology edge. It was a classic piece of "industrial policy"—but perhaps the fact that a Republican president had done it relieved it of some of its ideological opprobrium.

The North American Free Trade Agreement, which Clinton signed to take effect Jan. 1, 1994, was another piece of the response. By allowing American car makers to take advantage of both Canadian and Mexican suppliers and workers, the government helped Detroit in a major way.

There were other signs of response at the local and regional level. In 1992, we did a cover story called "Hot Spots." I organized and managed it. A team of reporters in different bureaus looked at regions in the United States that were displaying success in creating technology-based economic growth, as Silicon Valley had done. By tapping the technology coming out of research at key universities, these regions—like Salt Lake City or Austin, Texas—were creating start-up companies such as Novell and Dell Computer. This type of innovation is what Americans did better than anyone else in the world. If only we could spread the knowledge about how to do it. If only we could persuade more Americans that the old model—of getting a high school education and working in the factory until retiring—was evaporating.

To be sure, surprises emanated from Japan. Its financial markets, which had gone sky-high because of stock market speculation based on shady real estate loans, came back down to reality. Some Japanese companies ranging from Toyota to Toshiba suffered scandals and no longer seemed as invincible. Japanese consumer electronics companies missed the whole mobile telephone trend, as Nokia, Ericsson, Blackberry, and Motorola demonstrated.

Were the revisionists wrong? Not at all. We were right to express concern about the competitive imbalance and the loss of control of key industries, which were always more important than bilateral trade numbers.

So why did the Japan debate pass from the stage? The emergence of the "four tigers"—Hong Kong, Taiwan, South Korea, and Singapore—was one reason. But the single biggest explanation was the rise of China, which had ten times the population of Japan and far greater ambitions. In 1994, products started flooding into the United States from China in a way that they never had previously. American companies had invested and were manufacturing in China for the first time in a major way or else were procuring goods from suppliers. "A Tidal Wave of Chinese Goods," read the headline in a December 1994 story that I edited and contributed to. Toys R Us, Walmart, The Gap, and other retailers had started massive buying binges in China and were flying the goods to American stores in time for the holiday shopping season. "It seems that millions of Americans will enjoy bargain prices on gifts made in China," the piece concluded. "That may be just the beginning of a much broader China export boom."

The argument that Japan failed to embrace American ways and therefore has suffered two "lost decades" as a result is specious. Having traveled to Japan many times in the intervening years, and most recently in 2016 and 2017 to co-author a book on the ThinkPad (*How the ThinkPad Changed the World*), I can report that Japan is still one of the most sophisticated societies on the planet, with remarkable transportation and health care systems. Its cities have been transformed because Japanese engineers have learned how to give skyscrapers insulation against earthquakes, which are common in Japan and have constrained the building of skyscrapers for many years. Now the foundations of buildings can actually move in response to the quakes, sparing major damage. And the Japanese standard of living is world class.

True, China has outstripped it to become the world's No. 2 economy, but Japan is still No. 3. Japanese companies moved upscale to dominate fields such as special semiconductors, sensors, and capacitors. They realized they couldn't compete with China's low-cost labor, so they retreated from those fields and moved up the technology ladder. The single largest percentage of the value of components in an Apple iPhone, assembled in China, for example, is semiconductors from Toshiba, more than 30 percent of the value of an iPhone, according to one teardown analysis.

Unfortunately, American opinion of Japan has lurched from one extreme to another—from "Japan is a challenge" to "Japan no longer matters." American media organizations have pulled out dozens of correspondents from Tokyo. The prevailing view is that Japan is aging, and its population is in decline, so why bother covering the country? That's a terrible mistake. The Japanese see what's happening to their population and are responding by selectively allowing more foreigners to live in Japan, for example. The incredible irony today is that the United States very much needs Japan to help resist China's efforts to establish a Sino-centric world order. Japan also needs us. Neither of us can do it alone. How the wheel of history hath turned.

9 The Korean Miracle and Dr. Chin

The first time I went back to Asia following our return to the United States was when I flew to Seoul, South Korea, where I had never been. It was the summer of 1988, and South Korea was getting ready to host the Summer Olympics for the first time in September. We wanted a cover story to come out before the Olympics to address the question of whether South Korea could emerge economically, as Japan had.

Our stringer, Laxmi Nakarmi, had a fascinating personal story. He had been born in Nepal but was a second son and therefore would not inherit any of the family's property. Instead, his parents sent him to a Catholic school and then university in India. He ended up in South Korea. He married a Korean woman and learned to speak fluent Korean. Being from Asia and being brown-skinned, he really understood the Korean mindset. He knew that if he wanted access to a chief executive officer, he should give the appropriate gifts to their secretaries at New Year's. Laxmi might have gotten along better with the Koreans than he did with white Americans, whom he believed displayed racism toward him (as he later confided). But he was precisely the kind of bridge person I enjoyed, the kind who straddles multiple cultures. We struck up a partnership that endured for more than twenty years, even after we both had left *Business Week*. For the eight years we worked at *Business Week* together, I knew how to take his copy, which was rough, polish it, and extract the points I knew he was trying to make. Tokyo bureau chiefs didn't tend to have enough time to do that.

One of the best ways to understand Korea is to think of the game Risk. It's one of those countries, in the game, where invading armies go back and forth, attacking in force from multiple directions. Korea, a peninsula in real life, was invaded from both the north and the south over the course of its history. The Chinese and Mongols attacked from the north. The Japanese attacked from the south. Both China and Japan have much larger populations than South Korea. Japan actually tried to annex Korea from 1910 to 1945. It tried to eradicate the speaking of the Korean language and the sense of Korean nationalism, which obviously did not work.

You could get a sense of this history of conflict by climbing Namsan Mountain in the middle of Seoul, not from the Westin Chosun Hotel where I often stayed. I could jog to the top of the mountain from the hotel. On top, there were great big fire chambers. One could see other mountains to the north and south. A sign explained that when the residents of Seoul wanted to know about any impending attacks, they'd go to the top of the mountain and look at the fire signals coming from either direction. It was like Morse code, an early version of a telecommunications system. Altogether, Korea had been invaded four hundred times in its history.

I found that nothing I had done or learned in China or Japan helped me understand the Korean language, which was completely unintelligible. The Koreans used characters in their written language that appeared to be Chinese in origin but were actually phonetic. It was obvious that there had been deep cultural, linguistic, educational, and political exchanges between China, Japan, and Korea over the source of several thousand years and they were located in close geographic proximity. But they had developed their languages and cultures in a way that kept them very separate. You could almost feel yourself moving from one bubble to another, like different tennis bubbles, as you arrived in one of these countries from another.

The Koreans were much better drinkers of alcohol than the Japanese and most southern Chinese. Many Japanese and southern Chinese get red in the face after just one or two drinks and may have to vomit. Their systems seem to lack the enzyme that breaks alcohol down so that by the time it arrives in your brain, it feels pleasant. The Koreans and northern Chinese must have had Mongolian genes in their blood, because the Koreans, in particular, could drink like fish. As a result of my highly scientific survey of drinking practices in the three countries, I discovered one of the only linguistic commonalities among the three cultures. When you said, "Bottoms up!" in Chinese, it was *ganbei* (literally, "dry bottom.") In Japanese, it was *kanpai*, and in Korean it was *geonbae.*

My primary mission on this first visit was to get the business story, but Laxmi organized a very extensive schedule for me and provided translators. I went to a university in Seoul and interviewed students who told me they wanted to march north to the DMZ that separated South and North Korea to reunite with their northern cousins. That struck me as nutso. They would be shot down or killed by land mines. They also blamed the Americans for the division of the peninsula after the Korean War. The United States lost more than fifty thousand men fighting against a combination of North Korean and Chinese troops and agreed to draw a line 155 miles long across the 38th parallel to stop the bloodshed, cutting the peninsula into two countries. What were we supposed to have done? Lose another fifty thousand lives to push our area of control up to the Yalu River? The Chinese would have never allowed it, and they had millions of troops. We were vastly outnumbered.

My father had spent some time after World War II running an officer's club in Seoul. This would have been in 1945–46. He told me the Koreans at that time were so desperately poor and hungry that they were eating the bark off of trees. Adding to the misery of decades of Japanese occupation, the Korean War broke out. The peninsula was then ravaged by the push of Chinese and North Korean troops south almost all the way to the southern tip of the peninsula. Then the Americans counterattacked, starting with General MacArthur's famous Inchon landing, and started pushing north, inflicting another wave of death and destruction. The war lasted from 1950 to 1953.

On this, my first visit, I would say the Koreans were living on par with the Filipinos. The cars were small and cheap. There were a few skyscrapers in Seoul and a ten-lane expressway, but most of the rest of the country lagged far behind, perhaps a decade or more. The Koreans were completely dependent on the outside world for any advanced products. And they were living in the shadow of a North Korea that was armed to the teeth. The DMZ was only thirty-five miles north of Seoul. The North had hundreds of thousands of men, tanks, and missiles on their side of the DMZ, and it was assumed that they could rain destruction on Seoul at will. But South Koreans did not display much fear about a North Korean attack. Why would the North want to destroy the limited prosperity that South Koreans had created? Wouldn't they rather want to share in it?

I took a bus ride by myself to see the DMZ. Most of the passengers were Japanese men, who displayed distinctly un-Japanese behavior as we passed through checkpoints and military police boarded the bus to check IDs. The Japanese men—and they were all men—were openly dismissive of the MPs. Some of the Japanese men had frizzy hair, and they mostly wore white or light colors. I realized later that they were *yakuza*, the criminal gangs that dominate Japan's underworld.

The DMZ was deadly serious business. North Korean soldiers had tunneled into the US and South Korean side of the DMZ and killed GIs with axes. We could see big red concrete markers a few hundred yards from the actual border. US fighter pilots would engage in exercises in which they flew directly at the border at high speed to see if the US military could locate North Korean radar systems as they tracked the oncoming aircraft. The red concrete markers were there to remind the pilots that it was time to divert.

It was in the 90s Fahrenheit, and the heat was the sticky variety. Big, beefy US Marines were doing push-ups a few hundred yards from the border. "We're just here as speed bumps," one told me. If the North attacked, its tanks would roll over any defenders near the DMZ.

How was it possible that South Korea could stage a dash for prosperity under such circumstances? Korea's *chaebol*, the Korean equivalent of Japan's *keiretsu*, were the driving force. The largest of them were Hyundai, Lucky-Goldstar, Samsung, and Daewoo. They were younger than the Japanese *keiretsu* and were still being managed by their founders. The Koreans had obviously borrowed the model from Japan.

They wanted to emerge as major makers of steel. They wanted to develop a semiconductor industry and create an auto industry that could export to the world. In the West, there was deep skepticism that Koreans could do it.

I had a moment of truth when I went to visit a semiconductor factory that Samsung was building. I never wrote about this for the magazine, but this image still stands out in my mind. A diminutive young man was trying to get the Samsung memory chip factory up and running. Making semiconductors is a very precise and difficult thing to do. Chin Dae-Je had earned a PhD in electronic engineering at Stanford University and worked for IBM for a number of years in the United States.

It was morning when I visited, and he obviously had been up all night. The shadows under his eyes were pronounced. But he was absolutely determined. The determination, despite the odds and despite all the doubts, was what impressed me. I could feel it. I could taste it.

We at the magazine concluded that the raw drive for education and technology, combined with nationalism, would allow the South Koreans to emerge. We wrote that underlying all the conflicting forces among labor unions, student protesters, and regions "is one of the most intense stirrings of nationalism anywhere in the world. On morning radio talk shows, commentators urge Koreans to 'work hard to make our nation better.' Signs in the elevators at the Daewoo group's headquarters advise employees that 'the hand of the diligent shall rule.' Koreans work an average of 2,700 hours a year, 40 percent more than Americans and 25 percent more than the Japanese. The saying, *minjok chajon,* meaning, 'We can do it ourselves,' amounts to a national slogan." The joke at the time was that the only competitors in the world the Japanese worried about were the Koreans, because when the Japanese were playing golf on Sundays, the Koreans were still working.

I made several intervening trips over the years and charted Korea's stunning progress. The next time I met Dr. Chin was when I went to South Korea in 2002 for *Fortune* magazine to write about Samsung Electronics. The headline read: "Samsung's Golden Touch: Once a copycat, the Korean giant has money, market share and strong new products. Now it wants respect."

Dr. Chin was now one of the most senior executives at Samsung Electronics, which was part of the sprawling Samsung Group. He was head of the digital media division, which made computers and consumer electronics. "Five years ago, we had to buy chips from Sony or Matsushita, so we were always behind," he said. Now, he says, "We can be No. 1. There is no doubt in my mind."

We talked about the events of 1988 when I first met him. In trying to get the factory operating, he had run smack into the hierarchical and deferential Samsung culture, an imitation of Japanese management practices. Having spent time in the United States, Chin had been slightly Americanized. So he chafed when he was essentially told to remain quiet. "At strategy meetings, no one asked questions," he recalled. Asking unscripted questions can be considered rude: if the person does not have an answer, everyone loses face. "But I didn't understand things. So I asked questions. People blushed and turned red. They were upset. I didn't care. I just kept asking questions."

Dr. Chin told me a story he didn't expect me to use in the article, but it was so interesting and revealing about him and Samsung's driven culture that I did. It happened on a golf outing with CEO Yun Jong-yong. Whenever they finished a round, there would be an awards ceremony at which winners were encouraged to drink "atomic shots"—beer spiked with hard liquor. Yun offered to donate an expensive driver to the team of executives who could drink the most atomic shots. The bidding reached ten shots. Everybody thought that was the outer limit. But Chin, who hates to lose, upped the ante. He and six of his executives blew the other guys away by pledging fifteen—and then downing them. They might have puked for days afterward, but they had won.

Dr. Chin was so visionary and so well-respected that he was named the Minister of Information and Communications for the whole country. My next point of contact with him in that role was in 2005, when I was editor of *Chief Executive* magazine, and Laxmi also had moved on from *Business Week*. He was running a conference company and had maintained his relationship with Dr. Chin.

The three of us cooked up a plan to create the Seoul Digital Forum at the Shilla Hotel in Seoul in May 2005. This two-day conference was a money-making effort by Laxmi and my magazine, but Dr. Chin also would benefit by having me identify top technology executives to come to Seoul to meet him and other top officials. By this time Korea was among the heaviest users of the Internet in the world and was innovating on a global scale. The subject matter was cutting edge—we scheduled talks and panels on such subjects as broadband, digital broadcasting to mobile devices, open source software, global R&D strategies, and the like.

So in a spectacularly short period of time, South Korea had become a technology powerhouse. How did they do it? I would say the keys were an emphasis on education, as seen in

many other countries in Asia, and a flexibility to allow someone such as Dr. Chin to emerge and guide the whole country's
technology efforts. There was unity of purpose among companies and government ministries, which one does not necessarily
see in the United States. Despite a gulf between the *chaebol* and
left-leaning politicians, the society as a whole pulled together. The
Korean companies also were slightly more open to change than
the Japanese were. They embraced some foreigners into their
ranks but also a large number of Korean-Americans and Koreans
educated in the United States, such as Dr. Chin. And they worked
with a great sense of intensity and urgency, as if their national
well-being depended on it, which it did. There were lots of Chinese and Japanese tourists. The department stores were full of
luxury goods, and South Koreans were dressing in much more
fashionable clothing than ever before. Their use of cosmetics—
they were the largest per capital consumers of cosmetics in the
world—meant that they were attractive physically and respected
in other parts of Asia for their sense of style and beauty. That's
what technology-based economic growth creates.

It's interesting to speculate about whether Korea's transition from military rule to democracy helped or hindered its
economic success. Americans like to believe that democracy
helps breed economic gains, so it's important to re-examine that
assumption. (Chinese President Xi obviously believes that totalitarian control creates wealth.)

To put the Korean story as simply as possible, a military
president, Park Chung-hee, was assassinated and another military
man, Chun Doo-hwan, took charge. He gradually transitioned to
a former general who ruled as a civilian. In the early days, there
were fears that leftists and unions would take control of the society if democracy were introduced. Two presidents, Kim Young-
sam and Kim Dae-jung, were leftish, but they did not do anything
too radical. A conservative woman was elected, then another
left-leaning man. It became a true democracy.

There are still deep divisions in South Korea between the families who control the big business groups and the leftish voices who argue that they are evil and corrupt. But I'd say that the move to democracy encouraged all South Koreans to believe that they could push their causes and advance their interests. It allowed for the rise of people such as Dr. Chin. If the military had tried to maintain brute force control, I suspect more energy would have gone into resisting that and not into doing the necessary things to educate young people and work hard at creating wealth. On balance, I think the American belief in democracy and wealth creation was vindicated in the case of South Korea.

Very similar trends played out in Japan and Taiwan. After World War II, we wrote a new constitution for Japan and imposed it on them, but the Japanese learned to embrace the political concept called democracy and make it work for them, with a relatively free press and multiple political parties. Taiwan also moved away from the strongman rule imposed by Chiang Kai-shek after he lost the Chinese Civil War and fled to the island. His son, Chiang Ching-kuo, continued dictatorial rule but was eventually persuaded to allow democracy to take root. Taiwan is a thriving democracy today, perhaps the most open and robust in East Asia.

So there were reasons why many Americans believed similar trends could unfold on the Chinese mainland. It seemed to be the way history unfolded. No one thought it would be easy or quick, because the Communist Party had a long, proud history. But based on our experience in other countries in East Asia, if a country wanted to become prosperous, some form of greater pluralism seemed essential.

10 The European Front: Germany and Russia

Partly because my family incorrectly thought we were of German ancestry, I had always been interested in the country. Against the backdrop of the Vietnam War, I wrote a college paper about the experiences of two German intellectuals during World War I, philosopher Ernst Jünger and Erich Maria Remarque, author of *All Quiet on the Western Front*. That war shattered their faith in many of the institutions and beliefs that had formed the fabric of their lives, which was similar to what my generation was feeling about the Vietnam War. And I studied the rise of Adolf Hitler and his attempted "final solution," also known as the Holocaust.

In view of my interest, it is perhaps surprising that I did not actually make it to Germany until the late 1980s. But I was able to make a series of trips to Germany before the Berlin Wall fell in November 1989 and the two Germanies reunited in 1990, as well as afterward, up until 1993. I never lived in Germany, but once again, I stumbled into one of the greatest stories of the century.

Of course, the Soviet Union's collapse was precipitated at least in part by the fall of the Wall. There was a great debate at *Business Week* and throughout American policy circles about the new Commonwealth of Independent States and then just Russia. Could it adopt democracy and capitalism? I managed only one trip to Moscow in 1993, but that allowed me to form some impressions.

I'll tell these stories in three parts. The first is about the future of a united Germany. What kind of country would it become? Would it veer into a new kind of fascism? The second is about the agony of unifying the two Germanies from an economic perspective. I'll add a sidebar about what Americans can learn from Germany economically and educationally. The third and final part is about the theory that Russia could adopt democracy and capitalism "cold turkey," meaning overnight.

Overall, I became convinced that even if Americans preferred the charms of France or Portugal, Germany is the most important country in Europe for Americans to understand. When the United States and Germany drift apart, that sets the stage for world wars.

When I first visited Berlin in 1988, I particularly liked the neighborhood called Kreuzberg, which was smack up against the Berlin Wall. The wall was covered in bright graffiti and artistic drawings, even though there was a no man's land with barbed wire and armed guards on the other side. The locals had turned a symbol of oppression into a public mural. Kreuzberg felt a little bit like New York's Greenwich Village and was inhabited by a large percentage of Turks, who spoke fluent German and drove a lot of the taxis, and there was also a Jewish population. That was surprising to me. If Hitler had tried to kill Jews and Berlin was a living reminder of his evil, I would have thought the Jewish community would have left. But they didn't. Berlin also had an arts scene and displayed punk and gothic cultures. The nightlife was lively. It was a complete contrast with the absolutely antiseptic capital city of Bonn, way to the west on the Rhine.

History grabs at your ankles in Berlin like ground fog. Germans in other parts of the country say that everything bad in German history came from Berlin. Hitler's bunker was in the process of being demolished and covered by a large new office tower when I first visited. But the Bundestag, or German Parliament, where Hitler gave fiery speeches, still stood, and Checkpoint Charlie between East and West Berlin was still being used by traffic going both ways. The museum there displayed photographs of the incredible hardships that East Germans endured as they tried to escape. Families put children in suitcases. People tried to dig under the Wall. But the East German guards were brutally efficient, killing many of their own countrymen.

The best way to actually see East Berlin (before the Wall fell) was through the majestic Brandenburg Gate, which was on the border between the two Berlins. All the buildings on the other side of the gate showed a Soviet influence, meaning they were gray and drab and old. The East Germans drove Trabants, which were little cars so badly designed and manufactured that they were a kind of national joke. West Germans, in sharp contrast, drove Mercedes, BMWs, VWs, and Audis, which were international symbols of design and engineering excellence.

I was not present at the fall of the Berlin Wall, but it was simply stunning, even from afar. The German people literally tore it down. The joke at the time was that their thirst for blue jeans and bananas compelled them to rebel against the Soviets, and it seemed true that seeing the wealth of West Germany caused them to resent the Communist system for holding them back. President Reagan had also tried to gear up economic pressure against the Soviets by unveiling a Strategic Defense Initiative that would dramatically modernize the US military capability, forcing the Soviets to spend billions of rubles if they wished to keep pace.

I explored the theme of what kind of Germany would emerge in a "Letter from Berlin" I wrote on the basis of travel there in 1993. It was entitled "The Battleground for Germany's Soul." "Berlin has a hard edge of a kind a traveler doesn't immediately feel in Bonn or Cologne or Frankfurt," I wrote. "It is the edge of hate, expressed not only toward the 400,000 foreigners living in Berlin but also toward fellow Germans. One reason for the aggressive, confrontational tone is that Berlin is where the profoundly different psychologies of the former West and East Germanies butt heads.

"Westerners blithely dismiss the old East German system as having nothing worth preserving other than right-turn-on-red. Easterners say they've been invaded by greedy, materialistic Westerns. 'Spekulanten Raus (Speculators Out!),' scream the graffiti scrawled on a wall in eastern Berlin, attacking Westerns who have been snapping up apartment buildings."

I interviewed Jews who felt they were on the receiving end of discrimination, and I met the leader of the 137,000-person Turkish community, Turgut Cakmakoglu, who told me, "People get used to far-right attacks on foreigners. It becomes part of everyday life."

Far from Kreuzberg on the quiet, prosperous Kluckstrasse (*strasse* means street), I interviewed the leader of the right-wing Republican Party, Werner Müller, a former civil servant who took early retirement to take up the cause against foreigners. "The influence of the foreigners must be stopped," he said. "This is unbearable." He went on in tones that smacked of the medieval era. "Christendom" has to fight back against the "Turkish colony" in Berlin, he added.

What I did not include in the letter was that over this six-year period, I met dozens of students, elected officials, and average Germans in Bonn, Frankfurt, Cologne, Dresden, Kiel, and elsewhere who expressed revulsion about what happened in Germany from 1933 to 1945. It was the twelve years when Germany went crazy. They all knew the history, and they were determined to prevent it from occurring again. It's a great testament to German character that they elected Angela Merkel as prime minister. She came from the former East Germany, and she was the one who in about 2015 said Germany could handle another one million immigrants from such disaster zones as Syria. Germans may have grumbled about it, but they went along, and Merkel was able to win re-election. In general, the Germans have made it work, better perhaps than France or Belgium. The voices of division and hatred I heard in Berlin were never allowed to dominate the national conversation.

The second major theme was the enormous challenge West Germany faced in trying to absorb East Germany, probably the first and only time in history such a wealthy Western democracy took over a much poorer Communist society. Some experts said it would be impossible for the West to absorb the East.

In the East, it was like the COVID-19 pandemic hit. Suddenly, everything the East Germans thought they knew about how their companies worked and how their society functioned was radically changed. My first trip into the former East Germany was in 1992, when my *Business Week* colleague, Gail Edmundson, greeted me at Berlin's airport and then drove us to Jena, a center of East Germany's optics industry, with companies such as Carl Zeiss. I was surprised to see how primitive East Germany's roads and other infrastructure were compared to West Germany's. How could all the Soviet tanks have reached West Germany if the East German roads were in such awful condition?

But now the key questions were: What was anything worth in a hard currency? What was the value of a factory that made rail cars for the Soviet bloc? On the outskirts of Berlin in 1993, I visited Deutsche Waggonbau, one of the big Communist-style conglomerates that once had twenty-one factories and twenty-five thousand workers. It was now down to five factories and nine thousand workers. The firings had been massive. "All the structures we worked under for twenty to thirty years have been done away with by the stroke of someone's hand," said the head of public relations, Günter Krug. He said it amounted to "... the neocolonization of the West against the East."

One big piece in sorting all this out was the Treuhandanstalt, or "trust agency," created by the East German government before the official date of German reunification, October 3, 1990. It oversaw the restructure and sale of about eighty-five hundred state-owned companies with more than four million employees. It took ownership of everything from steel mills to film studios. It took over agricultural land and forests, and it took over the property of the former secret policy agency, the Stasi, and much of the property of the East German army.

The second head of the Treuhand, Birgit Breuel, (the first one had been assassinated by persons unknown) visited *Business Week* in New York, and I heard firsthand about the agonizing decisions she faced. Frau Breuel was a formidable, dour woman, probably in her fifties. It was her job to place a monetary value on all the former East German assets and to sell them to West German entities.

The human cost of all this was enormous, as I learned on that press trip in 1993 organized by the Atlantic Bridge, a nonprofit dedicated to German-American understanding. We interviewed Reinhard Kraetzer, who worked for the regional municipal council for social affairs in East Berlin. It was his job to try to preserve a social safety net for residents in his district. Who would pay the rent? Who would provide welfare? How can you create stability? "Nothing has stabilized," he told us. "We still have a decrease in jobs. We also have a high rate of debts." East Germans were surveying "the ruins of their lives," our translator said.

But collectively, the Germans did it. They figured out how to make unification work. How? One explanation is that they created institutional processes such as the Treuhand and stuck with them. They also demonstrated a great collective sense of being in it together, despite the heated rhetoric. And somehow they found the mutual trust that was necessary. They shared the cultural experience of being German—all good lessons for America as it wrestles with a highly divided society amid a pandemic.

***

Sidebar:
WHAT WE CAN LEARN FROM GERMANY
My starting point for understanding Germany's economic model was in 1991, when Gail Schares and John

Templeman in Bonn, Bob Neff in Tokyo, and I collaborated on a piece about Germany's small and midsize companies that are called the *Mittelstand,* which means medium-sized businesses in German in this context. I had been writing about how small and medium-sized US companies did not enjoy much support from government agencies or banks—or else faced a confusing thicket of conflicting advice. I wrote one story, "Why Johnny Can't Export." In retrospect, it's mildly miraculous that a news organization could have seasoned professionals on three continents who could drill in on a subject like the *Mittelstand.*

The story described how about three hundred thousand small and midsize German companies with fewer than five hundred employees produced two-thirds of Germany's gross national product, trained nine out of ten apprentices, and employed four out of the country's five workers. They made everything from motors and machine tools to camping equipment and high-fashion garments. They were all focused on their niches, much as the smaller American companies I had profiled were doing.

Part of their success stemmed from German business culture. The CEOs of these companies poured large portions of their revenues into research and development and were faster than large companies in introducing new products. These companies were run mostly by owner-managers who had their families' wealth on the line. They did not concentrate on quarterly earnings but rather on handing a healthy company on to the next generation.

But aside from culture, the Germans built an export infrastructure that assisted smaller companies. Former diplomats, bankers, and trade association officials collaborated closely with the smaller companies. Membership in industry associations was required, but those industry associations helped scout out export opportunities around the world. That was one stumbling block for US exporters—how could they tell where the opportunities were in distant lands?

Smaller German companies were eligible for up to $6 million in cheap funding from a government-owned bank, and the government reserved a slice of its research funds for *Mittelstand* companies.

Two other specific pieces of the German system remain relevant. One is the apprenticeship program. German employers maintained relationships with high schools and colleges and gave students the opportunity to work at the company for a summer. Some American companies also do this, but the Germans have institutionalized it. The net effect was that the quality of the German workforce was very high. Young people had a positive view of what they wanted to do with their lives and where they wanted to work. The German emphasis on education in general is something we could learn from. After all, they invented the concept of kindergarten.

The Germans also have many technical colleges and about sixty institutes whose purpose is to transfer technology to German companies, particularly small and medium-sized ones. That's one reason smaller German companies can be so competitive in the world. American universities and research institutes conduct R&D, of course, but they tend not to be as organized or as focused in transferring it to smaller companies. One reason is that technology licensing offices are often focused on protecting their technology, not promulgating it. Another is that larger American companies tend to have the resources to scout out what's happening at US research institutions and pay for access to it. Smaller companies are at a disadvantage in that regard.

So just as I saw the Chinese organize themselves for economic success, the Germans put specific institutions into place to help achieve more exports and technology-based economic growth, which translated into more wealth for all of German society. It was the devastation of World War II that forced the Germans to create many of these models. It was a time of "export or die." Some details of how the *Mittelstand* operates obviously have changed, but many lessons remain valid for Americans today.

End Sidebar

* * *

Of course, the really big story was the collapse of the Soviet Union, our archnemesis, against whom we had been fighting the Cold War since the end of World War II. I could taste the depth of the collapse in Berlin when I went to Brandenburg Gate on what had been the border between the two Berlins one day. Soviet soldiers were at the gate selling medals off their chests for hard currency so they could buy cigarettes. I bought several for a handful of coins.

Some *Business Week* editors back in New York, reflecting the wider debate around us, argued that the former Soviet Union should just go "cold turkey" and adopt Western-style capitalism and democracy overnight. That's what Harvard's Jeffrey Sachs argued. Similarly, Francis Fukuyama published a book entitled *The End of History* in 1992, proclaiming that Western values and ideals had won, and there would never be any values or ideals to compete with them.

Having lived in a Communist system in China, I did not buy it. I knew that Communist systems don't allow the emergence of the institutions that are necessary for genuine democracy—multiple political parties, think tanks, a free press and freedom of speech, academic freedom, business councils and industry associations, and the like.

On the last day of the German press trip in 1993, we went to a factory overlooking the Oder River, which marks the border between the unified Germany and Poland. The factory was decommissioning Soviet missiles that just a few years earlier had been pointed at the West. As a token of appreciation for our interest, they gave all of us gyroscopes that had been taken from the old missiles. Like everything the Soviets seemed to make, they were squarish and clunky—but effective. They were important parts of a missile, because the gyroscopes provided a sense of balance and direction. The gyroscopes were mounted on pieces of clear plastic with a few words written in German.

It just so happened that I had been given permission by *Business Week* to tack on a Moscow leg to this trip. Steve Shepard recognized it was valuable for editors in New York to get exposure to different stories we were involved in and to understand the challenges that our correspondents faced. At Moscow's airport, I could tell right away that things did not operate in Moscow the same way they did in the United States or Europe. Turkish diplomats and Korean traders flashed US dollars to bribe their way past customs and immigration officers at the airport.

Outside, I was met by bureau chief Peter Galuszka, who had been a friend and running buddy at *Business Week* in New York. On the drive in to his apartment and office, I was struck by all the traffic accidents we saw. Russians, as they were now called (not Soviets), had gone through an economic collapse and were just now getting access to new cars. Drivers lacked experience and were able to bribe their way into getting licenses. They had little respect for traffic rules. They also did not seem to understand that drunken driving was not smart, and they got very, very drunk. This period was called the *dikkiya vremya*, or "wild time." There was a whiff of chaos in the air.

Earlier in the month, before I arrived, Yeltsin had put down the so-called White House rebellion in the most brutal and bloody of ways. Several thousand Russians may have died as well as nine journalists.

On the way in from the airport that day, I mentioned to Peter that I was carrying a gyroscope from a Soviet missile in my suitcase.

He flipped. "Don't take that out of your suitcase. Don't talk about it to anyone, not at a restaurant, not in your hotel room, not anywhere." He was right, of course. I was back in a Communist society that, even if it were unraveling, still conducted massive eavesdropping. Who knows what would have happened if the KGB heard I was carrying around a Soviet gyroscope?

Adding to a sense of foreboding in Moscow were the presence of Chechens and other Central Asians in the markets. They were very tough-looking.

Even though Yeltsin had put down the rebellion, Russia was still in chaos. Yeltsin made noises suggesting he wanted to liberalize trade and embrace democratic reforms. He offered to stand for election. But he was resisted by hard-line Communists, by some in the military, and by the new incarnation of the KGB, called the FSB. They preferred the old model of Communist rule. It was just not clear where Yeltsin was going to lead the country. Russia did not have a West Germany to ride in to rescue it, as East Germany did.

I had one key interview with a new 35-year-old finance minister, Boris C. Federov, that revealed the depth of the problems. Yeltsin had appointed him. Walking into the heavily fortified and highly ornate Kremlin, the seat of Russian power since before the czars, was awe-inspiring. But Federov was candid in explaining that Russia was in a state approaching chaos. There was basic confusion over whether property, which was once owned exclusively by the state, could be privatized and sold. The government and parliament were deeply divided on the country's direction. The Central Bank refused to cooperate with Yeltsin's reformers, including Federov, the finance minister. It was not clear whether the Russian ruble would be made into a hard currency that could be traded with other currencies.

My most vivid experience was giving a talk at an academic institute. The bureau had previously scheduled it. This institute was in the business of starting to educate Russians about how things in the West worked. They wanted me to talk about financial portfolios. I was no financial specialist, but I had managed my own money and knew enough to fake it. I explained to forty or fifty attendees that Americans wanted different categories of assets in their portfolios to balance out the risk-reward ratio. Not everyone wanted 90 percent of their assets in equities. Some people preferred a guaranteed rate of return on Certificates of Deposit.

When I was finished, I expected to be peppered with questions. But there were none. The bilingual woman who ran the institute thanked me and people started leaving.

I asked her, "Why no questions?"

"Because," she said, "we don't have the words in Russian to understand anything you said."

By extrapolation, if they could not understand a simple talk on portfolios, how would they ever be able to develop the language to understand all the underpinnings of capitalism and democracy? I was a pessimist about Russia's future.

Apparently for good cause. It was not until Vladimir Putin, a former KGB officer, came along many years later that a new order clearly emerged. Essentially, he used former KGB people to solidify control. It looked a lot like the old Yeltsin order, except that the oligarchs who controlled much of Russia's economy were loyal to Putin and did his bidding. It was not a complete reversion to the centralized-planning model with five-year plans and such, but it became clear that any experimentation with democracy and Western-style capitalism was over. The Russians today are dedicated to trying to undermine American elections and American democracy. So much for embracing democratic capitalism "cold turkey."

11 The Roaring Nineties: The Media and Technology

I got my first desktop Apple computer in 1988. AOL (which stood for America Online) was just beginning. You had to hook your computer up to a phone line. Then the computer's modem had to dial up AOL. Once the modems on both ends made the connection, and after waiting several seconds, you'd hear the distinctive message, "You've got mail." It was decidedly clumsy.

There was no such thing as mobile computing. Computers started to get smaller, but moving a computer required some effort. People had to use little luggage carts, like the kind that flight attendants use for their baggage, to move their computers, earning them the nickname "luggables."

The first truly functional and widely accepted laptop was the IBM ThinkPad, which appeared in 1992. Arimasa Naitoh, the Japanese engineer credited with being the father of the ThinkPad, had to literally sleep in an IBM factory in North Carolina for days on end to coach workers on how to precisely assemble the machines, as he and I chronicled in the book, *How The ThinkPad Changed the World*.

In the beginning, the Internet was little more than a curiosity. Everyone made fun of Al Gore, the Tennessee senator, for talking about the "Information Superhighway." The way he said "superhighway" with a distinctive Tennessee accent made it easy to laugh off the implications of the Internet for those of us in the media business. It wasn't until 1993 or so that I looked around at a senior editors' meeting at *Business Week* and wondered, "What is going to happen to all of us if the big predictions prove correct?" We all had spouses and children and mortgages. Was it possible that the very foundations upon which we stood would be overwhelmed?

Of course, we were about to experience a period of upheaval. It's impossible to separate the two themes—media and technology—so I want to explore in this chapter how they were interwoven in ways that became clearer only much later.

By 1996, I had become frustrated at *Business Week*. The people above me on the masthead were of an age suggesting they were not going anywhere soon. I had the grand title of World Editor, but after eleven years had not been made a senior editor, which was a distinct management level. There was nowhere to go. It was the old "up or out" moment.

I heard that James Fallows was taking over as editor-in-chief of *U.S. News & World Report*. We had never met, but we knew of each other from the Great Japan Debate. I wrote a letter to him, asking whether he needed editorial help. I assumed he would want top editors. He did, in fact, offer me a job, but as a senior writer in the business department, reporting to James Impoco. "Just come in and write good stuff," Fallows told me.

So it was that I made another unusual career move—from being an international editor at a business magazine to becoming a writer at a news magazine with a primary focus on domestic US issues. *U.S. News*, or U.S. Snooze & World Distort, as we joked, was a distinct third in the general news magazine category, after *Time* and *Newsweek*. It was exactly the sort of challenge I relished—how could we position *U.S. News* to gain ground on the big boys?

One part of the answer seemed to be trying to be more intelligent about business and economics, which were not strong suits for the others. That meant that as a writer covering those subjects, I felt I was a central part of the challenge the magazine was mounting. The magazine was owned by Mort Zuckerman, the mercurial Canadian who had made his millions in real estate.

Okay, that's too polite. He was more than mercurial. He was a power-hungry egomaniac. But I was almost completely insulated from him. The magazine was headquartered in Washington, while the business news department where I worked was based in New York.

I now had a new platform to continue pounding away at how globalization and technology were transforming the American economy and creating challenges for average Americans. "Millions of Americans—economists put the figure as high as 80 percent of the population—are at risk of being left behind as the entire postwar manufacturing model is overhauled," I wrote in a piece co-bylined by Dan McGraw in Fort Worth, Texas, and Viva Hardigg in Los Angeles. The piece was designed to offer economic advice to Bill Clinton, who had just won re-election. "Some of the highest-employment industries, such as autos and auto parts, defense and aerospace, continue to undergo wrenching shakeouts. Old skills and work habits aren't needed anymore, thank you, as companies seek younger, highly educated, computer-literate, decision-making employees."

My reporting for the story took me to Bloomington, Indiana, where there was an old RCA television factory now owned by Thomson Consumer Electronics of France. There I met Bob and Sandra Griffin, ages 55 and 51 respectively, who worked at the plant along with thirteen hundred others. They were trying to hang onto their jobs for just four more years so they could retire. There were rumors that yet another buyer would take control of the plant and move the jobs to Mexico. This was the last television factory on US soil. All the others had shipped out.

The Griffins had no chance of understanding the forces swirling around them. They both had high school educations, but it was too late in life for them to be retrained for the "new economy," even if such retraining were available, which it probably was not. All the workers at the plant "are decent, hard-working people and they're scared," said John Fernandez, the 36-year-old mayor of Bloomington. "We have some responsibility to them. We shouldn't just write them off as structural change of the economy." But it was too late. The plant was closed, and everyone lost their jobs. Because of his understanding of the issues, Fernandez rose to a senior position at the US Department of Commerce in Washington.

* * *

I didn't realize it at the time, but the fact that I started concentrating on technology issues made me a different sort of China watcher. Many China observers understand the language or the history or the foreign policy issues, but relatively few understand the core technological issues today. I got a head start by starting to cover the tech beat.

That technology beat started heating up in 1997 as the underlying technologies of the first Internet bubble began to take shape. By now, Impoco and I had hired Fred Vogelstein as a writer in New York. A former colleague and friend from *Business Week*, Russ Mitchell, was hired in San Francisco to cover technology. Complementing my international experience, Impoco had worked for the Associated Press in Tokyo for four years and covered the Tiananmen Square massacre in June 1989 and Damon Darlin, managing editor under Fallows, had worked for *The Wall Street Journal* in Tokyo and Seoul. We were a highly experienced team. I co-wrote a great many stories with Fred. We joked that we were the Stein brothers. Impoco was the most talented editor I ever worked for. Our styles clicked.

Microsoft's antitrust case was arguably the biggest story of that year. The Internet was still building. People now had to have browsers on their computers to access the Internet. We were moving beyond dial-up modems. Small companies like Netscape Communications were coming up with browsers—pieces of software—that they sold separately to customers to give them access to the Internet.

Microsoft's Bill Gates, far from being the benevolent philanthropist he is portrayed as today, decided to start "bundling" Microsoft's own browser, Internet Explorer, with the Windows operating system. That means he started selling them together. Microsoft dominated one of the highest value-added pieces of the personal computer, namely the operating system. Intel dominated the other highly profitable segment, the semiconductor. Together they were called the Wintel duopoly, but Gates emerged as more of a lightning rod because of his personal style.

By bundling Internet Explorer with Windows, Microsoft's intent was to "choke off the air supply" to Netscape, which is how Microsoft executive Paul Maritz was alleged to have described the strategy in a meeting with Intel in November 1995. Maritz denied saying it, but it still made headlines.

Clinton had appointed a new head of the antitrust division at the Department of Justice, Joel Klein, who was angry about what Microsoft had done. In his first major action after ratification, he announced he would ask a federal court to impose fines of $1 million a day on Microsoft because it was a "monopoly" that was competing unfairly against Netscape. Bill Gates dismissed Klein's complaint, saying no "bureaucrat" should stand in the way of Microsoft customers getting what they wanted. "It's a confrontation between the world's most powerful government and the world's richest man, with implications for the world's strongest economy," I wrote with Mitchell and Vogelstein.

We got an interview with Klein, and Impoco and I flew down to Washington. His remarks that day were prescient and bear directly on what we see happening today with the FAANG technology platforms—Facebook, Amazon, Apple, Netflix and Google, a unit of Alphabet. Microsoft obviously remains a powerful platform. Call it FAANG plus M.

It was a brand new era, because antitrust policy had been applied to railroads and steel manufacturers, and the assumption was that combinations of companies in a certain industry would eliminate competition and therefore result in customers being charged more. But how would antitrust policy be applied in new technologies? "Klein," we wrote, "appears to accept the argument that an economy honeycombed by computers and fiber optics can create harmful monopolies even when prices are moving down. In this era, the key worry is not that robber barons will eventually gouge consumers but rather that digital monopolists will dominate a technology chain in a way that deters rivals and ultimately damps down the pace of innovation."

In the new vocabulary, a company such as Microsoft could "lock in" customers to its network, preventing others from competing. "What's different is that these industries are characterized by network effects," Klein said. "When you get an installed base, it's hard for people to penetrate that monopoly."

Although the courts supported Klein's case, in 2001 the company was ultimately able to negotiate a toothless resolution with a new Republican administration led by President George W. Bush. That clearly set the legal precedent for what Facebook and the others do today: if they see an emerging competitor in a space adjacent to their core businesses, they imitate that competitor's offerings and integrate it into their own platforms. That can drive the much smaller competitor out of business. Or they simply buy the competitor. The net effect is the same.

***

It wasn't clear at first that online retailing would ever work. The rap against online shopping was that it would remain a novelty, "the plaything of a few hard-core webheads," I wrote in a cover story entitled "Shopping on the Web" in December 1998 co-bylined with Susan Gregory Thomas and Fred Vogelstein.

Our hook was that it was the Christmas shopping season, and we suspected more people would be tempted to buy online. But there were hurdles. The spin against online shopping was that "... only the Internet fringe would have the patience to log into obscure Web sites and spend time navigating through poorly designed, repetitive screens," we wrote. "Ordinary people also would balk at providing credit card information to a faceless cyber-entity." This was a really big issue—what would credit card companies do if someone stole your information and made a purchase?

I found a retailer called Amish Acres in Nappanee, Indiana, population 5,500. It was a long, long way from Silicon Valley, and many of the locals were either Amish or Mennonites. Amish Acres was a complex of hotels, restaurants, and shops that catered to tourists. Richard Pletcher, founder and president of the development, had a General Store that he had just listed on Yahoo's newly expanded shopping channel. "I photographed my products digitally and uploaded them to Yahoo," he explained. "It's mind-boggling." He already could detect a pickup in orders for food, dolls, log cabin candy, and kitchen gadgets. His best-selling item was shoofly pie, a molasses-based treat that went for $8.95. He was getting orders from as far away as California. Imagine!

I asked Pletcher, "Do you really think this online shopping is going to take off?" He said, "I have no idea. But if it does, it could be big." We both were in a bit of awe.

In the article, we explained what we thought were some of the fundamental forces shaping the phenomenon. The fragmented nature of the Web was being consolidated by AOL, Yahoo, and Microsoft. "Their combined clout is beginning to change the economics of online shopping," we wrote. "As big online sites draw more visitors, or 'eyeballs' in E-speak, they are able to attract many more stores eager to list themselves." Amazon was still an obscure bookseller.

"In many cases," we added, "the online malls and shopping channels allow customers to enter their personal details and credit card information just once to make multiple purchases, improving convenience and safeguarding against credit card abuse."

All of this was genuinely exciting, and we were not the only ones writing about it. In fact, there was so much enthusiasm that it created an Internet stock market bubble. Stocks of companies that had virtually no sales or viable business models like Pet-Food.com soared. Millions of average Americans bought shares. Incredibly, AOL was able to leverage the value of its shares in 2000 to buy Time Warner, including Time Inc. and its stable of magazines. It was an astonishing moment. The new were buying the old.

Were we hyping our tech coverage? Those of us involved in this coverage were benefiting, because our skills, expertise, and contacts made us valuable to our organizations. Some news organizations benefited from advertising from tech companies. But we predicted in a cover story about the Internet stock market bubble that it would burst, which it did. The underlying technologies, of course, have continued to develop. Communications have gotten faster and gone wireless. The size of devices keeps shrinking, and they become more powerful. All of this has profoundly transformed the economy and society. On balance, I think our coverage was fair. A technological revolution was taking place and it continues.

I personally got caught up in the bubble. Zuckerman forced Jim Fallows out as editor in mid-1998. Then our business department started getting cherry-picked for talent in 1999 and 2000. *Fortune* hired Impoco and Vogelstein. A start-up magazine called *Business 2.0* hired Russ Mitchell as editor in San Francisco, and he recruited Damon Darlin as his managing editor.

There were several magazines like *Business 2.0* trying to make a run against the three established business magazines, *Business Week*, *Forbes*, and *Fortune*. There was the *Industry Standard*, *Wired*, *eCompanyNow* (owned by Time Inc.), and *Red Herring* in San

Francisco, and *Fast Company,* which was based in New York. The key editorial battleground was, of course, technology coverage.

I was left standing alone at *U.S. News,* or at least that's what it felt like. Mitchell tried to recruit me as an editor-at-large at *Business 2.0* with the same salary as his. At first, I resisted. He knew the magazine would have to be sold one day, because the founder, Chris Anderson, had mis-invested money that should have been poured into the magazine. Mitchell offered me a severance package if it all came crashing down. I took the leap, and what a glorious leap it was. For about six months.

It turned out that Time Inc. bought us for $100 million. At first, that did not seem like a bad thing. I assumed that what we were doing at *Business 2.0* was so valuable and exciting that Time Inc. would want to retain the editorial heart of our magazine. Time's intention was to merge our magazine with the wretched *eCompanyNow*, which never found its editorial groove. They were going to take our title, because it was so cool, and presumably would integrate some or many of us into a new editorial structure.

But Ned Desmond and James Aley, the top two editors at *eCompanyNow*, were given the job of integrating the two magazines. They decided simply to fire everyone at *Business 2.0.* It might have made sense on a personal level—we had been rivals. Why even try to manage us? Just get rid of everybody. But from a strategic point of view for Time Inc., it made no sense. I could write a Harvard case study on the dumbest magazine merger in history. Time poured another $100 million into the magazine trying to make it successful but finally had to close it. Blowing $200 million on *Business 2.0* is one reason Time Inc. no longer exists today.

The broader story is the meltdown that hit the whole industry. Even as the Internet was opening up new flows of communication and information, established media organizations were getting pummeled. Over the course of the years to come, *Business Week* was sold to Bloomberg News for pennies on the dollar. I primarily blame Terry McGraw, the lamebrain grandson of the founder of McGraw-Hill and the magazine's owner, for that disaster. Zuckerman closed the print edition of *U.S. News*, although something online still exists.

Fortune magazine was sold to a Thai chicken magnate, and *Forbes* was bought by a bunch of shady Hong Kong Chinese with connections to China. They closed the New York headquarters of *Forbes* and moved it to Singapore, effectively killing the magazine as it was known.

None of the other San Francisco-based magazines survived with the exception of *Wired*. Ironically, it was purchased by a Newhouse, based in the New York area. *Fast Company* had been based in New York, and it was purchased by Chicago-based mutual fund entrepreneur Joe Mansueto. It turned out that running a successful magazine required more than an exciting editorial product. It also required sophistication in circulation, sales, distribution, and all the business-side functions. Big established publishers knew how to do all that, or knew where to find the people who did.

The media meltdown had global implications, which were of concern to me from the OPC (Overseas Press Club) point of view. Newspapers such as *The Baltimore Sun, Chicago Tribune* and *Newsday* closed their foreign bureaus. Television networks greatly reduced their global footprints, shrinking to one bureau perhaps in London and one in Hong Kong. From those posts, they send out parachute-jumpers into the big breaking stories. True, Bloomberg has expanded globally and maintains a presence in more than 120 countries, but its information is limited to people rich enough to buy its terminals. *The New York Times* and *The Wall Street Journal* have retained strong global presences, but overall the American media retreated from covering the world with on-staff personnel.

The new pattern of coverage came to depend much more heavily on freelancers, both on Americans who chose to work as freelancers abroad or on local nationals who already spoke languages and had the right contacts. This meant that many people on the ground trying to cover the world's toughest stories did not necessarily have training at headquarters, as I had. They also might not be able to benefit from talking to the guys and gals with gray hair in the hotel bar—because those people were gone.

All this had big implications for the OPC Foundation and the OPC. The sort of young people the foundation identified and promoted were in hot demand from news organizations. The game became ever more dependent on young people. And some young freelancers were getting killed, such as James Foley and Steven Sotloff in Syria in 2014. We needed to invest more in security training, and we took part in the creation of an alliance, A Culture of Safety (ACOS), that specializes in security and safety training around the world. The OPC, for its part, started issuing very official-looking credentials to help freelancers get through checkpoints and such.

As the push toward youth occurred, the Baby Boom generation was almost completely pushed out. Over the years, I keep seeing new, younger editors and producers rediscovering stories and trends that we wrote about twenty-five years ago. Of course, there are new stories, such as massive human migrations and climate change. But on other stories, like North Korea, for example, the same patterns play out, year after year.

As for me, getting fired in the summer of 2001 was the end of my career as an on-staff journalist, with the exception of the years 2003-2007, when I was editor-in-chief of *Chief Executive* and then *Directorship* magazines. Otherwise, I had to assemble a portfolio of work to make ends meet—freelance gigs, corporate thought leadership projects, and books. It was a brave new world.

12 China: The Middle Years

Communism was in turmoil in 1989. Mikhail Gorbachev was losing his grip, and the Soviet Union was imploding. In China, students were occupying Tiananmen Square. The students said they wanted "democracy," but they did not seem to fully understand what that meant—it would have meant overthrowing the Communist Party. What they really wanted, it seemed, was for the government to listen to them more. They began to gather support from other constituencies, such as workers. The American media, particularly television networks, descended on Beijing, amplifying the protesters' demands to the world.

The one Chinese leader who expressed some support for the students was Zhao Ziyang, head of the Communist Party, but he was away on a trip to North Korea. In his absence, Vice Premier Deng Xiaoping, the paramount leader, came down on the side of repression and sent the army into Tiananmen. Thousands of unarmed civilians were killed.

At *Business Week*, we sent Dori Jones Yang from Hong Kong to Beijing. After covering the protests in May, she went back to Beijing just after the massacre on June 4th and took a taxi ride through the streets, surveying the incredible damage inflicted by People's Liberation Army tanks. Bicycles had been crushed. Twisted metal and burned-out vehicles littered the avenues. Bullet holes marked the buildings. It was the aftermath of massive brutality. I was her editor for a cover story, "The Great Leap Backward."

Americans were shocked by what had happened. But Deng's fear was that the entire Chinese population would start demanding democracy. He was quoted as saying that he had to "kill the chicken to scare the monkey."

Nearly everyone assumed that the massacre would interfere with China's efforts to modernize economically. But in one of the great twists of history, as Dori Jones Yang first pointed out to me decades later at an OPC event on the massacre's thirtieth anniversary, the massacre created certainty. The Communist Party's grip on power was certain. And certainty is what foreign business people needed to invest in China, and what Chinese people themselves needed to focus on: growth.

I had not been back to China since leaving in 1982, but starting in the early 1990s and up until 2008, I made about twenty trips back to China and watched how China's economic boom started to achieve momentum. I made the trips because news organizations including *Business Week, U.S. News & World Report*, and *Chief Executive* (and one book publisher) were willing to pay for me to go and continue to chart one of history's greatest stories.

Throughout this era, despite the Tiananmen crackdown, it appeared credible that American hopes of seeing a "peaceful evolution" of China's political and economic system were well-founded. It would have to happen very gradually. No one thought the Communist Party would disappear, but we could see how its grip was easing, and what we called a "civil society" was taking root. Dissidents were allowed to have lawyers to argue their cases, and a legal system at the grassroots level began to take hold. Western nongovernmental organizations (NGOs) were able to operate with relative freedom in addressing issues such as women's rights, religious freedom, and environmental problems. The authorities tolerated demonstrations by peasants angry that bureaucrats had stolen their land to build skyscrapers and factories, enriching themselves in the process. The Internet became available to many million Chinese during this era, and their wealth was increasing. Westerners thought that meant an increasingly prosperous middle class would be able to use the Internet to connect to the way things were done in the rest of the world—despite the gradual strengthening of the Great Firewall created by Chinese government censors. They would begin to demand more political rights.

There was no hint that China would attempt to project power on a world stage. The country remained largely silent on geopolitical issues, reflecting Deng Xiaoping's advice to his people: "Hide your capacities, bide your time." China appeared to accept the fact that the US Navy protected the sea lanes that supplied China with oil and food and essential raw materials. It still seemed reasonable to conclude that it would be a "responsible stakeholder" in the world order we had created, as diplomat Robert Zoellick put it.

Economically speaking, private companies began popping up in greater numbers, and Zhu Rongji, the vice premier in charge of the economy, started shutting down many state-owned enterprises (SOEs), which were the core of the party's command-and-control economy. Zhu was from Shanghai, where he had been mayor, and his brand of economic management over a decade displayed a distinct distaste for classic Communism. A thriving private sector, with companies such as Tencent and Alibaba, surely was a signal that greater pluralism would be inculcated into the fabric of Chinese society and economy.

It was in 1993 that lightbulbs went off in my head. In May, we geared up a cover story package, "China: The Making of an Economic Giant." The primary writers were Joyce Barnathan and Pete Engardio, both based in Hong Kong. (Dori Jones Yang had returned to Seattle.)

The story started off:

"To get a glimpse of China's economic boom, drive an hour north from the Hong Kong border and turn left at the giant stainless steel archway. You've just entered Changan Inc., population 30,000. Cruise the palm-tree–lined avenues, and you'll pass a gleaming new cultural center, office towers, and a sprawling public recreation complex with an Olympic-size pool and a golf course. More than one hundred two-story white townhouses with red tile roofs, sold for $100,000 to Hong Kong families, stand in neat rows, with scores more under construction.

"A decade ago, before the village's leaders traded their Mao jackets for Italian-styled suits, Changan was so poor that many of its people emigrated to Hong Kong. Now, the village owns nearly seven hundred factories employing 100,000 workers from other parts of China. Changan will bring in a cool $40 million this year renting the plants to foreign joint ventures making everything from Barbie Dolls to precision tools."

Airlines were springing up, and they were buying lots of Boeings. Motorola invested in a semiconductor plant in northern Tianjin. I was so pumped by it all that I wrote a book proposal, one of many that were never published. "It is only now that China's emergence is taking on the appearance of irreversibility," I wrote. "It has the smell of permanence."

The infrastructure boom was truly a thing to behold. In the summer of 1994 I went back to Asia to do a story on how all of East Asia was planning a major burst of spending to create airports, highways, ports, and other forms of infrastructure. I went to Seoul again, but also visited Shanghai and Shenzhen, just north of Hong Kong.

I interviewed a Guangzhou highway engineer in Shenzhen, which was now a sea of skyscrapers where the Hakka girls used to walk their buffalo. When I asked him what his ideal model was for how China would build its highway system, he said, "*Lo-san-gee.*" Meaning, "Los Angeles." The decisions the Chinese made about how to create a transportation system still reverberate around the world today. If they had followed a European or Japanese model of encouraging trains and making it expensive to own and drive cars, their consumption patterns would be very different today. Not to mention less pollution caused by heavy auto traffic. But the Chinese like the flash of fast luxury cars from Germany and big highways. So that's the way they went, at least at first. (They later built the world's biggest network of high-speed railways.)

One of the most vivid personalities I met on this journey was Shanghai's executive vice-mayor, Xu Kuangdi. In a sidebar, I called him "Shanghai's $100 billion man," because he was planning to spend that much on infrastructure in Shanghai and across the river in Pudong, a marshy, almost completely undeveloped tract of land with a few fishing villages and farms. Xu was planning roads, a port, and telecommunications links for Pudong. I interviewed him in English, which he had learned in Sweden, where he had spent two years.

"Xu's sophistication speaks volumes about the challenge foreign companies face in winning Asia's big deals," I wrote. "Decision-makers such as Xu, 57, combine the expertise of their native lands with that of the West. Hugely ambitious, they have access to world-class advice about how to make multinationals compete fiercely against each other. They also boast outstanding political connections."

It turned out that Zhu Rongji, the vice premier, had nurtured Xu when he, Zhu, was still mayor of Shanghai. While part of a delegation traveling in Europe, Zhu asked Xu to become director of Shanghai's planning commission.

"I don't believe in planning," Xu recalled saying.

"That's what I need," Zhu replied. "Someone with new ideas."

I found that openness completely refreshing. This seemed to be a dramatically different China than the one I had first encountered. (Xu was obviously involved in planning. I think what he meant by his remark was that he did not believe in the classic central government planning for the whole economy.) At the time, most foreigners thought that Pudong was going to be a white elephant, a giant failure. There did not seem to be logical or practical short-term commercial reasons to spend that much money. But Xu and other leaders had long-term vision. Build a field and the players will come.

I concluded the cover story by saying: "In short, Asia's infrastructure spending is shaping up as a massive transfer of technology and human capital. The Asian winners will set the stage for the next leg of their spectacular economic emergence—and foreigners who play it cleverly will enhance their global competitive clout."

It was also a personal thrill to get back to Shanghai. I wrote a note to my parents from the Peace Hotel: "Shanghai is once again destined for greatness."

***

Sidebar:
THE FATE OF HONG KONG

As president of the OPC, I was able to organize two study trips to Hong Kong in 1995 and 1996 for half a dozen OPC members, including myself. Each was organized in cooperation with different arms of the Hong Kong government and various foundations. On the first trip, in September 1995, we continued on from Hong Kong to see developments across the border in Shenzhen and Guangzhou. On the second trip the following September, we went to Hong Kong and then Shanghai, in part to see what was happening in Pudong.

I truly loved Hong Kong. It felt like home when I lived there, and I was comforted every time I went back. It was a crossroads, and pretty much the whole world was represented. Hong Kong operated on the basis of English and Cantonese, and its courts and governmental systems were based on the British model. It was rationally managed. And because of its location, it was a jump-off spot for all of China and East Asia.

So it was with some trepidation that we called on Governor Chris Patten in 1995. Earlier that year, the late Louis Kraar had written a cover story in *Fortune*, "The Death of Hong Kong." Kraar, whom I knew, believed that the transition back to Chinese control, scheduled for the summer of 1997, would quickly destroy Hong Kong's relatively open political system and dynamic economy. The Chinese and Hong Kong systems were completely different. That's why the Chinese agreed to the concept of "One country, two systems." Perhaps Kraar's story was one reason Hong Kong governmental bodies and foundations were willing to pay for our delegation to visit—to demonstrate to us that Hong Kong could navigate the transition.

During that first visit, we met attorney Martin Lee, the dynamic leading voice for democracy in Hong Kong. The Brits had never allowed full-throated democracy—it appointed the colony's governors—but the Hong Kong people had gotten a taste of it in terms of a lively press and local-level elections. The courts were fair and highly respected. Corruption was kept to a minimum by a powerful anti-corruption agency.

Chinese troops were scheduled to march in on July 1, 1997, and reporters descended on the border to watch the troops cross, expecting violence. I was watching from afar and thought the Chinese would avoid violence because Hong Kong was so important to them. I regarded Lee as the canary in the coal mine. If he got taken out, it meant that everyone else was in trouble. It finally happened twenty-three years later, during the meltdown in US-Chinese relations. The Chinese imposed a harsh new security law in July 2020. Martin Lee was arrested for sparking a demonstration and faced trial. The Chinese government started wiping out any semblance of pluralism, dictating that Hong Kong students would henceforth have to become Chinese patriots. It seemed like there was little that could be done to save the Hong Kong I adored. Louis Kraar may have ultimately (and posthumously) been proven right.

End sidebar

***

During the nineties, the American government had an argument each year about awarding "Most Favored Nation" trading status to China. Although my beat was primarily the US economy, I was able to stay involved with US-China issues. In 1997 for *U.S. News*, I tried to explain that America's perceptions of China had gone through wild swings. We were allies during World War II against Japan but then engaged in mutual "demonization" before re-opening relations in 1979. Deng Xiaoping amazed Americans by putting on a cowboy hat in his visit that year.

But the tone shifted after the Tiananmen Square massacre in 1989. Politicians lambasted "the dictators of Beijing" or "the butchers of Beijing." One author, Ross Munro, author of the book "The Coming Conflict With China," told me, "China identifies us as an enemy, and it's time we recognized it."

I quoted him but didn't buy it. Despite the ups and down in relations, I wrote, "American policy elites and business leaders have supported 'engagement'—diplomatese for maintaining open trade and security relations. The underlying idea has been that as China's power inevitably grew, economic and political interaction would be the most promising way to avoid showdowns or the emergence of a new cold war." Note the use of the term "new cold war." People have been talking about that possibility for decades.

I thought rationality could prevail. "The real issue now is how to manage these conflicts with China in a way that doesn't jeopardize US economic and geopolitical goals in the face of deep cultural and political differences," I wrote, with colleagues from Beijing and Tokyo.

When the debate rolled around again the following year, I came up with the idea of going to China to interview Eastman Kodak CEO George Fisher, who was planning a trip there. Even though Kodak had yet to recognize the arrival of the digital era, Fisher was working on the challenge and was a highly respected CEO. "Like a late twentieth-century Marco Polo," I wrote, "Fisher believes the streets of China are paved with gold—Kodak gold for that matter." (Kodak Gold was one type of film the company sold.) As they tasted wealth, Chinese were buying cameras for the first time and taking millions of pictures. They were absolute picture nuts.

Fisher was investing $1 billion to buy China's state-owned film enterprise in Fujian Province. In effect, he was buying the entire industry in China. His major competitor was Fuji Film of Japan, and China shaped up as a crucial battleground between the two. "Kodak's dealings with China reflect the kind of 'engagement through commerce' that President Clinton—who is in China this week—is trying to promote," I wrote. "The company's growing stake in China also shows why the administration's engagement policy is likely to remain intact—despite controversies over Chinese influence-buying and arms sales, and concerns about human rights abuses."

So in a balanced kind of way, I believed that engagement was better than attempting to isolate or contain China, and that conflicts in the relationship could be managed. The annual debates disappeared in 2000, when Clinton helped accelerate China's ascension into the World Trade Organization, reducing tariffs and other barriers to trade. The logic of engagement prevailed.

***

I had a unique insight into China thanks to a man named John Quincy Adams and his wife. No kidding. He was a direct descendant of the American president. He had been involved in importing Chinese-made goods into the United States, and he was married to Grace, who had been a schoolteacher in Tianjin, the port city located about a ninety-minute drive southeast of Beijing.

Adams was a big talker with big ideas, and I spent some time with Grace and him. The way things worked in China was through connections, and Grace had them in Tianjin. An institute was organizing a conference on Western financial systems. The Adams couple won a contract to bring in a panel of foreign experts. They knew two other genuine experts, but they included me as a third panelist because I guess they liked me. We all flew to Tianjin.

We spent two days talking about different aspects of how credit-rating systems worked and other subjects like that. It reminded me of the time I went to Moscow and tried to explain portfolios. The hundreds of Chinese attendees couldn't understand much of anything we talked about. The Chinese financial system worked on the basis of making essentially political decisions about who to lend to. They had no idea how to evaluate credit worthiness.

But it was the second trip to Tianjin a couple of years later that was most fascinating. By this time, I was editor of *Chief Executive* magazine, owned by an entrepreneur named Ed Kopko. Grace had maintained her connections and knew that the man in charge of the special economic zone in Tianjin was looking for conference ideas. His name was Mr. Pi. Grace knew a young man who was either part of Mr. Pi's wife's family or closely connected. He had the right *guanxi.*

Ed and I flew over to pitch the idea that *Chief Executive* could organize a conference that would attract foreign corporate leaders to Tianjin. Typically, the Tianjin authorities had built an enormous conference center but did not know what to do with it. Their "hard infrastructure" was way ahead of their "soft infrastructure."

When Ed and I arrived in Tianjin late at night, we were met by Mr. Pi's press secretary, a young woman. She spoke English, and we were surprised when she told us there was no opportunity for us to land a conference contract. That was precisely why we had come.

We met Mr. Pi the next day and spent a couple of days kicking around ideas, often with the silently hostile press secretary present. We finally figured out that the reason the press secretary was against us: she was Mr. Pi's mistress and was working on her on own *guanxi* to get the contract for someone else. Our *guanxi* was through Mr. Pi's wife. It turned out that both the women in Mr. Pi's life were trying to convince him to do business through them with their respective friends. Money was at stake for each of them. In the end, Mr. Pi made an offer to Ed, and Ed rejected it as being too low. But we learned a lesson about how things really worked in China, at least during that era.

There were a variety of other trips during these middle years, but I'll conclude with a 2008 visit to Shanghai to write a chapter about General Motors for my GM book. The Chinese, through some fluke of history, adored Buicks. At some point in history, Buicks must have been sold in China and become status symbols. GM's joint venture in China was an important piece of its international strategy and gave it access to what was quickly emerging as the world's largest market.

Pudong was now an incredible concentration of factories, office buildings, hotels, and other large structures. I stayed in a Marriott hotel in Pudong where the lobby was on about the thirty-fifth floor of the building. The lower thirty-four floors were office space. Pudong had an impressive skyline. And the GM factory, a joint venture with Shanghai Automotive Industrial Corp., owned by the city of Shanghai, was located in Pudong. What a stunning series of developments since interviewing Xu Kuangdi almost fifteen years earlier!

Prosperity was filtering down to people who used to live in villages but now worked at the GM plant. I spoke with Zhao Qingjie, a beefy 45-year-old group leader with a thin mustache. He was making a base salary of $500 a month, big money for China at that time.

Zhao was born in Pudong when it was nothing more than agricultural land with a few fishing villages. There was no mass transit, nor any bridges or tunnels to Shanghai, on the other side of the Huangpu River. Now the locals had factory jobs and were moving on up to nice apartments, a dramatic improvement from the old days. "If you wanted to buy anything, you needed to get coupons from the government," he recalled. "You had to stand in long lines to get those, and then you could bike to the market to get vegetables or eggs." It was a difficult life.

But now Zhao has purchased a Buick Excelle station wagon. He and his wife were able to buy a thousand-square-foot apartment with two bedrooms, and his wife no longer had to work. To top it all off, the Zhaos recently purchased a golden retriever.

What an incredible transformation they were living through. It felt like South Korea in 1988, some twenty years earlier. It appeared that China's emergence was good for China, good for the United States, and good for the world.

13 General Motors, Industrial Policy, and Globalization

The word "globalization" does not mean allowing "globalists" (i.e., foreigners) to take over American industries and throw American workers out of jobs. The original vision, rather, went like this: 96 percent of the world's population lives outside the United States. Americans can win in the world and achieve greater wealth when they learn how to export products and services. When they learn how to successfully manage corporations that research, manufacture, and sell around the world. When they learn how to innovate technologically and commercialize those innovations. When they learn how to educate and train themselves. All of it depends on having corporate, think tank, and university leaders and other elites who are sophisticated and worldly. All of it depends on having other countries adhere to essentially the same set of rules.

Where the original globalization vision went wrong was by assuming that as American companies kept moving up the technology ladder and concentrating on winning international strategies, all Americans would be able to keep pace. Some have—but not all. That has disenfranchised rural white Americans as well as some African-Americans and other people of color. As old factories were shuttered and their production shifted offshore, there haven't been enough new economic opportunities created. The people who have been left behind obviously blame "the system" for not taking them along for the ride, undermining their faith in their democracy and our form of capitalism. The winners enjoy upward spirals; the losers spiral downward into obesity, drugs, poor educations, and hate.

Technology has exacerbated the divide, as I first discovered in writing about the "digital divide" in Austin, Texas for *U.S. News* in 2000. West of I-35, the main north-south corridor, everybody was connected to the Internet and prospering. There were "Dellionaires" in the hills west of town, meaning people who had made millions working for Dell Computer, and who had built mansions.

But east of I-35, a much different population, weighted more heavily to African-Americans and Hispanics, did not have access to the Internet in their schools, homes or offices. The gap was painfully obvious. The coronavirus has greatly accelerated these trends that have been building for at least twenty years and been left largely unaddressed. As a society, we simply have not responded.

In this chapter, I will offer lessons about globalization and the American response to it through the lens of the huge political and ideological fight over the future of General Motors in 2009, just as my book, *Why GM Matters: Inside the Race to Transform an American Icon*, was appearing. These lessons will be important in the current debate America is having about how to respond to China.

The story starts in the spring of 2003, when I went to Detroit to interview General Motors Chief Executive Rick Wagoner for *Chief Executive*, where I had become editor-in-chief. From my years of living in Michigan, where the auto business permeates everyday life, and from my years of covering the auto industry at *U.S. News* and dating back to the Toyota cover story I had edited in 1985 for *Business Week*, I understood how cars are manufactured. It's a complex process involving multiple tiers of suppliers that feed into an assembly line where everything is bolted or screwed together.

GM had been a laughingstock for years as it lost ground to the Japanese and then Korean rivals. Wagoner was determined to turn it around and to get GM to move faster than it ever had.

I asked tough questions, but from an informed point of view rather than merely venting hostility, as some journalists did. I next interviewed Wagoner in 2005 for *The New York Times*, where I was a business columnist, and for *Chief Executive*.

So when the opportunity arose in 2008 to write a book about Wagoner's turnaround effort, I was primed. I was once again an independent writer. The company agreed to cooperate, but there was no financial support of any sort from GM.

The subject matter touched on so many aspects of American life. Under withering crossfire, could GM maintain its unionized work base, which consisted of many individuals who never advanced past high school and yet were able to afford homes, cabins by the lake, and college educations for their children? Could communities and states that were heavily dependent on making parts for GM survive? And what would happen to all of America's traditional manufacturing?

The main theme of the book was whether GM could improve its manufacturing methods. GM's learning curve started in 1983, when the company announced its NUMMI joint venture with Toyota. As mentioned previously, Toyota wanted help in learning how to manufacture in America; GM wanted to get a look at "sneaky" Japanese production techniques.

GM executives assigned to the joint venture were amazed to find that Toyota had built its just-in-time production system around the needs of workers. Toyota managers were using card-carrying members of the United Auto Workers to make better quality cars than GM could.

Waste was squeezed out. Parts arrived just in time. Workers could halt the production line to fix a problem rather than simply allowing a defective vehicle to move on down the line, which had been common practice in American auto manufacturing. The workers were organized in teams, another dramatic departure from American practices. One nickname for the Toyota method was "lean manufacturing."

The problem was, when GM managers came back from NUMMI to headquarters in Detroit and advocated adopting Toyota's practices, "immediately, they would be shot down by the GM establishment," auto analyst Joseph S. Phillippi told me. They were told to "go sit in the corner and shut up."

The Young Turks, let's call them, continued to push for GM to adopt the leaner manufacturing techniques. One of them, Wagoner, was dispatched to Brazil as a finance executive and, away from the gaze of headquarters, started pushing for leaner manufacturing. Certain techniques worked.

But it wasn't until after the fall of the Berlin Wall that the opportunity arose to fully implement Toyota's methods. It was a moment of complete panic for millions of East Germans, as described previously, including some ten thousand workers at the Wartburg auto factory in Eisenach in the province of Thuringia. Wartburgs were only slightly better than the much-maligned Trabants.

GM Europe bought the factory, once again away from the gaze of top management in Detroit, and proceeded to retool it to incorporate Toyota methods. I went to see it, crossing over what had once been one of the world's most heavily armed frontiers into the former East Germany. The German workers went along with the strange new practices. "We had to change our mindsets entirely," Harald Lieske, a toolmaker at the old plant and one of the first workers hired by GM in 1990, told me.

Results were impressive. Eisenach was able to achieve higher productivity levels than anywhere else in the European auto industry—or in North America. It was the proof of concept that the Young Turks needed. Plants in Argentina and Brazil were put through the same transformation with positive results.

Suddenly, the resistance at headquarters started to melt. When I toured the Cadillac factory in Lansing, Michigan, I could see how GM had taken Toyota's methods and supercharged them with wireless communications, for example. Rather than having workers orally communicate their needs for parts, that was now done wirelessly and automatically. GM had improved on the Toyota system.

There were other aspects to the turnaround Wagoner was attempting. The highly innovative OnStar communications system had been created. The Chevrolet Volt, a radical new concept called a hybrid, which lithium ion batteries, was under development. And Wagoner pushed the UAW into accepting a dual-tier wage system, in which new workers were paid much lower wages for a period of time before they were stepped up to higher wages.

Note the global aspects of the turnaround: America had allowed competition from Japan and South Korea, not to mention from Germany. That forced GM to respond, to start making better cars, which benefited millions of Americans. The foreign competition forced GM to alter its cost structure, which benefited consumers but hurt workers. And it was the ability to witness Toyota's techniques in California and then experiment with them first in Germany and South America that set the stage for the new methods to sweep into GM's domestic plants. China played a major role in all this. If you include the sales of its different joint ventures, GM sold more cars in China than it did in the United States. Wagoner at one point told me that profits from China helped the company make it through the grueling US financial crisis and bankruptcy. None of that might have happened if America had not accepted a globalized economic order.

As I was working on the book in 2008, US financial markets went crazy. In what developed into the worst financial crisis since the Great Depression, the financial system seized up. Young investment bankers were cleaning out their desks at Lehman Brothers and Bear Stearns as those institutions failed. AIG, the major insurance company, had to be bailed out by the US government. Credit froze. The auto companies couldn't tap their working capital lines; auto dealers could not borrow to put cars on their lots; and individual consumers could not obtain credit either. Sales cratered.

By the time I had to hand in the final manuscript in December, Barack Obama had been elected president, and I was confident he, as a Democrat, would act to preserve UAW jobs. But the way it all happened was bizarre.

After Obama took office in January 2009, a politically ambitious investment banker from New York, Steven Rattner, was hired by the White House as an adviser, and Obama tapped him to figure out how to save the auto industry. Rattner had probably never been in an auto plant, yet he was now going to be the "auto czar." My book emerged in February. I was out of the loop at GM, but I later learned that Wagoner was working on a doomsday survival plan with Jay Alix, a prominent Detroit-based consultant, in which GM would be divided into an "old" GM, with debts and bad assets, and a "new" GM that could survive. The number of brands would be cut from eight to four. Gone would be Saturn, Hummer, Pontiac, and Saab.

Amid a storm of controversy, Rattner started pushing to force GM and Chrysler into bankruptcy, which I feared would be a disaster, judging from how many years Ohio-based parts maker Delphi had struggled in bankruptcy. What GM and Chrysler needed was simple bridge financing to get them through to the other side of the crisis. Then, incredibly, Rattner started agitating to fire Wagoner, the very man who was transforming GM.

I wrote an op ed in *The New York Times* warning that too much of the wrong sort of federal intervention would have negative consequences. The talk from Rattner (and Obama) raised "... the prospect that the administration will intervene too deeply in the automaker, seriously jeopardizing a transformation effort that has come a long way."

I was caught in a bitter ideological fight. I was criticized or attacked in liberal media outlets because Wagoner had been tough on the UAW. One caller on a radio talk show on NPR told me I was a "shill," or stooge, for GM.

On the other end of the spectrum, I was criticized because more conservative journalists thought GM had been too soft on the UAW for years. I couldn't believe how the debate over America's largest industrial company was so completely clouded by ideology. No one seemed to understand that a turnaround was underway. None of the facts mattered. It was an early taste of the kinds of non-debates Americans are having today.

In the final analysis, Rattner prevailed in firing Wagoner and forcing the company into bankruptcy. He was able, in fact, to push the process through rapidly. But he claimed credit for the turnaround plan that Wagoner had developed with Alix. (Wagoner never said a negative word about Rattner. Ever loyal to his company, he was worried that the government would retaliate in some fashion against his beloved GM.)

Then Rattner saddled the company with a board of directors and a CEO who were mostly from the telecommunications and private equity industries—where Rattner had friends—and hence were completely unprepared to govern the world's largest automaker. The first chief executive officer appointed by Rattner was the former CEO of AT&T, Ed Whitacre, who even refused to move from Dallas to Detroit. That was a complete joke to everyone inside GM. It wasn't until Mary Barra emerged years later as CEO that the company once again had competent leadership at the top. She was part of the generation of emerging GM leaders who had watched the company suffer for decades. They were determined to turn it around. They have done it. But it was a close brush with disaster.

There are two major takeaways from this tale. First, only the federal government has the scale and the resources to respond to large crises. The private sector has traditionally been interested in achieving short-term profit increases and simply will not, and perhaps cannot, devote the resources to responding to such events as the near-bankruptcy of General Motors. No private sector lender would have even considered stepping up and supplying the capital that GM needed at a moment of complete panic.

This brings us to the issue of industrial policy, a highly loaded buzz phrase. We've seen the importance of government action time and time again, whether in times of war or peace. President Nixon declared war on cancer, and that led to the development of today's biotechnology industry. Military spending on satellites brought us GPS, and spending by the military and NASA brought us the semiconductor and the computer industry. The Internet was spawned at least in part by the Defense Department's decision to link its research institutes together in a network called ARPANET starting in 1969. No one understood the significance of that for decades. All this happened despite the refrain in American politics dating back to President Ronald Reagan that "government is the problem." As the Reaganites said, "Just get government out of the way, and everything will be fine."

That's wrong, of course, as we discovered during the pandemic. The key is that industrial policy has to be based on the facts and has to be conducted by people with specific experience in whatever field the government is addressing. And there's a difference between the government supporting promising technologies and the government seeking to support specific companies. There is some truth to the adage that government "shouldn't be picking winners and losers," meaning specific companies. The Obama Administration tried to create a solar panel power champion in Solyndra and a lithium ion battery champion with A123 Systems, at least partly in response to rapid Chinese gains in those industries. Both companies faltered amid a firestorm of Tea Party political opposition and ultimately failed after the administration withdrew funding. Which leads to yet another important piece of the equation—the process of supporting an emerging technology cannot be allowed to become politicized. Government strategies work only if they are consistent and long-term. Compounding the tragedy was that a major Chinese auto parts company was able to purchase A123 out of bankruptcy, obtaining full access to its technology.

The second major takeaway from the GM fight is this: globalization of the sort that GM embraced can work, to the benefit of large numbers of Americans, if other nations operate on roughly the same set of rules when it comes to the flow of trade, capital, and technology. GM was able to benefit from its presence in China, as have hundreds of other American companies.

But what if China decides it wants to change the rules of the international trade and investment game? President Xi Jinping increasingly sees American companies and others in China as strategic assets that can advance China's power and influence in the world. Can the United States continue to allow American companies to operate in China in a way that transfers technology to their Chinese competitors and allows them to become Beijing's pawns of influence? If their computer systems are penetrated and their secrets stolen? And is it wise for American companies to depend almost entirely on China for the supply of critical products, such as pharmaceuticals and protective medical equipment as well as a wide variety of other products?

The big question now is, how will America shift its thinking about globalization in response to China's rise? We can see that our concept of globalization needs to address the fact that so many Americans have been left behind. But if the second largest economy and the world's most populous nation with 1.4 billion people starts undermining how we believed globalization was working, as it is in the act of doing, we may need an even deeper rethinking.

That may extend to how American CEOs perceive their role in the world. A subcorollary of globalization was that companies existed to maximize earnings and could be geographically agnostic. Wherever they found markets or expertise or financial resources, that's where they went. This is the "stateless corporation" theory I wrote about for *Business Week*. But if one major government learns how to manipulate their technology and Information Technology systems, and indeed their loyalties, Americans will have to re-examine what these companies' responsibilities are to their native land.

14 How America's China Dream Turned Sour

When historians look back at what happened between the United States and China, they doubtlessly will zero in on one man—Xi Jinping. When he was consolidating power as president of the People's Republic of China and general secretary of the Communist Party in 2012 and 2013, he was portrayed as a compromise candidate among different factions within the party. He was billed as a moderate who would emphatically open up the Chinese system. Henry Paulson, the former Goldman Sachs chairman and Treasury Secretary, was particularly adamant in arguing that Xi would undertake Western-style economic reforms, including opening the country's financial markets.

But in fact, after a couple of years of cleaning out his predecessor's allies through an anticorruption campaign, Xi proved to be a Communist unlike any other. It's often said that Xi is the most powerful Chinese leader since Mao, but Mao wielded power in a very different way. He did not trust his governmental bureaucracy and instead incited the young to rise up against the old elites. In contrast, Xi has extended the tentacles of the Communist Party throughout government and the army, establishing the party as the only center of power. Whereas his predecessors had allowed other power centers to emerge, Xi has imposed a kind of totalitarian Communist orthodoxy, which has been reinforced by a sweeping technological control system, something Mao could never have dreamed of. Xi has become the emperor Mao could never become. Xi's ultimate role models have been Lenin and Stalin of the former Soviet Union.

Xi has sought to eliminate or absorb the Tibetan, Uighur, and Mongol minority peoples. He has imposed a draconian security law on the semi-autonomous Hong Kong, completely crushing any hopes of democracy. His military started building bases on atolls and islands in the South China Sea, seeking to control waters claimed by other nations, after promising not to. He inserted Communist Party committees in China's private sector companies, effectively nationalizing them. Dissidents and their lawyers were rounded up and, in some cases, disappeared. An embryonic legal system was shut down. There will be no rule of law. The law is what the party says it is.

Xi reinforced "the Great Firewall" that shields the Chinese people from information from the West. In fact, he has turned the Internet into a tool of massive control, dashing any illusions the outside world had about it becoming a tool of empowerment.

The same tools and same values are being exported as Xi seeks to achieve the Chinese "dream" of being the world's most powerful country. The American "dream" that China would emerge as a more pluralistic society, much as South Korea, Taiwan, and Japan did, has been shattered. As the old adage goes, the United States and China have been sleeping in the same bed but dreaming different dreams.

Xi's strategy is very sophisticated technologically, so sophisticated that even the United States has been late to recognize it. The thin edge of the wedge, so to speak, has been Huawei and its 5G wireless communications systems. The Chinese recognized, astutely, that if you can penetrate a society's communications, you can see and hear everything. They recognized it when Edward Snowden told the world what the National Security Agency was doing inside China in 2013—if they did not already know. They recognized that massive penetration of other countries' computer systems allows the systematic theft of data and technology secrets but also allows them to observe decision-making processes inside companies and governments.

There are clear military implications to this. "This is a battle for cyber terrain," a US military intelligence expert told me on the grounds I would not identify him or her. "Both the Chinese Communist Party and the US government recognize that cyberspace is a battlefield that requires taking and holding ground."

In other words, the battle over 5G is about more than just economic benefits. "Whoever writes the 5G standards and controls the infrastructure effectively controls the cyber terrain," my source explained. "China has made significant inroads in Africa, Asia, and parts of Europe through Huawei. This is where the US government and allies need to focus our efforts. If we lose, our ability to defend our interests in the cyber domain will be severely impacted."

The extent of Xi's ambitions, and the range of tools he uses, continue to surprise most China watchers. His government is taking advantage of the Chinese diaspora to recruit Chinese nationals or ethnic Chinese to steal technology. And he seeks to export Chinese methods of control even into the Western democracies of the United States, Canada, Australia, Britain, and Germany. In one shocking case, *The New York Times* disclosed in late September 2020 that Chinese diplomats based in New York had penetrated the New York Police Department to spy on Tibetan refugee communities. A Chinese-born Tibetan, Baimadajie Angwang, who worked for the NYPD, was arrested. Since at least 2018, Angwang had communicated regularly with two consular officials in New York, including one whose department was responsible for "neutralizing sources of potential opposition to the policies and authority" of the Chinese government, prosecutors alleged. China officially dismissed the allegation as an attempt to smear the country's diplomats.

Which was laughable. The penetration was completely consistent with other actions taken by Chinese diplomats. The "diplomats" coordinate with Chinese student and scholar associations at American universities to keep track of what some 360,000 Chinese students are doing, and who is saying what to whom. Chinese diplomats also work with the National Association for China's Peaceful Unification, which targets Chinese-Americans. They want to lure Chinese-Americans into cooperating with Beijing. Since writing *The New Art of War,* which appeared in May 2019, I've learned that Chinese diplomats also cooperate with the Thousand Talents Program, which is Beijing's effort to identify and recruit technical talents around the world and persuade them to move to China to conduct their research. On other fronts, representatives from China's Ministry of State Security directly approach some Chinese living abroad, in their schools or churches, to recruit them as spies.

The tools that Xi uses vary considerably, depending on the level of sophistication of a targeted country. In the developing world, Xi launched his Belt and Road Initiative (BRI), a hugely ambitious scheme to build ports, railroads, and cities everywhere from China through South Asia and Africa into ports in Italy and Greece. Latin America, although not on the route from China to Europe, has also received large-scale Chinese investments. Many countries borrowed more money than they could afford to pay for these projects, so they experienced "debt traps" and became ever more dependent on Beijing's tender mercies.

In many cases, Huawei signed secret deals with mostly autocratic rulers to build telecommunications systems and gave them voice and facial recognition tools to control their political opponents, thereby extending Xi's core values of corruption and control—and enrichment of China.

In short, Xi's emergence should have been seen as one of the pivotal events in history, a moment that galvanizes the world like the Soviet Union's launching of the Sputnik satellite did in the 1950s, or Japan did with the attack on Pearl Harbor. But not a single mainstream China expert foresaw Xi's aggressive, totalitarian strategies, and we have been slow to understand the threat they pose to the world order the United States and its allies established. Now that Xi has established himself as president for life, he could remain in power for ten or fifteen more years—or even longer. He is the world's first digitally enhanced emperor. No one saw it coming. As Jeremy Page recently described it in the pages of *The Wall Street Journal*, US officials who met Xi as he was consolidating power thought "… he likely shared (his predecessor's) commitment to stable ties with Washington and closer integration with the US-led global order. Some even hoped Mr. Xi would kick-start stalled economic reforms." But, the story concludes, "It was one of the biggest strategic miscalculations of the post–Cold War era." That's a truly sweeping statement.

It does not bring me any pleasure to describe all this. Imagine how painful it is to me, personally and professionally, to admit that an entire generation of China watchers, including me, have been surprised. I defended "engagement" for so many years. I believed that "integrating" China into the world economy would be positive for China and everyone else. Now it is my sacred duty to my fellow Americans to spend the rest of my days warning that China has emerged as an adversary far more than it has as a partner.

***

Sidebar:
AMERICAN TECH COMPANIES IN CHINA

For more than three decades, it was credible to believe that American companies could make money in China, and that the Communist system would evolve toward greater pluralism. Further, Beijing would become a "responsible stakeholder" in the world order created by America and its allies. The goals seemed compatible.

What has changed the equation is that Xi has imposed sweeping authoritarian rule at home while engaging in far more aggressive tactics in Hong Kong, Taiwan, the South China Sea, Australia, and inside the United States. The discovery that one thousand Chinese researchers inside the United States were apparently working secretly for the People's Liberation Army is merely the latest case in point.

Suddenly, there is stark conflict between traditional American goals vis-à-vis China and the role American CEOs are playing. A new book, *China's Quest for Foreign Technology: Beyond Espionage,* edited by William C. Hannas and Didi Kirsten Tatlow, explains how Microsoft has played a major role in training the leadership of China's artificial intelligence push at institutes in China. "It raises the question of what contribution the company's new China-based AI facilities will make toward U.S. security and prosperity," Hannas, formerly of the Central Intelligence Agency, writes.

The book and other published reports have also spotlighted how Intel, Nvidia, Seagate, and Western Digital have fueled the rise of China's Hikvision and Dahua, the world's largest players in the use of AI in facial recognition systems used to repress China's Uighur population but also being sold around the world.

American semiconductor makers and designers such as Qualcomm are coming under pressure for sales that end up in the hands of the People's Liberation Army. Thermo Fisher has been reported to be selling DNA-testing equipment to Chinese police, who have used it to build up an enormous DNA database of Chinese men as a tool of surveillance.

Apple, under pressure from Beijing, removed an app from its App Store that pro-democracy protestors in Hong Kong were using. Apple, for all intents and purposes, *is* a Chinese company, despite the fact that its headquarters is in California—it is so dependent on its manufacturing base in China that it dare not offend Chinese authorities, who could disrupt its supply chain or create endless complications in the ability of its main subcontractor, Foxconn, to assemble iPhones. "The CEOs of America's leading tech companies tend to be more concerned about what Beijing wants than what America needs," says Clyde Prestowitz, the veteran trade negotiator and author of *The World Turned Upside Down: America, China and the Struggle for Global Supremacy.*

As these revelations have come to light, American CEOs have maintained a code of silence about whether they bear any responsibility for how their products are used in China. And at home, national security is the government's problem, in their view.

The federal government will need to find a way to have deeply important conversations with tech CEOs, because they will inevitably be key to any real effort to moderate China's technological gains and help American technologies to either catch up or remain ahead. And they will be essential players if America is to find the will to harden its Information Technology systems and interrupt a pattern of deep and consistent Chinese penetration.

End Sidebar

***

The realization that the American dream about China was falling apart settled in on me in stages. I first got a whiff of this reality in 2013 by co-organizing a reunion of correspondents who had either covered China or currently did. We used the platform of the Overseas Press Club in New York for the gathering of seventy correspondents, who spent a whole day organized into panel discussions.

We recognized that our assumptions about the emergence of pluralism in China were being challenged by Xi, and we recognized that China might wield its power in the world in ways we never expected. One bright spot: we tended to believe—we wanted to believe—that the Internet would help give voice to hundreds of millions of increasingly affluent Chinese. One of our most distinguished correspondents, the late Seymour Topping, who covered the Chinese civil war in the late 1940s, argued that students at China's universities, empowered by the Internet, would prove to be a force for political change.

We organized that discussion into a book, *Has the American Media Misjudged China: Thirty-five years after China's opening to the world, some of the key assumptions that have guided coverage are being tested by the presidency of Xi Jinping.* The answer to the question of whether we had misjudged China's direction was, in a word, "Yes."

But the real turning point in my thinking came in writing *The New Art of War.* Friends who had visited Australia and seen the controversy there over how China was exerting influence over Australian politics suggested I look at what the Chinese government was doing inside America. I was skeptical at first that I would find anything and was reluctant to dig into a subject so sensitive because of the risk of being called "racist" if I questioned the loyalty of any Chinese-American or lost sight of the distinction between the Communist Party and the Chinese people.

But as I started to investigate, I was astonished. Chinese government-related entities had stolen massive amounts of data about Americans, which they were presumably using to create profiles of people of interest for possible approach or surveillance. A group called APT10 (APT stands for Advanced Persistent Threat), affiliated with the powerful Ministry of State Security, penetrated the cloud computing systems that major companies such as IBM had created, the US government alleged in December 2018. APT10 tricked the intrusion detection systems and were able to download malware that allowed them to capture the keystrokes of legitimate users. The Chinese hackers were then able to log in as legitimate users and remained inside these cloud computing systems for four years, "hopping" from one company to another that had entrusted their systems and their data to the cloud service providers. IBM was identified in media accounts as having its system compromised, but the company said it could find no evidence. That's how skillful the hackers were—they did not leave footprints.

There are clearly issues of national security involved in this. APT10 stole the names and personal information of one hundred thousand members of the US Navy, which means they might possess the personal information of a majority of naval personnel, when combined with the hack on the Office of Personnel Management in the 2013–2015 timeframe. And they stole ship maintenance logs. Why? "Ship maintenance logs are valuable to the Chinese for two reasons," the military intelligence expert told me. "First, it gives insight into the readiness level of each vessel. While we may have a two hundred–plus ship Navy, not all of those vessels are fully mission-capable, due to where they are in the maintenance cycle. Those logs give insight into how many ships the US could deploy in a 'fight tonight' scenario."

My source continued: "Second, the Chinese steal everything — technology, engineering specs, even uniforms. As a result, the PLA Navy does not have the resident expertise to maintain the technology they have stolen. Therefore, they also need to plagiarize our maintenance cycles and standard operating procedures. Those logs serve as a roadmap to maintain their own naval equipment."

Another shocking revelation with national security implications came from *Business Week* magazine, also in late 2018. In a cover story, the magazine disclosed that the People's Liberation Army had inserted tiny microchips on the motherboards that Supermicro, a California-based company, bought to assemble into servers, the building blocks of major computing systems. The magazine explained that big corporate customers such as Apple and Amazon were using those servers, as were both houses of Congress. These chips would allow the PLA to communicate with the servers and either extract information from them or shut them down. After *The New Art of War* appeared, other industry executives told me privately they also had problems sourcing computer equipment from China, because the Chinese would insert unwanted code into their devices—malware that could give them access.

What was striking about the reaction to the *Business Week* story was that Apple and Amazon went to extreme lengths to deny it. Why? I wondered.

A pattern began to emerge: big American companies may know that Chinese entities have penetrated their computer systems, or they may choose not to investigate, afraid of what they would find. After all, every computer sold in the United States has some Chinese componentry or was assembled in China. Every US company operating in China must allow the Chinese authorities to access its IT systems in China, as I discovered and wrote about for *National Interest*, which could easily allow them to leapfrog into systems based elsewhere in the world. The Chinese pattern has been to lurk inside US computer systems, quietly stealing intellectual property, but they do not disrupt the systems, as the North Koreans once did famously, attacking Sony's Hollywood studio.

(Nearly three years later, in February 2021, *Business Week* doubled down on its Big Hack story with another blockbuster demonstrating that the Department of Defense found thousands of its computer servers in its nonclassified networks were sending data to China—the result of code hidden in motherboards sold by Supermicro. The suspicion was that nearly every motherboard Supermicro had sold was vulnerable to malware, because the Chinese learned how to download the malware during periodic software updates. They no longer required physical chips. "Silicon Valley in particular needs to quit pretending that this isn't happening," the magazine quoted the former director of the FBI's national security branch as saying.)

In September 2020 the Department of Justice made another stunning revelation about Chinese government–affiliated hacking. Chinese entities supported by the Ministry of State Security broke into one hundred companies and agencies around the world, the Department of Justice alleged. One group called Wicked Panda targeted companies in the United States, Germany, Hong Kong, Japan, South Korea, and Taiwan in the agriculture, hospitality, chemicals, manufacturing, and technology sectors. China is quite literally hacking the world.

The Russians were identified as being behind a massive attack on American computing systems by penetrating the software supply chain that large companies and government agencies use. They got caught. But much of the Chinese penetration appears to be invisible. If the Ministry of Public Security can take over the Chinese-based computing systems of American companies and leapfrog to their global networks, the penetration would appear to be coming from legitimate users with valid passwords.

This is still speculative, but it's possible the sensational cyberattack that Chinese state-affiliated groups launched in the first two months of 2021 had their roots in the penetration of American tech companies' systems. Microsoft said it suspected that sensitive security details it shared only with its trusted partners involved in maintaining the company's Exchange email software around the world had been leaked, perhaps by one of its partners in China. And one reason the American government did not initially see the massive penetration of America's cloud computing systems was that the attacks were launched from inside the United States—in part on Amazon servers.

Is it possible that America CEOs are simply declining to respond to Chinese hacking in any significant way? I fear the answer is "Yes," for the following reasons. Executives are focused on making profits. If they tried to upgrade their systems to make them China-proof, it would cost millions of dollars and take years, hurting their short-term earnings. If they kicked out Chinese hackers, that might anger the Chinese government, upon whom they depend for access to the Chinese market. And if word about the penetrations surfaced publicly, CEOs and CIOs would lose their jobs. Shareholder lawsuits would be filed. Boards would be irate.

Better then to remain quiet about it. Because after all, isn't national security the government's problem, not that of the private sector? That's the traditional view. But China's pattern of actions, including the "civil-military fusion," makes it a dangerously old-fashioned one. If Chinese government-related entities penetrate America's cloud computing systems, as they have repeatedly done, they possess abundant information about our military and high-tech sectors.

I found similarly disturbing patterns in how the Ministry of State Security approaches Chinese nationals or Chinese-Americans working in US companies and persuades or forces them to reveal technical information. Only a handful of major US companies, most prominently General Electric, have publicly cooperated with the FBI and Department of Justice to investigate and arrest employees who provided information to the Chinese government. In one case, the Justice Department set up a sting operation in Brussels and arrested the official in the Ministry of State Security who was conspiring to obtain information about GE's jet engines.

Other companies appear to have quietly chosen not to cooperate with federal authorities because of the fear of public exposure. It might affect access to the Chinese market. It wouldn't look good to the board or shareholders. Better to keep it quiet. Besides, it would take two or three years for the Chinese to transform a stolen technology into an actual product. And by then, a new CEO would have arrived.

Aside from massive, systematic efforts to steal American technology, I discovered in writing *The New Art of War* that the Chinese were engaged in large influence efforts with Chinese-Americans and the 360,000 Chinese students enrolled at American universities. They were harassing survivors of the Tiananmen Square massacre and other critics and potential critics living in the United States. They had co-opted Hollywood studios and university presidents, who saw economic gain in maintaining their China ties even at the expense of artistic and academic freedom.

My major contribution was adding up these threads and asking whether the relationship was reciprocal and balanced. The answer: not even close. I was forced to conclude that even though we had a major business and economic connection with China—in effect, we have merged our economies—Xi's government was working to undermine American institutions and hence the American democracy itself. Xi is engineering all this because he thinks he can get away with it. This was a new kind of warfare, which is why I based the title of my book on *The Art of War*, by Sun Tzu, written 2,500 years ago. The Sun Tzu observation that struck home was this one: "The supreme art of war is to subdue the enemy without fighting."

The Chinese government–orchestrated patterns have intensified during the pandemic, as tensions between the two countries intensified. A prominent American chemist at Harvard University was caught taking money from the Chinese without disclosing it. The government has continued to make arrests of traitors who helped the Chinese break up the CIA's network of informants and operatives inside China.

The pattern of what the Chinese were doing in Xinjiang to the Uighurs was being exported to other countries. China was selling facial recognition systems relying on artificial intelligence to other governments. Huawei and other Chinese entities have been building "smart cities," or "safe cities," which rely heavily on cameras to observe and manage a city's flows of garbage and traffic, for example.

But they have a sinister dimension—the cameras are linked to centralized monitoring stations where computers analyze faces. According to a September 2020 article by Ross Anderson in *The Atlantic*, Chinese start-up Yitu is selling facial recognition technology to the Kuala Lumpur Police Department in Malaysia. Other such systems have been installed in Sri Lanka, Mongolia, and even as far west as Serbia. In Africa, Ethiopia, Kenya, Uganda, and Mauritius, Chinese state-backed companies have sold wireless networks with built-in backdoor access for those governments. And P.S., you can be sure that some of that data also flows to China, where it is being used as part of a "the Digital Silk Road" strategy.

I am indebted to an unlikely source for that phrase—the Gateway House in Mumbai, India, a think tank modeled after the Council on Foreign Relations in New York. It was founded by Manjeet Kripalani, who worked at *Business Week* at the same time I did. When I saw that her think tank had written an explosive report on China's digital penetration of India, resulting in the government's decision to shut down TikTok and nearly sixty other Chinese apps, I approached Manjeet about doing a video panel discussion with the Overseas Press Club in August 2020. We had six panelists on the call from Mumbai, the United States, and Europe. The discussion was entitled *China's Global Push: Is a Backlash Building?*

India took a particularly sharp turn in its attitudes toward China, starting with a border incident high in the Himalayas in June in which twenty Indian servicemen were bludgeoned to death. But then came the report by Gateway House showing that eighteen out of India's thirty most promising technology start-ups had taken funding from Chinese-related entities. Moreover, 80 percent of India's handsets were made by Chinese entities, and TikTok and other Chinese applications had grown very popular. The Chinese were trying to create an entire digital "ecosystem" of online commerce, social media, digital payment mechanisms, and the like in India—controlled from China.

Gateway House researchers concluded Chinese companies were sending data from this foothold back to China, where it could possibly be "mined" for names and personal information of prominent Indians.

One of the authors of the report, Blaise Fernandes, explained how building a Digital Silk Road was designed to complement China's Belt and Road Initiative. You can physically see the BRI, but you can't see the Digital Silk Road. Fernandes argued that Huawei's 5G wireless communications system was essential to building the Digital Silk Road. Beijing hopes that data communicated back to China will help ensure the success of its Made in China 2025 plan to dominate key technologies and products on a global basis. "The Digital Silk Road is the flag bearer for 'Made in China 2025,' because it will send them the data that will make those products competitive," Fernandes said. I had not fully understood the Digital Silk Road until Fernandes explained it.

It makes perfect sense—if China's goal is to dominate the world, then it needs a digital infrastructure to support it. It has such a large population and has educated so many engineers and other technology workers that it can manage such a sprawling telecommunications and computing network. Plus, it has emphasized the study of other languages.

It's not just India waking up to China's global ambitions. Even the Brookings Institution in Washington, DC, woke up. Brookings has been criticized for accepting funding from Huawei, and it has been curiously muffled on China issues. So I was struck by the testimony of Rush Doshi, director of Brookings' China Strategy Initiative. He appeared in July 2020 before a subcommittee of the US Senate Committee on Commerce, Science, and Transportation. "It is increasingly clear to most observers that China is pursuing a robust, state-backed effort to displace the United States from global technology leadership," Doshi said. "This effort is not driven entirely by commercial considerations but geopolitical ones as well. Beijing believes that the competition over technology is about more than whose companies will dominate particular markets. It is also about which country will be best positioned to lead the world." (Significantly, Doshi was tapped to join President Joe Biden's National Security Council to work on China issues.)

The sheer amount of data that China collects is staggering. Samantha Hoffman, an analyst at the Australian Strategic Policy Institute, and perhaps the world's top expert on the subject, told the *MIT Technology Review* that a Chinese entity called GTCOM is controlled by China's Central Propaganda Department and specializes in big data and AI. It has a product that collects ten terabytes of data a day from web pages, Twitter, Facebook, WeChat, and other sources. That's the equivalent of twenty billion Facebook photos. Among other things, the company has developed algorithms that look for military keywords, Hoffman explained. No doubt America's National Security Agency possesses similar capabilities, but China's capabilities are dedicated solely to promoting the Communist Party's power and influence.

China, in short, has a rival vision of the world from America's and is actively implementing it from a position of genuine technological and financial strength. Dictators and despots are reinforced. China's business deals usually are cut behind closed doors, raising the risk of bribery. The traditional American embrace of democracy and human rights and rule of law is undermined. Chinese diplomats have for the first time looked into the eyes of an American secretary of state and military chief and asserted that the United States lacks the moral authority to criticize anything that China does inside its own borders or elsewhere. They argue that their centrally controlled socialist system is better and more stable than our democracy, an argument we have unfortunately been helping them make.

To the voices who are warning that we are at risk of starting "a new cold war," I say we already are in the embrace of an adversary actively working to strip us of our technological

A Grand Strategy

advantage and undermine our democracy while at the same time seeking to impose a new China-centric world order. It is already a global confrontation.

It's a new kind of conflict, the likes of which the United States has never experienced. We think in binary terms. A country is either a friend or foe. But the Chinese are far more sophisticated. They have been able to develop a far more complex, multifaceted assault on American interests and values than the Soviets ever did.

Condoleezza Rice, the former national security advisor and Secretary of State, agreed with this assessment in a Crowdcast video conference in October 2020 cosponsored by the Hoover Institution at Stanford University. "This challenge with China is not just different but in many ways harder," said Rice. "The Soviet Union never accounted for more than 1 percent of world trade. It was isolated from the international economy. And though we thought of it as a military giant, it was actually a technological midget. That meant we were eventually able to defeat the Soviet Union because of our values, but also because its technological deficit eventually caught up with it. It was not able to sustain itself militarily against a revitalized American military under President Ronald Reagan. Fast forward to China. That's not the China we face."

The extreme choices that some policy gurus are offering—either war with China or complete "decoupling"—are simplistic in the extreme. A war isn't necessary and isn't either side's goal. The costs would be devastating to the whole world.

On the other end of the spectrum, the bilateral economic relationship would take ten years or more to unwind, at huge costs to both American and Chinese interests. There may be ways to build in protections for critical US technologies and no-go zones where Chinese technology players are not welcome. But the idea of a total "decoupling" of the economic relationship is naïve. The relationship is not just bilateral. It is global. Every region of the world is now a showdown between the American system and American values and the Chinese system and Chinese values. To truly decouple from China on a global basis, we would have to retreat to our own shores and hide behind sandbags. We are stuck in a messy embrace. We need to learn the new rules.

CHAPTER NOTES:

APT10: US Department of Justice, Office of Public Affairs, "Two Chinese Hackers Associated with the Ministry of State Security Charged with Global Computer Intrusion Campaigns Targeting Intellectual Property and Confidential Business Information." Dec. 20, 2018. https://www.justice.gov/opa/pr/two-chinese-hackers-associated-ministry-state-security-charged-global-computer-intrusion

Atlantic Magazine, The, "When China Sees All." By Ross Anderson, September 2020. https://www.theatlantic.com/magazine/archive/2020/09/china-ai-surveillance/614197/

Brookings—Yale fellow Rush Doshi. "The United States, China and the Contest for the Fourth Industrial Revolution." Senate Commerce Committee, July 31, 2020. https://www.brookings.edu/testimonies/the-united-states-china-and-the-contest-for-the-fourth-industrial-revolution/

Business Week, "The Big Hack." By Jordan Robertson and Michael Riley. Oct. 8, 2018.

Business Week, "The Long Hack: How China Exploited a U.S. Tech Supplier." By Jordan Robertson and Michael Riley, Feb. 12, 2001.

Gateway House. OPC and Gateway House Host Global Discussion on China Influence. Aug. 13, 2020. https://opcofamerica.org/Eventposts/opc-and-gateway-house-host-global-discussion-on-china-influence/

Harvard arrest. Department of Justice, Office of Public Affairs. Harvard University Professor And Two Chinese Nationals Charged in Three Separate China Related Cases. Jan. 28, 2020.

https://www.justice.gov/opa/pr/harvard-university-professor-and-two-chinese-nationals-charged-three-separate-china-related#:~:text=Charles%20Lieber%2C%2060%2C%20Chair%20of,false%2C%20fictitious%20and%20fraudulent%20statement.&text=Zaosong%20Zheng%2C%2030%

Hoffman, Samantha. "How China Surveils the World." *MIT Technology Review*. By Mara Hvistendahl. Aug. 19, 2020. https://www.technologyreview.com/2020/08/19/1006455/gtcom-samantha-hoffman-tiktok/

National Interest, "Is China Seeking a Secretive, Permanent Presence in America's Computers?" Nov. 30, 2020. https://nationalinterest.org/feature/china-seeking-secretive-permanent-presence-america%E2%80%99s-computers-173292

Paulson, Henry. *South China Morning Post*. "Beijing should use 'first rate' economic team to launch reforms, former US treasury secretary Henry Paulson says." By Robert Delaney. April 13, 2018. https://www.scmp.com/news/china/article/2141518/beijing-should-use-first-rate-economic-team-launch-reforms-former-us

Stanford University, Condoleezza Rice. Hoover Institution Discussion on China. Oct. 30, 2020. https://www.c-span.org/video/?477535-1/hoover-institution-discussion-china

Xi Jinping. *The Wall Street Journal*. "How the U.S. Misread China's Xi: Hoping for a Globalist, It Got an Autocrat." By Jeremy Page. Dec. 23, 2000.

Tibetans in New York. "N.Y.P.D. Officer Charged With Spying on Tibetans." By Nicole Hong. *The New York Times*. Sept. 22, 2020. https://www.nytimes.com/2020/09/21/nyregion/nypd-china-tibet-spy.html?searchResultPosition=1

Trump Administration speeches. "Stop Appeasing China, Barr Says, Urging U.S. Companies to Be Tough." By Charlie Savage, *The New York Times*. July 17, 2020. https://www.nytimes.com/2020/07/16/us/politics/barr-china.html?searchResultPosition=1

Wicked Panda. "Hackers Backed by China Had Broad Scope, U.S. Says." By Katie Benner and Nicole Perlroth. *The New York*

Times, Sept. 17, 2020. https://www.nytimes.com/2020/09/16/us/politics/china-hackers.html?searchResultPosition=1

American companies in China:

Researchers belonging to the PLA: https://www.washingtonpost.com/national-security/more-than-1000-visiting-researchers-affiliated-with-the-chinese-military-fled-the-united-states-this-summer-justice-department-says/2020/12/02/9c-564dee-34e1-11eb-b59c-adb7153d10c2_story.html

China's Quest For Foreign Technology: https://www.amazon.com/Chinas-Foreign-Technology-Security-Studies/dp/0367473577/ref=sr_1_2?crid=1EJYO3CR5ASUM&d-child=1&keywords=china%27s+quest+for+foreign+tech-nology+beyond+espionage&qid=1607264161&sprefix-=china%27s+quest+for+%2Caps%2C151&sr=8-2

AI facial recognition systems: https://www.nytimes.com/2020/11/22/technology/china-intel-nvidia-xinjiang.html

And: https://www.top10vpn.com/research/investigations/hikvision-dahua-surveillance-cameras-global-locations/

Qualcomm: https://www.washingtonpost.com/archive/business/2000/02/02/chinese-phone-firm-qualcomm-make-deal/25fb0331-95ff-4f50-9c48-5b77c1fcd8f7/

Thermo Fisher DNA equipment: https://www.nytimes.com/2020/06/17/world/asia/China-DNA-surveillance.html?searchResultPosition=2

Apple removes democracy app. https://www.reuters.com/article/hongkong-protests-apple/apple-removes-police-tracking-app-used-in-hong-kong-protests-from-its-app-store-idUSL2N26V00Z

Clyde Prestowitz book: https://www.amazon.com/World-Turned-Upside-Down-Leadership-ebook/dp/B08NZ5B1SL/ref=sr_1_1?dchild=1&keywords=prestow-itz+turned+upside+down&qid=1609167261&sr=8-1.

PART THREE

WHAT MUST BE DONE

15 Media and The American Democracy

Of all the countries and systems I have explored around the world, the one I find most mystifying and incomprehensible is my own beloved United States. Why are we allowing ourselves to be torn apart? You can't blame it solely on artificial intelligence or COVID-19 or Trumpism. Why are we not responding to obvious needs both internally and externally?

I am going to start Part Three by writing about the media, because it is the foundation for so many aspects of our democracy, our culture and essentially our ability to function. The next chapter will zero in on technology and the grand finale will be about China.

Analyzing the role of the media in American politics and society as a whole is exquisitely difficult. It's like trying to write about the ocean—there are different currents, different depths, different temperatures, different colors, and the like. No one simple statement can capture the entire complexity. So for purposes of this exercise, allow me to dwell on three currents—the impact of social media, which inevitably raises the question of what must be done about Section 230 of the Communications Decency Act; the rise of a new class of robber barons, who have completely altered the ownership structures of mainstream media organizations; and an erosion of trust and understanding between media practitioners and the broader public.

Social Media

One story in *The New York Times* in June 2020 encapsulated the absolute insanity taking place on social media. Most people have heard of Pizzagate. In 2016, baseless information suggesting that Hillary Clinton and Democratic elites were running a child sex-trafficking ring out of a Washington pizzeria spread across the Internet. A gunman in North Carolina actually believed it and drove to the pizzeria with an assault rifle and opened fire into a closet. No one was hurt. He surrendered to police. But he *believed* it.

Now, several years later, unknown young people using TikTok have resurrected PizzaGate, with a new twist. It isn't aimed at Hillary Clinton but rather at global elites, including Justin Bieber, Bill Gates, Ellen DeGeneres, and Oprah Winfrey. For groups like the right-wing anarchist group QAnon, PizzaGate has become a way to whip up discontent. TikTok posts with the #PizzaGate hashtag have been viewed more than eighty-two million times in recent months, the *Times* reported. Eighty-two million! The topic was taken up by bogus online publications on Facebook and Instagram. A former Hollywood stuntman even created a movie about it all that was released on YouTube. "It all becomes a game, and people are drawn in because it feels participatory," one conspiracy researcher was quoted as saying.

Note that no mainstream media gatekeepers were involved. The phenomenon completely bypassed the mainstream media until *The Times* reported on it. Why do millions of people allow themselves to be drawn into such mad games? The answer seems to be that many young people are not interested in real news provided by trained professionals. For them, social media are like video games, made to be played and shared. They perceive that government and other institutions are feeble and corrupt. They want to use the game of social media to get a response from others—whether outrage or amusement, they don't care. As long as it is a reaction of some sort. It's like Ivan Pavlov and his slobbering dogs.

It was the same pattern of misinformation and hate-mongering that led to the assault on the nation's Capitol on January 6, 2021.

Which makes it clear that the starting point for us trying to create a realistic and meaningful national debate—about any issue—is to start insisting that online platforms hire seasoned editors and create "safe zones." Facebook and the others say they have hired thousands of "monitors" and created specific guidelines to manage what appears on their sites, but that appears to be largely window dressing. They have resisted creating real editorial controls, because it would be hugely expensive and would hurt profitability. It's all about money. When Mark Zuckerberg told Congress he did not think a private sector organization such as his should be in the business of dictating truth, he failed to note that's precisely what newspapers, radio stations, television stations, and other established forms of media do every day. They employ people who are trained. They have methods and systems in place to assure that the information they distribute is of the highest possible quality.

Zuckerberg also has expressed a deep commitment to freedom of expression as a reason he should not seek to modulate Facebook's content. But that sentiment seems to have far more to do with the profit motive than any deeply held philosophical conviction. It would eat into his profits if he were to impose legitimate parameters. Zuckerberg's arguments are nonsensical. Yet they have gone largely unchallenged.

Facebook took out full-page newspaper advertisements in July 2020 to tell the world that it had tripled the number of safety and security teams to thirty-five thousand people and removed billions of fake accounts. If they have thirty-five thousand monitors, why cannot it not somehow modulate the flow of dangerous and often violence-inspiring communications? And how was it possible for *billions* of fake accounts to be established in the first place?

It was only in reaction to the insurrection attempting to block the Electoral College results from being approved that Facebook, Twitter, and the other tech platforms, including Alphabet's Google, appear to be facing up to the central reality— they have created algorithms that are completely out of control and are damaging America's democracy.

They are damaging the democracy because they exaggerate our worst tendencies rather than our best. "There are bad people doing bad things on the Internet—QAnon, white supremacists," Hany Farid, a computer science professor at the University of California, Berkeley, told *The Wall Street Journal*. "It's not that Facebook, YouTube, and other social-media sites allow it on their platforms. It's that they amplify it."

After years of insisting they did not have the power to monitor the content that appeared on their platforms, within the space of two or three days, Facebook and Twitter either suspended or shut down former President Trump's access to his accounts because of his role in fomenting the insurrection. Apple and Google removed a right-wing conspiracy platform, Parler, from their app stores. And Amazon said it would no longer host the Parler site, because it had not sufficiently policed posts that incited violence and crime.

Big Tech clearly had an incentive to take such forceful action—with antitrust actions pending, they feared being blamed for a fundamental breakdown in American democracy. The tide of opinion shifted. They could no longer simply allow their platforms to be highly profitable cesspools.

The big tech platforms could take further steps by hiring editors, not just monitors, for certain areas, perhaps starting with politics. I realize millions of messages and videos are posted in a very short period of time. Editors could use human judgment to delay certain postings for a precious few minutes to try to stop obviously false or hate-filled postings. There is no reason everything has to be posted immediately. Editors also could identify persistent violators of the standards they establish and take appropriate steps to restrict or impede their access. Perhaps other safe zones where editors could buffer the avalanche of postings could be health and science, where accuracy is vital. People could still post videos or pictures of themselves dumping ice water on their heads without interference. Or talk about Pizzagate. We just need clearer boundaries concerning what's real and what's unreal. There must be more warning signs about people who have become dangerously unmoored from reality. The social media giants have to take some measure of *responsibility*.

Google's YouTube has a "three strikes" strategy that might help show the way. Each time a major account with a large following shares discredited information or comes even close to abusive behavior, that account gets a warning. Three warnings and it faces a lengthy suspension or outright ban. A small-time crackpot with fifty followers would not be affected.

Which raises the question of what must be done with Section 230 of the Communication Decency Act of 1996. All this is tricky, because we do not want the government to dictate the outcome. But Section 230 has helped the big social media platforms by absolving them of any and all legal responsibility for their user-generated content, including any threat of being held responsible for libel, which mainstream media organizations worry about whenever they handle sensitive stories about powerful people.

We don't want to completely destroy social media, but we would like to channel it in more positive directions. The law should be tweaked to advocate for safe zones, or "guardrails," and to create more avenues to obtain redress from the sites when they post particularly virulent and inaccurate content. And social media sites should be held responsible for allowing hate that inspires violence. Senators Mark Warner, Mazie

Hirono, and Amy Klobuchar introduced the SAFE TECH Act in early 2021; it would strip away some of those protections. Immunity would not apply to online speech that violated civil rights or cyberstalking laws, for example. Some experts said the legislation was imperfect because the big tech platforms will be able to manage the new environment, but smaller social media outlets will be squelched. Altogether, some twenty bills to amend Section 230 were introduced.

On balance, I think it is better to do something than nothing. If enacting any new law has unintended side effects, they can be amended once those side effects become clear. There is no immediate, perfect, silver-bullet solution to a problem that has been brewing for twenty years. The devil will truly be in the details.

Ultimately, the only way our society can understand what the social media algorithms are doing is if we hire experts to analyze them. Which again gets us into very difficult territory. Can the government demand to see a company's algorithms? The only way to know for sure whether the social media platforms are intentionally exaggerating the worst content would be to understand the feed-ranking and recommendation systems contained in their algorithms.

Could an independent algorithm review board be created to examine the algorithms of a company found to be fanning the flames of hate? Some countries have debated doing this. In the US context, it should comprise top experts from academia, the technology world, and perhaps a smattering of experts from the Federal Communications Commission. It should not be a full governmental body. It needs to be independent but possess real stature and prestige. If a social media company's algorithms are identified as violating norms that the panel establishes, the panel would have the bully pulpit to publicize it and perhaps spark governmental action. If nothing else, the threat of creating such a body could be held over the heads of recalcitrant social media tycoons.

The ideal way to create a new social compact, so to speak, with Big Tech would be to create a dialogue between them and major mainstream media organizations, journalistic unions, press nonprofits, journalism schools, advertisers, and perhaps other constituencies. The goal would be to persuade Big Tech that it needs to start fulfilling its responsibilities and willingly agree on standards and procedures that would cost it money but which would buy it a measure of protection from harsher governmental action.

Part and parcel of any such grand reckoning would a greater sharing of profits with established media organizations. Their "content" is being distributed by the Apple News app, Google, and others, and the original creators of that content are not being adequately compensated for it. That's wrong and needs to change. (In an example of how the tech giants can be played against each other, Microsoft in February 2021 called for competition laws that would force Facebook and Google to share more revenue with publishers. "The tech sector is not a monolith," Microsoft President Brad Smith was quoted as saying.)

If Big Tech stonewalls, then it's time for greater government pressure. The FCC has to issue licenses for radio and television stations (because there is a finite amount of frequencies available in a given area without causing interference to another station's signal). That's another ultimate threat to Big Tech—forcing it to get licenses. But I think the momentum has shifted—Big Tech might be persuaded voluntarily to take the right steps.

Ownership Structures

The second major ocean current is, can the media find an ownership structure that allows the pursuit well-balanced, conscientious coverage? There are challenges in this regard from multiple directions. It appeared at one time that online news organizations would simply blow away the likes of *The New York*

Times and *The Wall Street Journal*. It would be BuzzFeed for everyone, and "clickbait" lists about "The Ten Best Cat Somersault Tricks" would dominate our attention spans.

But a funny thing happened on the way to the future. Partly because of investments from technologists such as Jeff Bezos and Patrick Soon-Shiong, *The Washington Post* and *Los Angeles Times* appear surprisingly solid. The *Times* and *Journal* also seem certain to endure. *The Atlantic,* with funding from Steve Jobs' widow, will clearly endure.

The way these organizations have resisted being destroyed is that, at least in part, they borrowed tools from the online world. A subscriber to both the print and digital editions, I've watched what *The New York Times* has done with its digital operations. It sends out daily briefings. It has video and highly informative graphics on its website that present data in very interesting ways. They've developed apps for their crossword puzzle followers. They have a cooking site. They have created a much deeper conversation with their readers and viewers, or rather a series of conversations, such as "Modern Love" and a jogging blog. They have created a series of communities. It's a far cry from the days when the newspaper was known as the Gray Lady that printed "All the News That's Fit to Print."

As a result, digital advertising now exceeds print advertising revenue. *The Times* has seven million subscribers, with more digital subscribers than print subscribers. And its core editorial operations are proving to be an advantage against online start-ups that tend to hire younger, less experienced editors, producers, writers, and so forth. In the final analysis, experience matters. (I also subscribe digitally to *The Wall Street Journal, The Washington Post* and *South China Morning Post* of Hong Kong.)

Some two thousand other daily newspapers have gone out of business, however, as previously noted. It is an absolute disaster. In most towns now, nobody is covering the water commission or the planning board. People simply do not know what is happening in their own towns and regions.

Aside from the pressures of the Internet, the core problem is ownership structure. The Gannetts and GateHouses and McClatchys, in tandem with their "vulture" capital friends, such as Alden Global Capital, have bought newspapers and gutted them. That starts a death spiral. Locals don't care to read the papers, because they are so awful. Many Americans no longer believe that reading really matters, and the poor quality of newspapers reinforces that belief. Classified advertising, once a key source of revenue, is just a shadow of what it once was. Like a vulture feeding on a carcass, McClatchy has now been taken over by a New Jersey-based hedge fund, Chatham Asset Management. In a new book called *Ghosting The News: Local Journalism and the Crisis of American Democracy*, Margaret Sullivan calls the actions of the financial raiders "strip-mining" that has created "news deserts."

Ever since my days watching UPI be sold out from under us, I have believed that journalists should do a better job of understanding their ownership structure and trying to find ways to influence it for the best editorial outcomes. We are, after all, skilled at shaping opinions.

On a national scale, what Alden is doing seems particularly pernicious. Through its MediaNews Group, it controls about two hundred publications, including *The Denver Post* and *Boston Herald*. It also owns 32 percent of *The Chicago Tribune* and announced it was bidding for the remainder of the shares—and hence full control. These are major newspapers that could be in the hands of completely irresponsible owners who have a single objective—stripping them further to make more money. Chatham had much the same strategy. We don't want government to intervene directly, but a congressional committee should hold hearings on this issue just to apply pressure on the manipulators and to draw wider public attention.

One of the most agonizingly difficult things for journalists to do is get involved in newspaper purchases at the local level. That is outside their comfort zone. But journalists need to create conversations with local businesses, religious figures, and educational leaders to ask: what is the quality of the media in our city or region? And if Gannett (now owned by GateHouse) or Alden (or Rupert Murdoch) come sniffing around to buy newspapers or radio or television stations, what are the alternatives?

Similarly, if the rapacious media giants already have secured control, how can a community communicate its expectations about the quality of coverage? It might be possible for journalists to create local media councils that include the different constituencies and try to shape the outcome of some of these fights for control. It is tricky, to be sure. Journalists don't want to allow governments or wealthy families or large corporations to tell them what to do, but if the dialogue can be constructed in the right way, it could be useful. Readers and listeners could be galvanized to support local control of media institutions.

One very positive model is that of *The Salt Lake Tribune*, which turned itself into a nonprofit institution in late 2019. The move to nonprofit status was spurred by the newspaper's owner, Paul Huntsman, who gave up his sole ownership. "The current business model for local newspapers is broken and beyond repair," said Huntsman. Something called the Utah Journalism Foundation is creating an endowment to fund independent journalism in Utah, with *The Tribune* being one major cause. This kind of rational strategy might not be possible in every part of the country, because not every state and city possesses the cohesion that the Mormons do, but it's an interesting model. So too are proposals to make the paying of subscriptions to newspapers tax-deductible on state and federal tax returns.

Rebuilding Trust Between the Mainstream Media and Its Public

The media's popular image has been under assault from a president who shouted "Fake News" and called journalists "enemies of the people." Enough people believed Trump that violence against journalists rose to an all-time high, particularly in covering the Black Lives Matter protests and riots and in the January 6 violence at the Capitol. "Murder the media," one protestor etched into a door inside the Capitol. The combination of economic crisis, the pandemic, and rising violence against journalists has made this one of the most difficult moments in the profession's modern history.

Once again, I think journalists need to emerge from their traditional roles to become more active in shaping the climate around them. Most journalists just want to get the story before the competition does and go home (or, in the old days, to the bar). But that is no longer good enough. Journalists need to overcome their institutional rivalries to realize they have common interests.

By way of one small example, I have sought to do that with the Overseas Press Club and its sister organization, the OPC Foundation. I was president of the OPC from 1994-1996 and remain on the board. And I became president of the OPC Foundation in 1996 and remain in that role.

Together, these organizations support the world of foreign correspondents, which is admittedly just one piece of the broader challenge of rebuilding trust. But it's an important one. The OPC gives awards annually for the best international news coverage in print, photography, television, books, cartoons, and other categories. Winning an award is a major affirmation of a news organization's decision to spend money to hire seasoned editors and put correspondents on the ground. It serves as kind of a networking mechanism for correspondents at major organizations as well as for freelancers. At a deeper level, the OPC developed legitimacy as a platform—and platforms are essential to create meaningful discussions about the big issues. And it has emerged as a bastion of strength in helping freelancers based abroad who have been caught in the worst professional and economic crisis they have ever faced because of the pandemic.

The foundation, for its part, identifies college students who want to become foreign correspondents and conducts an annual competition to select seventeen of them. We bring them to New York to expose them to decision-making editors and producers. We place ten to twelve each year in the foreign bureaus of the Associated Press, Reuters, *The Wall Street Journal,* and others. We've launched the careers of hundreds of journalists over twenty-five years.

All this set the stage for another example of the impact journalists can have outside the newsroom without betraying their sacred principles. After the beheadings of James Foley and Steven Sotloff in Syria in 2014, the profession was, of course, shocked. What could be done? Three journalists I know—Charlie Sennott of the GroundTruth Project, John Daniszewski of the Associated Press, and David Rohde, then at Reuters, started holding a series of conversations with the Frontline Freelance Register in London, an association of freelancers, and with nonprofits such as the Committee to Protect Journalists in New York. As noted previously, they came up with the idea of creating A Culture of Safety Alliance (ACOS,) an alliance that would fight to establish principles that hiring editors and producers would accept in deploying freelancers in conflict zones.

But how would they establish themselves as a legal entity? Jane Reilly, executive director of the Overseas Press Club Foundation, conceived the idea that our foundation, which enjoys 501(c)(3) tax status, would become the financial sponsor for ACOS. It helped that Sennott, Daniszewski, and Rohde already were on the OPC Foundation board. I was able to persuade the full board to accept that sponsoring ACOS reflected an expansion of our mission to launch the careers of foreign correspondents. ACOS accepted the fact that we control the flow of money to them from the John D. and Catherine T. MacArthur Foundation and the Open Society Foundations.

The results have been powerful. Dozens of media organizations have embraced ACOS principles, such as providing proper protective equipment to freelancers and planning their trips so that they have clear evacuation protocols and access to medical care. ACOS has galvanized news organizations, freelancers, and NGOs to become part of a coalition aimed at making sure no freelancers are ever again placed, or place themselves, in situations in which their lives could be in danger. Hundreds of journalists have now been trained. Both Diane Foley, mother of James, and Art Sotloff, father of Steven, sit on the ACOS board, as do I. The memory of what happened to their sons hangs in the air.

In effect, we have built institutions to defend the causes we believe in, which is not what most journalists ever get involved in. They think it's someone else's job. But as a result of what these organizations have done, aspiring and midcareer journalists can obtain the encouragement, mentoring, training, and support of a sort I once enjoyed. And the profession that covers the world and translates events into a framework that Americans can understand has been supported and defended. As a result of the ACOS alliance, the news industry's behavior has changed. Freelancers got smarter and were better supported. No Western freelancer has been killed since the grizzly 2014 murders, although local journalists who work for international news organizations are frequently killed or imprisoned. And we saw a surge of nonlethal violence against American journalists *inside* America, which was shocking.

At the highest level, we in the media need to take the lead in fostering a debate about the quality of our democracy and our role in it. Have we held the middle ground? Even before the January 6 insurrection, pressures were mounting from multiple directions. In the emotional aftermath of George Floyd's shocking death in Minneapolis, voices from the liberal end of the spectrum were forceful in pushing for an end to a deep pattern of racial segregation and discrimination.

But they risked showing a degree of intolerance for other viewpoints. As I discovered in Vietnam War protests, simply shouting slogans does not change society. Shouting "Black lives matter" and "Defund the police," and then calling anyone who does not agree a "racist," is not the way to engage in the sustained and genuine dialogue our society needs. A letter entitled, "A Letter on Justice and Open Debate," signed by 153 prominent intellectuals and artists, appeared in *Harper's Magazine* and then on the front page of *The New York Times*. "The free exchange of information and ideas, the lifeblood of a liberal society, is daily becoming more constricted," the letter said, citing "... an intolerance of opposing views, a vogue for public shaming and ostracism, and the tendency to dissolve complex policy issues in a blinding moral certainty." I particularly like that last phrase, "blinding moral certainty."

The American media, writ broadly, should be pointing out examples of situations in which Americans are cooperating to create futures for themselves—across races, Republican and Democrat, rural and urban. It is the responsibility of the American media to stand radically in the center of our society and help chart a course out of bitter ideological divisiveness rather than catering to the extremes. Rather than wrapping ourselves in the sanctity of the First Amendment, we should rededicate ourselves to that proposition.

Instead, journalists have teetered on the edge of advocacy in what should be rigorously balanced news sections. *The New York Times*, in particular, has become an open advocate in its news columns, not just on its editorial pages, of greater racial justice and greater rights and recognition for the LGBTQ community. CNN and MSNBC are also clearly catering to one end of the political spectrum, and their ratings soared as they offered nearly nonstop negative coverage of Trump. Even after his defeat and the swearing in of Biden, CNN and MSNBC continued to harp on the themes of division.

But by far the worst transgressions came from Rush Limbaugh and Fox News, who created the narrative that the coronavirus was a Democratic scheme to undermine Trump after the first impeachment effort failed. Even further to the right, Newsmax and One American News Network sprang forth. Thousands of Americans died because of the misinformation spewed by these news organizations. That is not an opinion. It is a cold, hard fact. Thanks to this right-wing echo chamber, many people were able to live in their own make-believe worlds, where COVID did not represent a threat. Paradoxically, Fox's ratings surged, because that's what Fox viewers wanted to hear.

In journalism school, we were taught that we should be "objective." Of course, it's impossible to be completely objective. If your brain were completely empty, you would never be able to find the thread of a story or develop a line of analysis. I think of being objective as trying to remain in the center of the issues, so that a journalistic platform can foster real debate, not merely preach to the converted, and not merely drive up one's ratings or hits.

On balance, the mainstream media performed an incredibly useful role in spotting the coronavirus outbreak in Wuhan at a time when the Communist Party was trying to hide it. The fact that American news organizations had seasoned, Mandarin-speaking correspondents on the ground in China who could follow Chinese social media accounts before censors removed them was essential. (Many of them are now gone after being expelled.) In the absence of any clear and decisive action by the Trump administration, the mainstream media as a whole also served as an early warning system for Americans who would listen, and it promulgated the best practices for avoiding the virus.

The media isn't the only institution that has suffered in the minds of the American people. Entire books have been written about how Americans do not trust experts of any sort (*The Death of Expertise: The Campaign Against Established Knowledge and Why It Matters,* by Tom Nichols, 2017), and how we can no longer establish the facts in any given situation (*The Death of Truth: Notes on Falsehood in the Age of Trump,* by Michiko Kakutani, 2018). Science is not really science. And because we cannot agree on the facts, our democracy has been crippled. Lives have been lost. Never has the need for credible information, and indeed expertise, been more urgent.

***

There are also actions that a public concerned about its quality of information could take. In schools, at all levels, we need to teach media literacy. In the old game Telephone, a group of eight or ten people sit in a room. The first person whispers a story to a second person, who then repeats the story as best he or she can. By the time the story has reached the final person, and he or she repeats it aloud, inevitably it has evolved or morphed into something slightly different than when it started, perhaps even significantly different. The purpose of the game is to show just how devilishly difficult accurate communication is.

We should teach Americans starting in elementary school to ask questions such as, "What is the source of information?" "Where does it come from?" "Is it from a primary source or secondary source?" "Are their multiple sources or just one?" "Did the person providing the information actually go to where something happened, or was the person speculating from afar?" "What is the background of the source, and what is their motivation?" "What is disinformation?" Disinformation is emerging as an entire academic discipline. Platform manipulation, in which powerful groups flood Twitter or Facebook with thousands of posts, is another phenomenon that bears deeper examination.

We need to teach people what data really is, and why it can be so valuable. What is Big Data? What is data mining? What is an algorithm, and how does it work? What is a "recommendation tunnel"? (I've also heard it called a "recommendation engine.")

If people are becoming choosier about what kind of water they drink and want vegetables straight from a farm, why don't they apply the same efforts to understanding and managing the sources of their information? That question is becoming increasingly urgent, as computer-generated graphics and other powerful tools allow bad actors to create completely fake images or video. "Deep fakes" are so well done that even experts can't be sure about their authenticity. Women who are active online have even been subjected to "deep fake pornography." Harassers post real pictures of women that have been altered/manipulated so that the women appear to be engaging in pornographic activities.

And now, a new software program from OpenAI called GPT-3 has "learned" how to write humanlike text, opening up new possibilities for misinformation and fraud. Grammarly.com uses what appear to be AI tools to help people write better, which means it soon could become impossible to know if someone really wrote something without assistance. (No, I have never used it and never will.) Music can be generated by computer and "married" to computer-generated music. An entirely new field called "ethical deep fakes" has emerged to counte the unethical deep fakes.

In response, we need to teach people how to use Snopes.com and other fact-checking services to sniff out the real from the unreal. Other Internet-based services inform us about the authenticity of websites, providing the modern version of the Good Housekeeping Seal. One of those is NewsGuard, which monitors the trustworthiness and transparency of more than four thousand news sites. This service offers a "nutrition label" that lists nine specific criteria for sorting out trust scores. I do not think that similar services are widely available to analyze whether a video or text is real or not, but they should be developed and made more widely available.

Journalists also should become more vocal in articulating why what we do is important. *The New York Times* has started a column on page 2 of the physical newspaper talking about how decisions are made internally to cover certain stories. That helps readers understand that real people are involved in trying to figure out how to tell the truth. *The Times* also has started advertising on television, with slogans such as "Life Needs Truth." *The Washington Post* has adopted the motto, "Democracy Dies in Darkness." I think journalists have assumed that the larger public understands the importance of what we do and we don't need to explain it. But in today's climate, we do. We need to persuade people to subscribe to newspapers and magazines, not just stare at their phones. We need to give more talks to high school and college students to teach them why the quality of their information is critical.

We also should have a philosophical debate about communication itself, something I've been thinking about since reading the early media critics such as Liebling and McLuhan and then finding myself at the heart of UPI's real-time global operations. Aside from long-form written communication, which I obviously espouse, the medium that allows for the highest quality of communication is the old-fashioned, face-to-face meeting or interview. Many dimensions of truth are communicated spontaneously by tone of voice, posture, gestures, and the like. Conference calls with multiple people on, whether on video or just phone, become political. Gamesmanship increases. Candor is lessened.

The Internet allows certain new forms of communication that are truly awesome for sharing messages or videos with a wide circle of people around the world instantaneously. It allows research powers of a sort that never used to exist.

But email is inherently scattershot, particularly if multiple people are cc'd or bcc'd. If I ask someone three questions in an email, they can choose to answer just one. They can say they never got the email because it went to their spam folder. Or they can say that they have been "drinking from a firehose" and simply could not respond. Texting is even worse. But the ultimate nadir in my humble estimation is the use of emojis and memes and TikTok videos, which may communicate a fleeting feeling but do not reflect any real thought process. They are not true communication in the richest sense of the word.

As McLuhan, the media theorist, wrote, "We shape our tools, and thereafter our tools shape us." I suspect that the newest forms of communication prevent us from having meaningful, rich discussions. Instead, they encourage snap judgments of "blinding moral certainty" and "delegitimization."

I also have detected a pattern I call "device arrogance," or, alternatively, "app arrogance." If people use their devices and apps in very sophisticated ways, they confuse that skill with the real meaning of what they are communicating. They think they're smart just because of the way they use their devices—even if what they say is disjointed or poorly constructed.

Discussing media and communications leads directly into a discussion about values. It's fashionable these days to attack institutions such as the media, Congress, the federal government, and corporations. But I believe in the power of institutions. We can shape our society and our relations among ourselves if we build better institutions, particularly if we find ways for those institutions to have overlapping interests with each other. Institutions transmit values. I was struck by what James Bennet, the editorial page editor of the *New York Times*, wrote in a piece describing the role of the editorial board, which is distinct from the newsroom. "I've always believed that strong institutions, like strong families, are meant to transmit principles across generations," he wrote, referring specifically to his editorial board. (Bennet was drummed out of the *Times* because of an op-ed his department ran by an Arkansas politician who thought military force was justified to suppress Black Lives Matter demonstrations. That was an example of an intolerant backlash from people inside *The Times* who possessed "blinding moral certainty." The precise reason an op-ed page exists is to explore different opinions.)

On another front, we need to do a better job of teaching civics, even at a time when the educational system is in a COVID-induced crisis. In my high school, the class was taught by the football coach and was something of a joke. But the course appears to have disappeared almost entirely from most high schools. That's a mistake. Americans seem to have forgotten a great deal about how our democracy is supposed to function. We are not supposed to involve foreign powers in our domestic politics. We are supposed to respect a system of checks and balances against absolute power. The three branches of government (legislative, executive, and judicial) need to engage with each other on the basis of long-established principles. Peaceful transfers of power are one of the bedrocks of our system. And what is the meaning of the First Amendment and press freedom, and why are those concepts so important?

Language is important. Some leftish voices in 2020 called for "socialism." Did they really know what socialism is? They may wish for a kinder, gentler form of capitalism as practiced in Japan and Europe, but calling for outright socialism reflects a complete lack of understanding about how their country's economy functions. This also needs to be taught at all levels of the educational system. Our capitalistic system is not perfect and needs constant adjustment, but it cannot simply be thrown out the window.

Another value that our educational institutions and media should promote is that the collision of cultures and religions can be enriching, not threatening. Differences should not be an automatic cause of conflict. Trying to learn a language or understand a foreign culture or system does not make us less American. I suspect some Americans might think I must have been corrupted by the Chinese Communist Party because I studied Chinese in Beijing. Far from it. My understanding of the language and culture enables me to conclude that the current form of authoritarianism is not in keeping with the best of Chinese culture. In fact, knowing how other societies functions allows us to better understand our own systems and values.

The trends that have dramatically impacted the media's central role in our democracy have been building for decades. It will take time to repair. And there is no one easy solution—rewriting Section 230 or breaking up Big Tech are not panaceas. Forcing Alden Global Capital and Gannett into the court of public opinion is only part of the solution.

To revitalize and strengthen the American debate, it will take a village—media practitioners, journalism schools, local communities, politicians, responsible corporations, and educational leaders. Renee DiResta, research manager at the Stanford Internet Observatory and an expert in online disinformation, was quoted by the *MIT Technology Review* as saying we should be "rethinking the entire information ecosystem."

This would not represent an effort to turn back the clock to the 1950s–1960s and the *Leave It To Beaver* and *Gilligan's Island* era. But it would be a start in re-establishing a healthy national discussion. Many things have changed—but not the enduring values that define us as Americans. One of those values is a commitment to genuine dialogue and compromise.

CHAPTER NOTES:

Alden Global Capital. "Hedge Fund Is Seeking Full Control of Tribune." By Michel J. de la Merced and Mark Tracy. *The New York Times*. Jan. 1, 2021. https://www.nytimes.com/2020/12/31/business/media/tribune-alden-global.html?searchResultPosition=1

A Culture of Safety. www.acosalliance.org.

DiResta, Renee. "It's Too Late to Stop QAnon with Fact Checks and Account Bans." By Abby Ohlheiser. *MIT Technology Review*. July 26, 2020. https://www.technologyreview.com/2020/07/26/1005609/QAnon-facebook-twitter-youtuube/

Facebook and hate speech. "Facebook Lets Hate Flourish, Report Finds." By Mike Isaac. *The New York Times*. July 8, 2020. https://www.nytimes.com/2020/07/08/technology/facebook-civil-rights-audit.html?searchResultPosition=1

Facebook boycott. "Did the 1,000-Advertiser Boycott of Facebook over Hate Speech Work?" By Tiffany Hsu and Eleanor Lutz. *The New York Times*. Aug. 2, 2020. https://www.nytimes.com/2020/08/01/business/media/facebook-boycott.html?searchResultPosition=1

Google antitrust suit. "Publishers Feel Validated by States' Google Antitrust Lawsuit." By Keach Hagey, *The Wall Street Journal*. Dec. 22, 2020.

GPT-3. "Meet GPT-3. It Has Learned to Code (and Blog and Argue)." By Cade Metz. *The New York Times.* Nov. 24, 2020. https://www.nytimes.com/2020/11/24/science/artificial-intelligence-ai-gpt3.html?searchResultPosition=1

Kakutani, Michiko. *The Death of Truth: Notes on Falsehood in the Age of Trump.* Tim Duggan Books. 2018. https://www.amazon.com/Death-Truth-Notes-Falsehood-Trump-ebook/dp/B077LS52P5/ref=sr_1_1?crid=2U2SAA9MYAER-Z&dchild=1&keywords=the+death+of+truth+by+michiko+kakutani&qid=1610132696&sprefix=death+of+truth%2C+mich%2Caps%2C159&sr=8-1

Microsoft. "A Look Back at Microsoft for Lessons on Antitrust." By Steve Lohr. *The New York Times.* June 24, 2019. https://www.nytimes.com/2019/06/23/technology/antitrust-tech-microsoft-lessons.html?searchResultPosition=1

Microsoft supports revenue sharing. "Microsoft Supports Proposal For News Revenue Sharing." By Cecilia Kang. *The New York Times*. Feb. 12, 2021.

The New York Times. "New York Times Amasses Over 7 Million Subscribers." By Edmund Lee. Nov. 6, 2020. https://www.nytimes.com/2020/11/05/business/media/new-york-times-q3-2020-earnings-nyt.html?searchResultPosition=1

News deserts. "The 'News Desert' is Growing. So is a Tiny Upstart." By James Dobbins, *The New York Times.* Jan. 2, 2021. https://www.nytimes.com/2021/01/01/us/del-rio-texas-newspaper.html?searchResultPosition=1

Nichols, Tom. The Death of Expertise: The Campaign against Established Knowledge and Why it Matters. Oxford University Press. 2017.

Overseas Press Club. www.opcofamerica.org

OPC Foundation, www.overseaspressclubfoundation.org

Pizzagate. "In TikTok Era, New Life for a Conspiracy Theory." By Cecilia Kang and Sheera Frenkel. *The New York Times.* June 28, 2020. https://www.nytimes.com/2020/06/27/technology/pizzagate-justin-bieber-QAnon-tiktok.html?searchResultPosition=1

SAFE TECH Act. "How a Democrat plan to reform Section 230 could backfire." By Robbie Johnson, *MIT Technology Review.* Feb. 8, 2021. https://www.technologyreview.com/2021/02/08/1017625/safe-tech-section-230-democrat-reform/

Section 230 of the Communications Decency Act. "How the Biden Administration Can Help Wean Americans from the Scourge of Hoaxes and Lies." By Kevin Roose. *The New York Times.* Feb. 4, 2021. https://www.nytimes.com/2021/02/02/technology/biden-reality-crisis-misinformation.html?searchResultPosition=1

Section 230. "How Do You Solve a Problem like Online Speech?" By Christopher Mims. *The Wall Street Journal.* Feb. 13-14, 2021.

Social media algorithms. "Social-Media Algorithms Rule How We See the World. Good Luck Trying to Stop Them." By Joanna Stern. *The Wall Street Journal.* Jan. 18, 2021. https://www.wsj.

com/articles/social-media-algorithms-rule-how-we-see-the-world-good-luck-trying-to-stop-them-11610884800?page=1

Social media crackdown. "A Web Haven for Trump Fans Faces the Void." By Jack Nicas and Davey Alba. *The New York Times*. Jan. 11, 2011. https://www.nytimes.com/2021/01/10/technology/parler-app-trump-free-speech.html?searchResultPosition=1

Sullivan, Margaret. *Ghosting The News: Local Journalism and the Crisis of American Democracy*. Columbia Global Reports. July 14, 2020. https://www.amazon.com/s?k=ghosting+the+news&ref=nb_sb_noss_1

YouTube practices. "Trump Isn't the Only One Typing Away." By Shira Ovide. *The New York Times*. Jan. 10, 2021. https://www.nytimes.com/2021/01/08/technology/trump-misin-formation-superspreaders.html?searchResultPosition=1

16 Taming the Tech Giants and Managing Technology

Mobile computing changed the world. In co-writing the ThinkPad book, I helped chronicle how profound a revolution mobile computing has been. For decades, computing was static. You had to physically go to a computer center and hand over your programming cards to attendants, who took them into the back room where the computer was. You came back the next day for your results.

The PC was a great invention, but it didn't allow complete mobility. It was still too heavy and bulky. For a period of time, there were "luggable" computers you had to wheel around. But the ThinkPad, introduced in 1992, followed by smart devices from Motorola, Blackberry, Nokia and Ericsson, untethered the computer. The iPhone was a relative late arrival to the party, appearing in 2007.

Wireless communications enabled these devices to be mobile and connected to the Internet at the same time. We were able to have devices in our pockets or on our laps that had the computing power a mainframe computer once had and be seamlessly connected to a worldwide communications network. Music, photos, and video could magically fly through the air and do so globally.

It has been one of the largest economic and social transformations in history. It has changed human behavior. There are more people in the world using wireless devices than there are people using toothbrushes, according to Ericcson, the big Swedish phone and telecommunications equipment maker.

And COVID-19 has accelerated it. Anything that could be moved online has been moved. We have developed a heavier reliance on artificial intelligence and voice recognition systems. You can hear it when you call a bank or a credit card company or a health care provider on the telephone. The machines that answer the phones—and that's what they are, machines—can recognize what you are saying, thanks to much improved voice recognition technology, and attempt to answer questions without any human involvement. Functions that could not be performed safely during the pandemic, such as sorting packages in crowded distribution centers, started relying more on robots.

I can sense the rapid pace of change on my Apple iPhone with Siri. Siri's voice recognition technology is impressive, because it seems to have been enhanced with some form of AI. As I ask a question, I can see Siri repeating in words on my screen what it thinks I am saying. It keeps adjusting the words it thinks it heard me say until it can decipher my meaning. It goes through very rapid iterations until the logic is found.

Think also about how the nearly ubiquitous presence of video cameras is reverberating through our society, sending people into the streets or into the Capitol. What if the videos get faked? Would people respond in the same way?

There's also been a revolution in music and television. The way I listen to music now is through Spotify on my phone linked by Bluetooth communications to an eight-inch-high, conical speaker called Ultimate Ears. The net effect is sound quality as good as, if not better than, what I was able to produce with the turntable and giant speakers that I lugged around as a college kid. And I can barely keep pace with the explosion of streaming services on television. I used to know where to look to find out what was on television. But now, most movies and TV series are available at any time. Newspapers have stopped trying to list television schedules. The notion that I would speak into my television's remote control to find channels would once have been considered pure science fiction. Yet it is a reality today.

You also can feel rapid shifts in technology when you punch out a text message with your fingers, and the phone tries to anticipate what you want to say. That's also AI at work. It's called "autocomplete."

As a result of all this, the digital divide, which I first wrote about twenty years ago in Austin, has deepened. Some people do not have access to the Internet, perhaps because they cannot afford computers or high-speed communications. Older Americans are at a particular disadvantage. It gets harder and harder for them to keep track of user IDs and passwords. People with high school educations or less may not be able to exploit the full functionality of the Net. All these people are simply being left behind as the rest of society races forward.

That obviously accentuates racial, class, and age divisions at a time when we surely do not need new, deeper divisions. One class of people rely on technology to do their jobs and obtain all the services they need, whether financial transactions or telemedicine or entertainment. The other class cannot do those things. In some cases, they have to risk their lives to achieve what others can do online.

The sheer speed at which all this happened and continues to happen has clearly overwhelmed our ability to fully digest the implications. I was struck by what the top lawyer for the National Security Agency, Glenn S. Gerstell, wrote in September 2019. Referring to the explosion of digital technologies, he wrote, "Other transformational technologies, such as railroads, electricity, radio, television, automobiles, and airplanes all took several decades before they reached that comparable level of ubiquity. Society had the time to sort out the norms, rules, and laws governing those technologies and the respective roles of government and the private sector." Obviously, the digital revolution has occurred too fast to digest.

And the pace of technological change is not even close to being over. 5G communications will be another game changer, because it will increase the speed of our communications by a hundredfold. The 5G service that Verizon and AT&T are now heavily promoting is really just an enhanced version of 4G. True 5G has not yet arrived. History teaches us that every time we increase the speed of communications, new ways of using information are either discovered or enhanced. Autonomous driving, for example, would be greatly assisted by more rapid wireless communications.

Virtual reality and augmented reality will further obscure the differences between what is real and what is not. The gaming industry is using these tools to create ever more lifelike games that young people are playing for endless hours. Imagine what VR and AR will do for the pornography industry.

Quantum computing alone would change the world. Every existing computer and every existing algorithm would become obsolete if quantum computing can be made to work. The country that masters it first would be able to penetrate the encrypted computer systems of every other country on earth. Genetic editing and 3D "additive" manufacturing are both transformative. And artificial intelligence is finding rapid adoption in fields such as medicine, where it is used to scan MRIs to detect cancers.

This is an enormous subject, and to make it comprehensible, I'll again break it into three subthemes: redefining the relationship between government and Big Tech; developing technology with a greater focus on ethics and human needs; and attacking the digital divide.

Redefining the Relationship Between Government and Big Tech:

It is in the US government's best interest and in the best interest of society as a whole that the technology platform giants be coaxed and nudged into behaving better. They ought to bring some of their hundreds of billions of dollars of profits home from offshore and pay taxes on them. They ought to be encouraged to recognize that they have to differentiate between material that is "news" and material that is plain drivel. That will cost them money. And, as noted in the previous chapter, they should share more revenue with existing mainstream organizations whose content they distribute, as major news organizations including *The New York Times* and *The Wall Street Journal* have demanded. If they took those steps, they'd have fewer billions to throw at acquisitions. Their behavior would be modified at least somewhat.

I do not think attempting to break them up would be successful. It would create years of litigation and cause a complete collapse of trust between the government and the companies—a trust that is becoming more essential, not less, in view of China's gathering momentum.

But perhaps their aggressive expansion into different fields could be moderated. One way to start would be to rewrite American antitrust laws, which were designed for a different era. They were written in a day when if one steel company bought another steel company, it might cut production and raise prices for customers. Or if one railroad bought another and raised prices. That was clearly anticompetitive behavior.

The tech giants, however, have moved into adjacent fields, as evidenced by Amazon's purchase of Whole Foods, or Microsoft's purchase of Skype, or Facebook's purchase of Instagram. There is no evidence that those acquisitions resulted in price increases. In fact, one could argue that Amazon's entry into the grocery business has helped Whole Foods maintain the line on pricing and quality, and put pressure on the rest of the grocery industry to move into the twenty-first century. The result of some mergers has been to offer consumers more choices either for very little money or for free (in exchange for their data.)

It's simply stunning that even though Joel Klein started talking about "network effects" and "installed base" nearly twenty-five years ago, we have not modernized our antitrust laws in response to the technological change that has washed over us. The testimony of the CEOs of Amazon, Apple, Facebook, and Microsoft before Congress in late July 2020 was more political theater than a serious intellectual effort. We need to put our best minds to work on creating an antitrust framework that checks the power of Big Tech without halting genuine technological progress. We need to define the behaviors that are not acceptable and therefore are anticompetitive. A variety of authorities—federal watchdogs, state attorneys general, and Congress—have been investigating and suing Big Tech, but it seems to me they cannot be truly effective until they have clarified the legal underpinnings.

I cannot possibly provide the full answers, but one issue would be what happens when an established tech platform sees a smaller competitor that has a useful idea which leads to a viable product. In our system, the dominant player should be allowed to pay a fair price and acquire that company. But it should not be allowed to imitate what the smaller guy is offering and then drive the start-up out of business, which is what Microsoft did to Netscape. Rigorous competition is one thing, but if there is *intent* to undermine a company's business fundamentals for the purpose of buying it lock, stock, and barrel, that's another.

It continues to happen. According to subpoenaed emails and texts from the past fifteen years that Congress demanded in connection with the July 2020 hearings, Big Tech was consciously trying to drive small competitors out of business. An email from Facebook's Zuckerberg suggests that starting in 2008, he developed a method to crush "nascent" companies that posed "very disruptive" threats to Facebook. "It is better to buy than compete," he wrote.

One proposal aimed at halting that practice is legislation introduced by Sen. Amy Klobuchar, who became head of the

Senate antitrust subcommittee. Her bill would shift the ground rules for deciding whether an acquisition is anticompetitive. Rather than the government having to prove that a merger substantially lessens competition, the companies themselves would have to prove that a proposed acquisition does not "create an appreciable risk of materially lessening competition." That's still imperfect, because many deals, such as Amazon's acquisition of Whole Foods, actually intensified competition in the grocery sector. But the legislation would be a step in the right direction.

Another way to chip away at Big Tech's power would be to require it to pay some consumers for at least some of the data they collect, as proposed by Democratic presidential candidate Andrew Yang. He put forth the idea of a Data Dividend Project, which was modeled on the California Consumer Privacy Act. That program seeks to "… pave the way for a future in which all Americans can claim their data as a property right and receive payment" if they choose to share their data. That would help restore a measure of privacy at a time when massive amounts of data are being collected about users. It would also, once again, put a curb on the profits the tech platforms are making.

Clearer rules about which forms of data collection are legal and which ones are illegal would also help. I used to like using Siri on my iPhone to conduct research on crossword puzzles. But then I looked at the types of data that Siri collects, according to its privacy policy on my phone:

—"contact names, nicknames, and relationships (e.g., "my dad"), if you set them up in your contacts;
—"music, books, and podcasts you enjoy;
—"names of your device and your Family Sharing members' devices;
—"the names of your photo albums, apps installed on your device, and shortcuts you added through Siri."

Why does Siri need to know all that? Is it to help me, or is it to help Apple compile a portrait of me as a consumer? It's obvious it is aimed at marketing to me or selling information to others who will market to me. Siri allows Apple to engage in "social mapping," meaning understanding my network of personal and professional contacts, which Facebook and Google and Amazon also are capable of doing. My disenchantment with Siri only intensified when I discovered that even when I'm not using it, it is listening to every sound I make or someone near me makes. It analyzes my environment, listening for key words. Amazon's Alexa does much the same, as does Google Nest.

Clearly, these are disturbing practices, and I stopped using Siri for anything. This is far from legal language, but it seems to me that the standard for allowing a company to collect data is whether it benefits the consumer in a tangible way. I can understand that Amazon collects information on my previous book purchases (and books I've considered buying) and makes recommendations, on the basis of that knowledge, about new books I might find interesting. There is value to me in that. But collecting random data about me and my entire sets of contacts to create marketing opportunities does not benefit me in the slightest.

There are also big questions about who should have access to all the data that is being collected. People should have the power to know what major technology platforms know about them, and what they are doing with the information. But sadly, no policy framework has ever been put in place. One positive signal is that people in at least some cities can now request and watch the videos recorded by body cameras on police officers.

One obvious data abuse that is occurring: a facial recognition company called Clearview AI has "scraped" billions of photos of people from platforms such as LinkedIn and Instagram and from employment sites. It then sells access to its database of images to hundreds of law enforcement agencies. When a police officer uploads the image of a suspect into the database,

Clearview can match the face to any other images of that face it has, providing clues and context about the person's identity and location. Complaints and lawsuits were filed against Clearview. Its defenders argued that it was an issue of freedom of speech subject to the provisions of the First Amendment. Malarkey, I say. It was, and remains, a massive invasion of privacy.

There are also big questions about the laws surrounding search engines, the most powerful tools for navigating the Web. If I do a search on Google for "antitrust cases against Google," the company has the right to first present clearly identified ads, but then it should find relevant articles and present them in a dispassionate way. If we learn that dominant search giants are consciously skewing our search findings in any way, that strikes me as anticompetitive behavior.

Google certainly demonstrated monopolistic behavior in Australia in January 2021 when it threatened to shut down its search engine there because of pending legislation that would require it to pay publishers for the news they published. Imagine if Google threatened to shut down its search engine in American states or in the United States as a whole. As a society, we would be enraged.

All of which raises the question: what happens when a tech giant creates a powerful platform that exceeds purely private-sector interests? This is why the concept of "network effects" is so important. As more and more people use a particular service or platform, it can take on outsized power. How can that be measured? At what point does the tech giant have to adopt a higher standard in managing such a dominant platform rather than simply seeking to maximize profit?

Search engines are one type of those platforms; so is Apple's App Store. Apple allegedly discriminates against third-party creators of new programs created for iPhones. Apple created this platform, so on one level, it seems like Apple should be able to manage it as it sees fit. But at what point does a platform created by a private-sector company become more like a public utility?

This is not a theoretical question: In August 2020 Epic Games, the maker of Fortnite, one of the world's most popular video games, sued both Apple and Google (whose Google Play Store for Android phones is also quite powerful) for violating antitrust laws. Both Apple and Google take a 30 percent cut of whatever money Epic Games makes when it sells its games through their app stores. When Epic attempted to circumvent the big platforms by encouraging users to buy the games directly from Epic, both dropped Epic from their app stores. (Apple, under pressure, has agreed to cut in half the 30 percent fee it charges.)

Achieving and maintaining a newly rebalanced relationship between government and the tech giants will require great dexterity. The government and country as a whole need their expertise and technology to continue advancing and to help us compete against China, as I will argue in the next chapter. The argument from some of the tech CEOs that taking any actions to guide or mitigate their conduct would merely benefit Chinese competitors is specious and intended to confuse their critics. We also need them to take more seriously the pervasive hacking and espionage by China and other countries that undermines American national security and democracy. We want them to remain at least modestly profitable. The goal is not to drive them out of business.

Developing and managing a successful, balanced strategy would require the US government to get smarter and more cohesive. The White House Office of Science and Technology Policy is one body that could start demonstrating this type of leadership. It has shrunk in recent years and was led during the Trump era by an Oklahoman weatherman, but it could be revitalized and given the best possible leadership, drawn from government, universities, and the private sector. Another recommendation, made by

Clyde Prestowitz in his book, *A World Turned Upside Down*, is that the National Security Council and National Economic Council— both located within the White House apparatus—be merged. I cannot define the precise bureaucratic mechanism. But only an office at the White House level, with access to the president and his team, could command the range of resources necessary to do the job of better managing relations with the tech giants, in cooperation with other government agencies and indeed with other governments. It boils down to: who's in charge? Have the tech giants become governments unto themselves? I'll touch on this theme again in the final chapter.

Build in Ethics to The Innovation Process

More broadly, we need to have a debate about why some technologies are being developed and how. I am indebted to the *MIT Technology Review,* to which I subscribe (both in print and digitally), for much of this thinking. The vast majority of new technologies have been created to make money. They have not been created primarily with an eye to human needs. Venture capitalists and others invest in technology start-ups because they want a rate of return. They want to make their "exits" with fat profits in hand, meaning the start-up either goes public or is purchased by a larger company. That's fair.

But as technology plays a bigger role than ever in the fabric of our society, we also need to ask ourselves if there are technologies that should be developed because they serve a broader social agenda. If so, how do we fund their creation and development? Tools that help us recognize deep visual or textual fakes would be an example of what we need, but perhaps market forces are not strong enough to give birth to them.

I don't think we need to wipe out or eliminate Silicon Valley's hard-charging, individualist, Ayn Rand-ish style, if even that were possible. But we need to supplement it with more people who are trained in ethics and the implications of the technologies being developed. Rather than inventing technologies such as drones, for example, and then waking up to the fact that they can be misused, the thought process involved in creating them ought to include people who can identify possible patterns of abuse and demand solutions before the technology is deployed. Rather than designing algorithms and then discovering that they reinforce a user's underlying prejudices and contribute to our national discord, shouldn't they be designed to be dispassionate and balanced? Bias in, bias out.

It has to be more than just a public relations exercise. The fact that Google apparently fired Timnit Gebru, the co-lead of its ethical AI team, was a case in point. Google hired Gebru, a highly visible woman of color, to colead this effort, and she wrote a report warning that the AI systems underpinning Google's search engine and other services contained harmful racial biases.

The fact that Google parted company with her established that it was not really serious about addressing ethics, at least not yet. They did not want ethics to interfere with development of a tool that might make a great deal of money. But addressing ethical issues is going to be crucial. AI used in medical diagnosis may be a clear 100 percent win. But what about AI used in facial recognition technology, as Clearview does? That is good for nabbing criminals and international fugitives, but it also could be used to target peaceful protesters or others with legitimate grievances, as Chinese authorities did in Hong Kong. And as previously argued, it is a massive invasion of privacy.

Or consider AI's growing role in corporate human resource departments and the identification and hiring of new employees. Do those AI programs have a built-in bias against certain ethnicities or cultures? The only way to make sure they do not is to have someone involved in creating these programs who is sensitive to the broader social implications. AI also is being used in "predictive policing," or trying to understand who is likely to commit crimes. Again, critics have suggested racial bias has played a role in shaping those algorithms.

I doubt that laws can be enacted to govern AI, because it is evolving so rapidly. But it would be helpful if government, educational leaders, nonprofit groups dedicated to various forms of justice, and technology leaders created a platform that can generate loose guidelines for the use of AI. Such a platform could be a consortium of interested parties who debate guidelines and issue their findings. It would have to be truly independent to be credible. The Technology Policy Institute, a nonprofit research and educational organization affiliated with the Aspen Institute, is one interesting model. Another is the Stanford Institute for Human-Centered Artificial Intelligence in California.

Attacking the Digital Divide

When I was a kid, interstate highways were being built through the forests and meadows near where I lived in Ohio and Kentucky. (They were already present in Los Angeles—though not as jammed as today.) Although these roads were conceived by President Dwight Eisenhower for possible use in military conflicts, they opened up the not-insignificant possibility for millions of Americans to get into a car with friends or family and drive straight for twenty-fou hours, covering an enormous distance. The highway system opened up America to all Americans.

I look at broadband, or high-speed, communications in much the same way. Just as anyone could get on the interstate as long as they could afford a car and gasoline, they could go anywhere. It was an enabler.

But somewhere between twenty and forty million Americans do not have access to broadband. Predictably, the areas with the poorest-quality service are remote rural areas and the inner cores of major cities. Estimates about how much it would cost to get everyone connected range from $80 billion to $100 billion. "People are afraid of the price tag," said Rep. James Clyburn, a Democrat of South Carolina, who introduced a bill to rectify the situation. "We can't afford not to do it."

I think that's the most persuasive point—we can't afford not to do it. To allow further fragmentation of our society along social, class, and ethnic lines is exactly the wrong direction to be going. Add in the China factor, and the argument is even more compelling. Chinese use of the Internet and communications networks around the world has exploded in sophistication and sheer volume. As with so many other issues involving China, there is a domestic, internal challenge that is connected to the external challenge. If we wish to shape American society in a positive way at the same time that we compete against China, we need to get serious about improving our communication systems.

There is more to it than just building the networks, as my former *Business Week* colleague Chris Farrell argued recently on the Marketplace radio program. "There are also going to be subsidies in terms of computers, support training, no question about that," he said. "And big service providers (like AT&T and Verizon) aren't going to like this idea. But I still think this is a critical step for an economy that, as we emerge from the pandemic recession, shouldn't be like the old one. It should be better."

By definition, this network should be a 5G network, the most advanced possible. This obviously touches again on China-related issues. Thanks to their long-term strategic thinking, and massive support from their government, Huawei and to a lesser extent ZTE came up with 5G wireless systems and software before anyone else in the world. Clearly, we cannot allow more of Huawei's systems inside the United States (and preferably not in any of our key allies, an enormously important battle). And we need to eliminate Huawei from rural networks in some parts of the United States.

But what have the Americans done to come up with a competitive product? Very little. It is simply shocking that our system, writ large, has failed to respond. I'll address this further in the next chapter.

Taming technology so that it advances our social and political well-being will require an all-of-government and all-of-society response. Government has to establish a framework of acceptable behavior and be able to decide when Big Tech has crossed a line in the sand. As for society as a whole, our educational system needs to be teaching about the waves of technology that have washed over us, and how we have responded—or haven't. It needs to be teaching people about their privacy and their data. And it needs to be rapidly increasing the sophistication of students, so that they can understand how to shape technology toward accomplishing societal goals. We need more research institutes specializing in these fields. And we need more enlightened commentary in our media.

It may be human nature. Or it may be the profit motive. But Americans have been quick to embrace the easy, fun, and convenient aspects of new technologies without understanding their downsides and risks. Companies have exploited the short-term profitability of large computer systems, but haven't properly safeguarded them against state-supported intruders. We need to create a society-wide conversation about these issues.

CHAPTER NOTES

Antitrust legislation: "Klobuchar to Introduce Antitrust Bill Raising Bar for Technology Deals." *The Wall Street Journal*. Feb. 2, 2021.

Apple cuts fees. "Apple, Under Antitrust Scrutiny, Halves App Store Fee for Smaller Developers." By Tim Higgins. *The Wall Street Journal*. Nov. 18, 2020.

Artificial Intelligence. "Can Artificial Intelligence Be Bias-Free?" By Cade Metz. *The New York Times*. March 21, 2021.

https://www.nytimes.com/2021/03/15/technology/artificial-intelligence-google-bias.html?searchResultPosition=3

Data Dividend Project. "Andrew Yang is pushing Big Tech to pay users for data." By Makena Kelly. *The Verge.* June 22, 2020. https://www.theverge.com/2020/6/22/21298919/andrew-yang-big-tech-data-dividend-project-facebook-google-ubi

Ericsson statement on toothbrushes. "Mobile radio access networks: What policy makers need to know." By Rene Summer. Sept. 17, 2020. https://www.ericsson.com/en/blog/2020/9/ran-what-policy-makers-need-to-know

Facebook. "In Suits, U.S. and Over 40 States Ask Court to Break Up Facebook." By Cecilia Kang and Mike Issac. *The New York Times.* Dec. 10, 2020. https://www.nytimes.com/2020/12/09/technology/facebook-antitrust-monopoly.html?searchResultPosition=1

Gerstell, Glenn S. "I Work for the N.S.A. We Cannot Afford to Lose the Digital Revolution." Glenn S. Gerstell, *The New York Times.* Sept. 10, 2019. https://www.nytimes.com/2019/09/10/opinion/nsa-privacy.html

Google threatens Australia. "Google Threatens to Cut Off Australia." By Mike Cherney. *The Wall Street Journal.* Jan. 23-24, 2021.

Google fires Timnit Gebru. "Google hired Timnit Gebru to be an outspoken critic of unethical AI. Then she was fired for it." By Nitasha Tiku. *The Washington Post.* Dec. 23, 2020. https://www.washingtonpost.com/technology/2020/12/23/google-timnit-gebru-ai-ethics/

Stanford Institute for Human-Centered Artificial Intelligence. https://hai.stanford.edu/

Technology Policy Institute. https://techpolicyinstitute.org/

Venture capital: "Why venture capital doesn't build the things we really need." By Elizabeth MacBride. *MIT Technology Review.* June 17, 2000. https://www.technologyreview.com/2020/06/17/1003318/why-venture-capital-doesnt-build-the-things-we-really-need/?

Zuckerberg, Mark. "Zuckerberg: It's better to buy than compete. Is Facebook a monopoly?" *TRT World.* Dec. 10, 2010. https://www.trtworld.com/magazine/zuckerberg-its-better-to-buy-than-compete-is-facebook-a-monopoly-42243#:~:-text=In%20one%202008%20email%20highlighted,first%20 place%20%E2%80%93%20and%20that's%20true.

17 A Grand Strategy to Resist Xi Jinping

We need to frankly acknowledge that the American system has not responded well to a China that is actively putting measures in place to dominate much of the world and to exercise growing influence over the United States. We must close the gaps in our pluralistic system that are allowing a centrally orchestrated, sophisticated Chinese government to drive through the cracks. The Chinese party-state has been exploiting the open model we celebrate so much. The only rational conclusion: we need to improve our model without sacrificing the values we hold dear.

We need to create a stronger framework for cooperating—with each other. One of the most important fissures has been between the US government agencies that are worried about China's tactics (the intelligence community, FBI and Justice Department, Homeland Security, and the military) and the agencies that depend on continued business ties—Commerce and Treasury. The Treasury Department has borrowed tens of billions of dollars from China, which holds roughly $1 trillion of government debt.

The hawks under President Trump imposed tariffs on goods being made in China and shipped to the United States, but that had almost no impact on the underlying technological or national security issues. The moves announced against Huawei and other major China tech players were more cosmetic and defensive than they were part of a deeper, systematic response. In the absence of coordination with our allies, cutting off supplies of equipment to China's largest semiconductor maker meant that it merely turned to other suppliers in Japan or South Korea or the Netherlands.

Simply "calling out" Chinese espionage and hacking did not work and will never work. Some very sophisticated people within the US government seemed to believe that if they publicly identified the practices, the Chinese party-state would stop doing them. This was the "name and blame" theory. Show the public FBI wanted posters with the names and faces of Chinese hackers, and they will be quaking in their boots. But that did not reflect an understanding of the values of the Communist Party. If it can continue to get away with it, it will.

The Biden administration has so far proceeded cautiously in carving out a China strategy, which has been sensible. It has not appeared that Biden would revert to the relatively naïve policies of Barack Obama or the showmanship of Donald Trump, and would instead concentrate on a deep structural response to China, in cooperation with key allies.

But creating a coherent US government strategy over the long term will require very sensitive, ongoing conversations between government and Big Tech. Our most important technology companies have enormous stakes in China. Microsoft, Cisco, Oracle, and Intel have enormous sales there. Google's Android operating system is used on Chinese smartphones, and Amazon web services division has a big presence in China. Only Facebook appears to be left on the outside looking in. Any US president and his team must develop and maintain relationships with the tech giants, where concern can be expressed about technology being transferred to or being developed in China. And how can they help the US government, including the Pentagon, develop and retain a lead in crucial technologies? The gap between Washington and Silicon Valley must be gently but firmly narrowed. Perhaps just ten CEOs of major tech firms, if sufficiently motivated, possess sufficient power to achieve such a goal.

The appointment of the first national cyber director, Chris Inglis, could be the beginning of a conscious effort to harden the sprawling array of government systems. But the government also needs to work more closely with all businesses, and those businesses must work with government, to stop the penetration of computer systems and a widespread pattern of China's Ministry of State Security recruiting agents. We must harden our targets. The Chinese are forcing the realization that business and national security are firmly linked. I don't think business leaders are "kowtowing" to Beijing. They are stuck in incredibly difficult situations, with such large market shares or business relationships in China that they cannot afford to just walk away from them. No one could have foreseen the day that the Chinese government would use those relationships to force American airlines and hotel companies to change their maps and drop Taiwan as a separate country.

Even if some CEOs think of their companies as being "stateless" or "citizens of the world," as Dow Chemical's Carl Gerstacker told me back in the 1970s, they need America and the American government. They need a home government to protect them from other governments, to create a flow of well-educated students, to build infrastructure, and to create a rational regulatory and legal climate. So while respecting the fact that government and CEOs have different interests, it's essential that they find ways to cooperate to moderate China's ambitions.

The first piece of the argument that the federal government should make to leaders of American technology companies should be strategic: The Communist Party is playing a long-term game against you. It is sucking out your technological lifeblood and preparing to leapfrog you with products that have gone through "indigenous" innovation in China—meaning the Chinese developed the stolen ideas faster than Americans could, because of huge government funding. That's the reason the Chinese government is suddenly serious about protecting intellectual property—it wants to protect Chinese products that were developed on the basis of other people's ideas. Once Chinese enterprises have leapfrogged American companies, as Huawei, Zoom, and TikTok have done, your futures will have been compromised. Once you are no longer useful, the Chinese will destroy you, as they did Canada's Nortel, an event that largely escaped attentions south of the border. When the company was forced into bankruptcy in 2010, it was revealed that Huawei and hackers affiliated with the People's Liberation Army had penetrated the company's internal systems and stolen its technology development plans. They had penetrated the company's email system all the way up to that of top company officers.

At the tactical level, the US government should establish a mechanism that can track China's technology gains at the same time that it facilitates Manhattan Project–style initiatives to help American companies rev up 5G and 6G wireless communications technology, AI, quantum computing, and other fields Biden has identified.

This body should be to use a combination of "sticks" and "carrots" to gradually bring American tech companies into positions more agreeable with US governmental goals. Such an entity at the White House level could bring to bear the full force of the US government.

The "sticks" could be:

—The companies' multimillion-dollar IT and defense contracts with the government could suddenly come up for review.

—Antitrust pressures could be dialed up.

—Export licenses for dual-use technologies could suddenly become more difficult to obtain.

—Obtaining H-1B visas to fly in software engineers from India for short-term assignments could suddenly become more difficult.

—The practice of parking billions of dollars of profits in offshore tax havens could come under assault from the Internal Revenue Service and the Treasury Department.

The "carrots" could be:

—Provide the opportunity to get involved in government-supported projects to rapidly develop and commercialize new technologies that would offer profit opportunities.
—Help in reshoring some activities, meaning to bring them back manufacturing from China. In view of the pandemic, even the most gung ho CEO must recognize that over-dependence on China is not a healthy corporate strategy.
—Provide reassurance that the US antitrust policy climate will not threaten their very existence.

I can already hear howls of outrage coming from corner offices throughout the land. These tactics would be a violation of the norms. They play favorites. They're un-American. We'll take you to court. But they are precisely the kinds of tools that Beijing uses against our companies operating in China, and there are no courts in China that can stand up to Beijing. Much tighter US policy coordination will be necessary if America is to confront a monolithic Communist Party. Only a truly resolved president and his team can forge the common vision and integrated strategy that allow for a truly effective response to Xi Jinping.

***

There are at least two big areas of technology we need to get right. The first is 5G wireless communications, because the Chinese already have it, and the second is semiconductors, where we still have a dominant position. What the Trump

Administration did was to punish Huawei and cut off its access to the vast majority of American semiconductors for use in its handsets and networks, which caused the company to build up a massive inventory of chips and chipmaking equipment, often purchased from non-American companies.

But the ultimate goal should be to create an American version of 5G and then 6G. AT&T, Verizon, and T-Mobile have started building what they describe as 5G networks in major cities, working with Nokia and Ericsson, but they are still embryonic. What they are marketing so heavily is a slightly enhanced version of the previous generation of technology. 5G is going to require a complete rebuild of our wireless communications infrastructure. Base stations and towers are going to have to be closer to each other to handle 5G signals. New phones will be necessary.

The Federal Communications Commission has recently completed the sale of more than $80 billion worth of C band spectrum rights to the telecom providers. But is that enough? It turns out that the Pentagon dominates and controls spectrum that might be most effective for 5G and allow the system to be built out less expensively, says Eric Schmidt, the former chief executive of Google and former chairman of the Defense Innovation Board. He emerged as an important voice on the subject. "There is generally an accepted sweet spot for 5G, which is frequencies below 6 gigahertz," he told a *Wall Street Journal* forum. "It's a trade-off, because the higher the frequency, the more bandwidth that you can provide, but the less capable it is to go through walls—furthermore, the more towers that you need, because the waves are essentially shorter," he said. He believes there is a way the military can continue to own the frequency but share it with the telecommunications companies through something called dynamic spectrum sharing. I have no idea what that means, but if it is coming from Eric Schmidt, it is an idea worth exploring. (He shaped up to be an important voice in the Biden Administration's overall efforts to create a response to China. As a former CEO, he seemed uniquely capable of speaking the language that the business community could understand and respect.)

Aside from allocating spectrum, a key question is how all the 5G equipment will be manufactured. One broad guiding principle is that American companies would not necessarily have to make all of it. Sweden's Ericcson and Finland's Nokia already make the equipment and could be brought into a consortium or partnership with US companies to get the job done. The Pentagon also could consider making the nation's telecommunications system part of its Defense Industrial Base, ensuring that funding is available to help manufacturers make the necessary gear. And the United States should make the equipment as software-intensive as possible, because that's where the American advantage lies.

Ultimately, the private sector should be in charge of picking exactly the right technology, building the networks, and managing them, because it will be extremely complex to maintain the security and privacy of users' data. It is extremely important to establish an American standard for 5G. If we want other countries to buy our 5G systems, international standards should be compatible with the American system. China is trying to establish its version of 5G as the world standard, effectively cutting everyone else out, as it is attempting to do in many of the industries of the future.

All this is extremely complex, but public support should be built for it. We could rally behind slogans such as, "Stand Up to China," or "5G for All Americans." If we could arouse interest and indeed excitement, the government might be able to issue bonds that the public would buy to help finance the effort, just as millions of Americans bought war bonds to support the national effort in World War II. Some of the programs that Franklin D. Roosevelt unveiled during the Great Depression might be worth reexamining and repurposing.

The second technology we must get right is semiconductors, which are the brains of all computerized devices. China buys

$300 billion worth of microchips each year from foreign producers, mostly for products it then exports. China is dependent on our semiconductor makers and designers, such as Intel, Nvidia, Micron, and the wireless chip company Qualcomm.

Cutting Huawei off from American semiconductors will hurt it in the short to medium term, but there are possible downsides. The first is that Huawei and every other Chinese company and government ministry involved have already redoubled their efforts to establish independence from American-related suppliers. They are pouring billions more into the effort, and they will also probably redouble their efforts to steal semiconductor know-how and to recruit Chinese or Chinese-Americans who have access to that know-how. American companies and government agencies should prepare for that.

It might be a smarter strategy to keep China dependent on American semiconductors, if indeed that is still possible. Chips are one of the last points of technological leverage we have. Under this scenario, American-related semiconductor companies might slow down the speed at which innovations are passed along to the Chinese. The products would be just a half step behind the cutting edge. This would have to be coordinated between the US government and the chip companies, and that would have to be done very quietly. There also should be a conversation about how the semiconductors are being used—do we really want to sell into the facial recognition systems being used to oppress the Uighurs or send Chinese rockets to Mars? And there must also be a conversation about how the Chinese military uses American semiconductors. It might be possible to slow the speed and limit the volume of chips going to the People's Liberation Army, even though the system of middlemen in China would make that difficult.

The upside of this strategy is that American chip companies could continue to make money in China, pleasing American investors, suppliers, employees, and shareholders. But we would slow the pace just a bit to maintain a strategic advantage, discourage Chinese efforts to reach parity, and learn how to direct the flow of chips away from certain sectors. It would take industry and government to trust each other and cooperate, a radical idea in today's environment. But that's what it would take.

At the same time, we need to accelerate the development of new generations of chips here. One looming issue seems to center on Intel, for decades the gold standard of the American semiconductor industry. The company stunned investors in July 2020 by announcing that it was running behind in perfecting the manufacturing of its latest chip, whose circuits are only 7 nanometers wide, and was considering turning to other manufacturers, known as chip foundries, to make the chips. Those foundries are either in Taiwan or South Korea. Intel seems to be reeling from the resignation of one CEO for having a consensual relationship with an Intel employee. He departed, and then the next CEO arrived and departed. A new one has arrived and pledged to continue manufacturing in the United States, but it's not clear whether it can be done. One problem is that investors seemed to be urging Intel to get out of manufacturing and adopt a more profitable, "asset-lite" business strategy.

Where Intel makes the next generation of chips is not just a business decision. It has strategic and national security implications that far outweigh Wall Street's desire for quarterly earnings increases. We have to figure out a way to make the next generation of chips in the United States, because if that manufacturing goes offshore, it will be far more vulnerable to being imitated or stolen by the Chinese government.

Intel and federal agencies last year persuaded Congress to subsidize US chip factories and chip research, and the new administration and Congress appeared, as of this writing, to be moving forward on a $50 billion package, a positive development indeed.

All these proposals suggest that Americans, under pressure from China, are beginning to have to overcome the perennial argument about having an "industrial policy." There are right ways and wrong ways for government and industry to work together. The right ways, as argued in Chapter Thirteen, are to take politics out of the process and bring in seasoned technologists and educators who help make decisions using solid business logic. Government agencies might fund two or three different technology approaches in each field and let the private sector sort out which one is best. Government cannot play God, but it can encourage businesses to explore the right paths.

There are many such straws in the wind. In late 2020, Sen. Chuck Schumer of New York and Sen. Bob Menendez of New Jersey introduced a bipartisan bill to spend $350 billion over a decade to build a comprehensive strategy to confront and compete with China. Hundreds of bills related to China were introduced but not enacted. In October 2020 the White House's National Security Council released a proposal called the National Strategy for Critical and Emerging Technologies. It urged a "markets-oriented approach" rather than the top-down, statist approach being taken by China. But the proposal came just weeks before national elections and was lost in the political roar.

There are other signs, however, that this logic was beginning to take hold. The Defense Department awoke to the dangers of depending on China for 80 percent of all the rare earths the United States uses, including in its weapon systems. The key company trying to establish the ability to take rare earths mined in California and process them into forms that can be used in industry is MP Materials of Mountain Pass, California. The Pentagon allocated $125 million for funding rare earth projects, and the Energy Department also offered nearly $160 million for rare earths research and development. Several companies vied for the funding. Buoyed by the new support, MP Materials was expected to be able to raise $490 million in private sector investments. (The Pentagon should evaluate its entire supply chain to identify other vulnerabilities.)

The White House Office of Science and Technology Policy also started to address the need to compete in advanced technologies by increasing funding for artificial intelligence and quantum computing by 30 percent. Its proposal would develop AI research institutes formed by the National Science Foundation and other government agencies. The Energy Department would get $25 million to build an early-stage quantum Internet.

So there appeared to be broad, bipartisan support to launch a genuine competitive response to China. The challenge was to organize, fund, and manage these projects over the long term while avoiding the partisan wrangling that sank Solyndra and A 123. There is more than one precedent; an example is the War Production Board during World War II. The American military needed a massive expansion in the production of hardware, so private and public sector interests agreed that the War Production Board would be established and led by a top executive from Sears, Roebuck and Co., then a major corporation. It coordinated the flow of raw materials into producing the hardware that the US military needed, which was one of the crucial factors in winning the conflicts in Europe and Asia. When Americans agree that they face a challenge, they can overcome the distinctions between the public and private good.

One major piece of the challenge is to start rebuilding a computer industry inside the United States. It does not have to happen overnight, and it's foolish to argue that we could become completely self-reliant. But government and the private sector have to commit to this cause, because as long as our computer equipment is built either in China or assembled with Chinese parts, we are going to be vulnerable to the penetration of our IT systems. Foxconn, Apple's lead contractor in assembling its iPhones in China, made a big splash about creating a liquid crystal display factory in Wisconsin, but it has yet to materialize. Taiwan Semiconductor Manufacturing Corp. (TSMC), which has a dominant position in chip manufacturing, was said to be considering building a major semiconductor facility in Arizona. That is precisely the kind of cornerstone investment that could help revive an American computer industry. In addition to maintaining Intel's manufacturing inside the United States, those types of investments should be a national priority.

We need to revive manufacturing across the board. The pandemic revealed that we are completely dependent on China in many sectors. China has taught us that manufacturing represents national power. I've been impressed with the work of the nonprofit Reshoring Initiative, which seeks to help American manufacturers analyze the cost structure of manufacturing in China and decide what makes the most economic sense in bringing back, or "reshoring," to America. CEOs do not need to bring all their manufacturing home—just a percentage to avoid being dependent on a single source, which in many cases is China. They should diversify their supply chains, because is the strategically sound thing to do for the long term. CEOs should also become a larger part of the solution by deepening their ties to universities, high schools, and training institutes to make sure Americans, young and old, learn what they need to find roles in the rapidly evolving economy.

All this is going to cost money at a time when US government debt has eclipsed the size of the national economy, a key benchmark. It's the first time that has happened since World War II. Adapting to the realities of China's ambitions is also going to affect short-term corporate profits. Stock prices will suffer if Wall Street maintains its insistence that a company increase profits every quarter. It will be a period of shared sacrifice.

Thus a complete and coherent strategy toward China would focus on critical technologies and attempt to ensure that American companies remain in the lead, that critical manufacturing remains here or returns, and that Chinese hacking and espionage are greatly reduced.

None of this will work unless we can secure control of our own IT systems, including all communications networks and computing systems. If Chinese government ministries such as the Ministry for State Security and various hacking groups are deeply lodged inside corporate and governmental networks, much as the Russians seem to be (as evidenced in the Solar Winds hack), there is no way our decision-making processes can be secure. Our intellectual property can never be safe. This is not wild-eyed paranoia. In a September 2020 report that was almost universally ignored, our own Cybersecurity and Infrastructure Security Agency, in cooperation with the FBI, described how China's state security ministry uses open-source tools to scan American networks for vulnerabilities, and then enters those systems before their software can be patched. The ministry is quite literally roaming through America's IT systems. We Americans believed in our inherent superiority when it came to computer systems; Xi Jinping is seeking to prove us wrong. We are more vulnerable than any of us had recognized.

Aside from spending the money and training the talent, we need to eliminate obvious Trojan horses. Zoom Video Communications became hugely popular during the pandemic and theoretically is a California-based company, but it is still controlled from China, as federal prosecutors charged in December 2020. Engineers in China shut down at least four video meetings that were scheduled to be held to discuss the Tiananmen Square massacre.

TikTok also has become wildly popular, attracting as many as one hundred million American users. But it too is a tool for collecting data about the networks and email addresses for anybody related to a TikTok fanatic. The Trump Administration should have shut it down, but TikTok was able to argue that it was subject to American legal protections. What rubbish! The Chinese have learned how to game our system. They have learned the art of creating front companies, mostly in California, to pretend to be American, when in fact their data and algorithms are controlled from China. That has to be stopped.

And I don't see how the United States and its closest allies can take part in the 2022 Olympics in Beijing without it representing a huge propaganda victory for Xi Jinping on par with the image boost that Adolph Hitler enjoyed in hosting the 1936 Olympics.

***

There are at least three other elements of a grand strategy. The first is to rebuild our intellectual common ground to better understand the sophistication of China's strategy, and the second is to create a global response to China. The third is to strike the right balance in communicating with Chinese-Americans.

First, the intellectual piece. We have allowed ourselves to become intellectually colonized. Indeed, we have welcomed it. Universities and high schools have entered at least one hundred deals with the Confucius Institutes, which are managed by China's Education Ministry. The ministry funds Chinese studies at American educational institutions but insists that they obey Chinese law, which forbids the discussion of anything remotely controversial.

We need to wean ourselves off these institutes and devote resources to building our own, more balanced China studies programs, including language training.

Universities also have gotten hooked on having 360,000 Chinese students enrolled in the United States, because they pay top dollar. University presidents are putting their financial interests ahead of the interests of academic freedom. Some professors of Chinese studies have been banned from going to China because of research that was critical of the Communist Party. Any self-respecting university president should see that as a violation of academic freedom and attach a higher value to that than to the flow of Chinese funds, but none has.

One side effect of how universities are mismanaging their China studies programs is that very few young Americans are going into the field. I made appearances at Columbia University and New York University to promote *The New Art of War* and was exposed to dozens of graduate students in Chinese studies. The overwhelming majority were Chinese. Not a single American-born student was present. Chinese and Chinese-American students have obvious linguistic advantages over non-Chinese speakers, and they may not be as worried about paying off their student loans. But we are allowing a dangerous dependence to emerge. The Chinese government has been able to devote far more human talent and financial resources to this effort than the Japanese ever were. The Japanese might have endowed a chair in a university department; the Chinese can flood the department with students and seek to dominate future generations of the China-watching profession. And it can co-opt university presidents by directing large numbers of Chinese students to them and by allowing them to operate highly profitable campuses in China.

Incredibly, universities have allowed Chinese students who are secretly officers in the People's Liberation Army to study the most advanced technologies. That is madness and must be stopped. It seems unavoidable—for universities to do a better job in protecting their research, they must admit fewer Chinese students.

Secondly, the global response. FBI Director Christopher Wray has advocated the use of "all tools" in "all sectors" for a "whole of society response" to China. That's good, but it's not enough. It has to be international in nature. The United States has started to identify Chinese practices that violate international norms and to oppose them, and that effort must be sustained. The United States needs to fight to maintain the neutral role that organizations such as the World Health Organization are designed to play. The Trump Administration started pulling the United States out of WHO, but that was precisely the wrong thing to do. We should increase our commitment of human resources and money to maintain a strong US role at WHO rather than allowing it to tip into China's hands.

We are in a global battle, and we have to re-establish a global presence and alliances with key partners. An alliance among the United States, Japan, Australia, and India called the Quad, or Quadrilateral Security Dialogue, is still embryonic but could be powerful. A first virtual summit meeting has been held.

Across the other ocean, deep wounds have been inflicted on the trans-Atlantic alliance, by such acts as attacking NATO and threatening to pull troops out of Germany without any discussion or negotiation. Repairing those ties has begun and must remain a top priority, because if the United States and Europe agree on an issue, that creates a globally significant force.

We need a nongovernmental Global China Institute, which would be a mechanism for tracking and understanding what China is doing around the world, and communicate those findings internationally. It should cooperate with other leading research institutions, such as the Australian Strategic Policy Institute and the Mercator Institute For China Studies in Berlin. If all the countries in the world understood that China has a strategy to dominate them, they might resist Chinese blandishments.

It will obviously take years, but the United States needs to re-establish a sense of leadership that the world trusts, and a sense that we remain true to our values—and that those values are more enduring and attractive than the ones being promoted by Xi Jinping.

Thirdly, Chinese-Americans. We need to have a conversation with, and about, the presence of about 3.8 million Chinese-Americans among us, according to the 2010 census. They can be highly effective in understanding the pattern of what the Chinese government is doing and help stop it. I suspect that only a tiny fraction wish to see the Communist Party triumph. Many Chinese-Americans came to these shores generations ago, have lost any family connections, and perhaps don't even speak Mandarin, the official national language. Even some Chinese-born, Mandarin-speaking Chinese I have met want nothing to do with the Communist Party. We need their help. We don't want to turn them into more tempting targets for hatred. And we don't want to send a flood of highly talented Chinese back to the mainland.

***

Critics have said that I am just trying to create a foreign enemy, a bogeyman, when the real enemy is here at home, in the form of obesity, ignorance, poor infrastructure, and surprisingly deep inequality, among other problems. Yes, I agree, domestic and foreign challenges are connected. The reason the Chinese have such momentum at the moment is because of things they have done in their own society. They've trained hundreds of thousands of engineers and scientists. They take STEM education seriously. Millions have learned English and other languages. They've achieved an incredible infrastructure buildout. They've made a major commitment to information technology. They possess an appetite for rapid technological change. They share a vision of China as the world's most powerful nation, as it once was. The Silk Road existed because poor Europeans hungered for the silk and porcelains only the Chinese knew how to make. The Chinese also invented gunpowder, the compass, and paper. They understand technological dominance. Xi Jinping has stated that China should once again achieve that goal by 2049, the one-hundred-year anniversary of the Communist victory in the Chinese civil war.

We are weakened because we haven't chosen to organize ourselves to compete, and we have not created a society that all participants believe in. We don't educate and train our people well enough. We don't study the Chinese language in any serious way. We don't build new infrastructure on any meaningful scale. We are like deer in the headlights. But to pretend that our problems are purely domestic in nature is to ignore the fact that the largest nation on earth, with 1.4 billion people, is seeking to undermine us, at home and abroad, and has become increasingly open in denying the validity of American values.

As a student of Chinese propaganda, I am amused to hear spokespeople for the Chinese government say the United States is trying to "hold China back" and is trying to "contain" China. Really? We were the ones who engineered China's entry onto the world stage, and we actively cooperated in building the world's largest manufacturing platform in China. The reason for our shift in thinking is that Xi Jinping shattered our "dream" about China and launched his county onto a different path than anyone anticipated. He became aggressive, as his "wolf warrior" diplomats made abundantly clear.

I've also had people ask me if we shouldn't we be more worried about our own tech companies gathering our data than the Chinese. I agree that limitations should be put in place on Big Tech, as argued previously, but their collection of data does not threaten military secrets, national security, or our intellectual property.

And doesn't our government, in the form of the FBI and Homeland Security, surveil us? Yes, that obviously happens. But I have more confidence that that surveillance is at least partly based on court orders and is governed by a body of law. It isn't perfect, but it's a far cry from what the Chinese are doing. The fact that Apple defied the FBI's request to unlock an iPhone belonging to a suspected criminal was a case in point.

In this book, I have outlined responses to what I think are three major challenges that our society faces. They are clearly related. And there are clear steps that can be taken from the center of the political spectrum. We desperately need to rebuild that political center. Bipartisan agreements on responding to China could help achieve that.

That would help set the stage for the next phase of American democracy, one where there is rational dialogue and that can shape technology in directions that are in better harmony with national and societal goals.

Can it all be realistically accomplished? Or is the game already over?

This "game" will never be over. This is a multigenerational challenge we will hand down to our children and grandchildren. Even if it takes four or five years to restore a genuine national conversation and create a national strategy, we will have turned the corner on one of the darkest moments in American history. We will have proven that the concept of America remains valid. When galvanized and when focused, I remain confident that the American model is the most flexible, resilient—and effective—in the world.

I didn't set out in life to become a curmudgeon. I was fueled by a thirst for adventure, a burning curiosity, and raw determination. What I have learned during the journey, however, is that different peoples in the world make decisions about how they organize themselves, and that those decisions are hugely important in creating wealth and opportunity—and perhaps even happiness. To do that, they have to create strategic visions that are shared by a majority of their populations. Call that patriotism or nationalism, but the net effect is the same. They build institutions and systems that concentrate on the long term. They work with each other in a rational way. They don't seek quick fixes or magic bullets.

I hope I have convinced and inspired my fellow Americans to learn those lessons and once again pursue a winning pragmatic path—together.

CHAPTER NOTES

Artificial intelligence, quantum computing funding. "Big Boost for A.I. and Quantum Computing Research." By Cade Metz. *The New York Times.* Feb. 11, 2020. https://www.nytimes. com/2020/02/10/technology/white-house-earmarks-new-money-for-ai-and-quantum-computing.html?searchResultPosition=1

China's semiconductor purchases. "China to import $300 billion of chips for third straight year: industry group." Reuters staff. Aug. 26, 2020. https://www.reuters.com/article/us-china-semiconductors/china-to-import-300-billion-of-chips-for-third-straight-year-industry-group-idUSKBN25M1CX

China's semiconductor development efforts. "China's Frenzy to Master Chip Manufacturing." By Raymond Zhong and Cao Li. *The New York Times.* Dec. 28, 2020. https://www.nytimes.com/2020/12/24/technology/china-semiconductors.html?searchResultPosition=1

Cyber Czar. "N.S.A. Veteran is Chosen to Lead New Cyber Effort," by Michael D. Shear and Julian E. Barnes. *The New York Times.* April 13, 2021. https://www.nytimes.com/2021/04/12/us/politics/chris-inglis-cyber-director.html?searchResultPosition=1

5G: "5G Rivals Face an $81 Billion Tab After Spectrum Buying Spree." By Drew Fitzgerald and Sam Goldfarb. *The Wall Street Journal.* Jan. 17, 2021.

FBI Director Christopher Wray. "The Threat Posed by the Chinese Government and the Chinese Communist Party to the Economic and National Security of the United States." A speech at the Hudson Institute. July 7, 2020. https://www.fbi.gov/news/speeches/the-threat-posed-by-the-chinese-government-and-the-chinese-communist-party-to-the-economic-and-national-security-of-the-united-states

Intel. "Intel: Sorry, But Our 7nm Chips Will Be Delayed to 2022, 2023." By Michael Kan. *PC Magazine.*

July 23, 2020. https://www.pcmag.com/news/intel-sorry-but-our-7nm-chips-will-be-delayed-to-2022-2023

Ministry of State Security presence in American computers. "Chinese Ministry of State Security-Affiliated Cyber Threat Actor Activity." Cybersecurity and Infrastructure Security Agency. Sept. 14, 2020. https://us-cert.cisa.gov/ncas/alerts/aa20-258a

National Strategy for Critical and Emerging Technologies. "White House Strategy Names 20 Emerging Technologies Crucial to National Security." Nextgov.com. By Aaron Boyd. Oct. 15, 2020. https://www.nextgov.com/emerging-tech/2020/10/white-house-strategy-names-20-emerging-technologies-crucial-national-security/169293/

Nortel: "Exclusive: Did Huawei bring down Nortel? Corporate espionage, theft, and the parallel rise and fall of two telecom giants." By Tom Blackwell. *National Post*. Feb. 20, 2020. https://nationalpost.com/news/exclusive-did-huawei-bring-down-nortel-corporate-espionage-theft-and-the-parallel-rise-and-fall-of-two-telecom-giants#:~:text=In%202008%2C%20the%20Chinese%20firm,together%20a%20buy%2Dout%20bid.

Pentagon support for rare earths. "U.S. Companies Vie for Funds in Race to Build Rare Earths Industry." By Zach Montague. *The New York Times*. Aug. 14, 2020. https://www.nytimes.com/2020/08/14/us/politics/rare-earths-american-companies.html

Reshoring Initiative. www.reshorenow.org

Restricting China's largest chipmaker. "U.S. Restricts Chip Maker in China, Citing Risks." By Ana Swanson and Raymond Zhong. *The New York Times*. Sept. 27, 2020. https://www.nytimes.com/2020/09/26/technology/trump-china-smic-blacklist.html?searchResultPosition=1

Senate competitive plan. "Senate Democrats Present $350 Billion Strategy to Counter China." By Catie Edmondson. *The New York Times*. Sept. 17, 2020. https://www.nytimes.com/2020/09/17/us/politics/democrats-china-strategy.html

Eric Schmidt and 5G. "Should the U.S. Change How It Doles Out Airwaves for 5g?" *The Wall Street Journal.* Nov. 10, 2020.

Supporting U.S. semiconductors. "Debating U.S. Support for the Chip Industry." By Shira Ovide. *The New York Times.* Feb. 8, 2021. https://www.nytimes.com/2021/02/05/technology/computer-chips-government-help.html?searchResultPosition=1

TikTok. "Trump Administration Prepares Forced Sale of TikTok." By Russ Mitchell. *Los Angeles Times.* July 31. https://www.latimes.com/business/technology/story/2020-07-31/trump-administration-prepares-forced-sale-of-tiktok-national-security-threat

Zoom. "Federal prosecutors accuse Zoom executive of working with Chinese government to surveil users and suppress video calls." By Drew Harwell and Ellen Nakashima. *The Washington Post.* Dec. 18, 2020. https://www.washingtonpost.com/technology/2020/12/18/zoom-helped-china-surveillance/

ACKNOWLEDGMENTS

In rough chronological order, I'd like to thank John Moody for helping me recall details of our days together at United Press International. Bradley Martin and Tony Walker read portions of the manuscript dealing with our time in Beijing. Dori Jones Yang was particularly helpful in checking my Chinese language references.

Sally Fitton made a number of corrections in the chapter about Afghanistan. Former *Business Week* colleagues Peter Galuszka, Jonathan Kapstein, Patricia Kranz, and Russ Mitchell read portions of the manuscript and shared their insights. Toshio Aritake read portions related to Japan. Steve Shepard fact-checked my descriptions of *Business Week*.

Offering general advice and support were family, friends, and associates: Abe Benyunes, Bill Collins, Sonya Fry, Thomas Goltz, Lindsay Sara Krasner, Marcy McGinnis, Jane Reilly, Genevieve Stroh, and Portia Sweet.

But of course, the greatest source of support was from my wife, Rita Sevell, who helped me survive the emtional rollercoater ride called "writing a book." I heartily recommend that all journalists and authors marry their own psychotherapists.

Lightning Source UK Ltd.
Milton Keynes UK
UKHW021552150921
390625UK00010B/1903